# CRIMINAL CAPITAL

# CRIMINAL CAPITAL

## HOW THE FINANCE INDUSTRY FACILITATES CRIME

## STEPHEN PLATT

palgrave
macmillan

First published 2015 by
PALGRAVE MACMILLAN

Palgrave Macmillan in the UK is an imprint of Macmillan Publishers Limited, registered in England, company number 785998, of Houndmills, Basingstoke, Hampshire RG21 6XS.

Palgrave Macmillan in the US is a division of St Martin's Press LLC, 175 Fifth Avenue, New York, NY 10010.

Palgrave Macmillan is the global academic imprint of the above companies and has companies and representatives throughout the world.

Palgrave® and Macmillan® are registered trademarks in the United States, the United Kingdom, Europe and other countries

ISBN: 978–1–137–33729–0

This book is printed on paper suitable for recycling and made from fully managed and sustained forest sources. Logging, pulping and manufacturing processes are expected to conform to the environmental regulations of the country of origin.

A catalogue record for this book is available from the British Library.

A catalog record for this book is available from the Library of Congress.

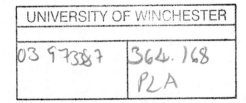

*For Joshua & William*

# CONTENTS

# FOREWORD

By the winter of 1988 I had just finished several years of deep undercover work, living as a money launderer for Pablo Escobar and his closest associates. My covert life had taken me to many interesting places including the boardroom of what some have described as the dirtiest bank of all time – the Bank of Credit and Commerce International. BCCI was the seventh largest privately held bank in the world, a global powerhouse that catered to drug lords, arms dealers, terrorists and big-time tax evaders. As gatekeepers for the fortunes of the underworld, BCCI bankers taught me every money laundering trick they knew. The investigation resulted in nearly 100 drug traffickers, money launderers and bankers being arrested. The scandal made the headlines for years as everyone, including governments, reeled from the shock that one of the world's largest banks was inextricably intertwined with some of the world's most toxic individuals. Shortly afterwards, death threats forced me and my family to go into hiding.

While preparing to testify in the resulting criminal trials in the United States and Europe, I noticed an unfamiliar face at the US Customs office in Tampa. A young student from London had been given a once-in-a-life time opportunity to study our work in pursuit of his university thesis. My stints in the office were short and guarded, so I observed him only from a distance. That student was Stephen Platt. Twenty-three years later, I met him and realised that he was the student I had seen in Tampa all those years before. His decision to pursue a career in law and financial crime prevention in particular was, it transpires, strongly influenced by the BCCI case. I am grateful for that because his journey since has been remarkable. It has imbued him with a deep expertise of the criminal vulnerabilities of financial services in both on – and offshore financial centres. He is now justifiably regarded as one of the world's leading practitioners in the field, trusted by governments and regulators alike to undertake highly sensitive investigations which are often systemically important to the jurisdictions concerned.

In *Criminal Capital*, Stephen has given us an invaluable gift. He catapults the reader's knowledge about the methods used by criminals to commit crimes and launder their proceeds with the help of the finance industry. He examines a range of different predicate crime types and explains how they generate vast fortunes that are retained by criminals who exercise enormous leverage over banks and sometimes the jurisdictions in which they operate. Guiding the reader through some of the biggest bank laundering scandals of the past decade he considers why money laundering is causally linked to a range of other harmful behaviours in finance, including excessive risk taking, mis-selling and rate rigging.

This is a well-researched and powerful book. It should be a required reading for compliance professionals in finance as well as policymakers charged with implementing meaningful reform of the banking industry.

Robert Mazur
Former US Federal Agent
Author of *The Infiltrator*

# PREFACE

For much of the last 20 years, I have sifted through thousands of files relating to hundreds of relationships involving financial institutions in different parts of the world that have either facilitated crimes or laundered the proceeds of crimes on behalf of customers. I have tried to maintain a balanced perspective, recognising that many financial institutions are committed to the prevention of illegal activity and not its facilitation. Yet, my experience, synthesized with the ever-expanding list of financial institutions embroiled in scandalous conduct, has persuaded me that change is required. I do not subscribe to the view that there is an innate toxicity at the heart of the financial services industry but I do believe the industry needs to take tougher action to address its susceptibility to the facilitation of crime and the laundering of its proceeds and that to do so meaningfully it must recalibrate its values. To encourage it, prosecutors and regulators must begin to wield bigger sticks.

My motivation in writing this book is to inform both the professional and lay reader about the excesses of the financial services community by cutting through industry jargon and looking at abusive products, services, arrangements and relationships for what they really are. I attempt to boil down what appear to be highly complex concepts into basic digestible components, and to analyse different predicate crime types and the ways in which the financial services industry helps in their commission and launders the proceeds generated by them.

Client confidentiality is non-negotiable. I reveal nothing about particular clients or matters that I have been called upon to consider. Instead, I draw upon what I have observed over the course of my career to illustrate, through fictitious scenarios, the vulnerabilities of the financial services sector to criminal abuse in the hope that they will serve the dual purpose of helping the industry take more effective preventative action whilst also assisting the authorities to hold the industry to greater account.

*Stephen Platt*
*July 2014*

# ACKNOWLEDGEMENTS

This book is the product of the collective efforts of a number of colleagues to whom I am indebted: my editor Pete Baker for his guidance; Colleen and Charlotte for their research and attention to detail; Tom for keeping the home fires burning and Bob for the Foreword. My career was made possible only because of the sacrifices of my loving parents. Finally, thanks to my wife without whose love and support this book would have remained a fanciful notion.

# 1

# HARMFUL PRACTICES

Risk is synonymous with banking. Every loan and refinancing arrangement is an exercise in risk management undertaken by banks in the knowledge that without risk there can be no reward and that there are as many dangers in not taking enough risk as there are in taking too much.

In recent years, the fact and consequences of excessive risk taking by banks has been thrust into the spotlight – and rightly so. As the 2008 banking crisis revealed, the systemically important nature of large banks and the interconnectivity between them, markets, and governments had created a situation in which some financial institutions were crippled as a result of excessive risk taking. Yet, these institutions were seen as 'too big to fail' – that is to say, their collapse might have risked catastrophe, not only for their own customers, but for the entire international financial system and all that depends upon it.

A degree of risk taking by banks is, however, necessary for the continued health of the global economy. Businesses require capital in order to start up and to expand, much of which is drawn from bank lending. Individuals benefit from access to finance for house purchases and from income accruing to their pensions from investments in bank stocks. And national treasuries benefit from the taxation of bank profits (at least when they are not bailing the banks out). In short then, public interest demands that banks take risks, but not so much risk that taxpayers have to foot the bill.

Recognition of the stake that society has in the behaviour of banks is only one reason why there is now a strong public interest in the way financial institutions take and manage risk. Before 2008 I had formed the view that some of the behaviours of the financial services industry were contrary to the public interest, and not only because of an unhealthy general approach to risk taking. Two further crucial, but underrated, reasons stood out, both of which were ultimately linked to excessive risk taking: the role of the industry in laundering the proceeds of crime, and the role of the industry in the facilitation of crime itself. Extreme risk taking, along with other damaging activities such as product mis-selling and rate fixing, have dominated public discourse since 2008, whilst money laundering and the associated facilitation of criminal activity by financial institutions have been relegated to a less prominent position. There has, in addition, been scant recognition of the commonality of causes lurking beneath all these types of misconduct, an understanding of which is essential to changing attitudes and reform.

Money laundering and the facilitation of crime by financial institutions are two of the great evils of our age. They enable drug dealing, human trafficking, tax evasion, corrupt payments, and the commission of acts of terrorism all over the world. Laundering and facilitation lie behind the infliction of misery and suffering on countless millions of people, and allow the perpetrators to get away with and retain the proceeds of their crimes. Very few bankers knowingly assist such people (albeit there are some notable exceptions); the vast majority would be aghast if confronted with the results of the abuse of their institutions by criminals. The fact that such abuse is more likely to result from negligence on the part of the banks than from a deliberate policy to facilitate crime and launder money ultimately, however, matters little – the end effect is much the same.

This is not a book about how to 'fix' the finance industry in a broad sense. Rather, it seeks to advance three propositions. First, that there are multiple common causal factors behind reckless risk taking, various forms of harmful behaviours, and the facilitation of crime and money laundering by financial institutions. Second, that policy-makers and bankers need to study all of those related causes before shaping responses to the 2008 financial crisis, in particular those conduct types that indicate the most reckless disregard for the law. Thus far they have failed to do so. Third, that the traditional model of money laundering – which continues to form the bedrock of the industry's attempts to prevent financial crime – is flawed; this has resulted in a great deal of avoidable harm caused by financial institutions failing to detect money laundering and the facilitation of crime because they were not looking for it in the right places. A new model is needed, which this book proposes.

The industry is a sick patient whose symptoms range from excessive risk taking, rate fixing, and mis-selling financial products to breaching sanctions laws, laundering money, and facilitating crime. These harms are all given cursory examination in this chapter, but it is money laundering and the facilitation of crime – the most heinous symptoms of the industry's malady – that the majority of this book is devoted to.

## EXCESSIVE RISK TAKING

It is widely acknowledged that reckless risk taking was key among a nexus of factors that precipitated the financial crisis in 2008. The report published by the US Senate Permanent Subcommittee on Investigations in 2011, drawing from millions of pages of documents and numerous interviews, examined the causes of the collapse, placing its origins in: 'high risk lending by U.S. financial institutions; regulatory failures; inflated credit ratings; and high risk, poor quality financial products designed and sold by some investment banks'.[1] The central role of risk taking in the triggering of the downturn becomes all the more clear when we consider the use of the word 'risk' 1,200 times throughout the report's 639 pages.

The cumulative consequences of excessive risk taking manifested themselves most dramatically in the collapse of Lehman Brothers and the UK government bailouts of Northern Rock, Royal Bank of Scotland, and HBOS shortly thereafter. Despite all of the macroeconomic contributing factors including the asymmetry between the capital deficits of the West and the surpluses in emerging markets, the crisis at its core is a tale of capital and liquidity indiscipline and risk taking on an epic scale. Banks had leveraged their capital bases so highly that even small movements in the value of their underlying assets could have catastrophic consequences. By the time that Lehman Brothers filed for Chapter 11 bankruptcy protection on 15 September 2008, its leverage ratios were sky high; with its assets taking a tumble in value, so followed the rest of the bank. Lehman's own reporting to the Securities and Exchange Commission showed that towards the end of 2007, the bank's leverage ratio (a figure which pits assets against owner equity) was 30.7:1. This ratio was a steady increase on previous years – 26.2:1 in 2006, 24.4:1 in 2005, 23.9:1 in 2004 – and exposed the bank to extraordinary vulnerabilities, especially in the housing-related market where it had a substantial portfolio of mortgage-backed securities.

To the uninitiated, the world of packaged mortgages, collateralised debt obligations (CDOs), and credit default swaps (CDSs) seems impenetrable. In fact, if we ignore the self-serving investment banking jargon the products involved are relatively straightforward and, pre-2008, many of them essentially involved banks taking a punt on whether or not home-owning members of the public would meet their mortgage repayments.

CDOs gained notoriety from the financial crisis, and they even garner a fleeting mention in Martin Scorsese's 2013 film *The Wolf of Wall Street*. The principle behind them is simple: CDOs are forms of security against certain kinds of debts that can be traded. Owners of and investors in CDOs are entitled to receive income arising from the repayment of the loans underlying the security. In the run up to the crisis, banks lent money to borrowers and then sold the ownership of the right to receive the repayments to third parties in the form of CDOs. Because the lending banks were able to offload the mortgages through the sale of CDOs, they had little interest in whether the loans were going to be repaid. As a result, they lent recklessly, including to borrowers with little ability to repay (referred to as 'subprime'). This system incentivised banks to lend as much money to as many borrowers as possible, paying little heed as to whether or not mortgage repayments could be met.

Recognising that for there to be an active and continuing market in CDOs, they had to sell AND buy CDOs, the banks which were engaged in the origination of the loans and the structure and sale of CDOs also bought CDOs from other lenders thereby merrily engaging in a game of pass the parcel with ticking time bombs.

CDOs were supplemented by CDSs. A CDS is akin to an insurance policy, whereby the seller of a CDO is obliged to compensate the buyer in the event of a default in the underlying loans. Investors in CDOs bought CDSs to hedge against the risk of default by the home-loan borrowers underpinning the CDOs. Speculators (including banks) with no interest in the underlying loans began to buy CDSs as a means of betting on whether those loans would be repaid.

Several banks structured and sold CDOs for the express purpose of buying CDSs to bet against them, assuming (rightly as it turned out) that borrowers would fail to repay their loans. Banks were actually creating and selling securities so that they could profit by betting that they were worthless. When the US housing bubble burst the party came to an abrupt end, and sellers of the CDSs were left with a very serious hangover. In some cases, chief among them American International Group (AIG), they were so undermined they either went bust or required government bailouts. In a nutshell, the wheeling and dealing of these products led to massive increases in national deficits and a global economic downturn.

You may well wonder how CDOs and CDSs fit into the high street banking landscape? The answer is of course that they bear very little relation to the traditional model of borrowing from depositors and lending to homeowners but, since the 1990s, significant profits have been generated from these more exotic investment banking activities that allowed the lunatics to take over the asylum. Just as nobody at Barings condescended to ask how Nick Leeson was generating such enormous profits out in Singapore over a decade earlier, so bank directors and risk departments, as well as other market participants including the lawyers who structured the instruments and the accountants who audited them, seemed blind to whether the CDO/CDS merry-go-round had any sound basis in logic. Bank of America paid the steepest price yet for alleged behaviour of this kind after federal prosecutors and state attorney generals said that two of its divisions knowingly misrepresented the toxicity of mortgage-backed securities and other financial products to investors and the US government in the run-up to the financial crisis. In August 2014 it agreed a $16.6 billion civil settlement to resolve the accusations, the largest fine of its kind in the history of the United States.

You would be forgiven for thinking that financial institutions took a long hard look at the weaknesses in their systems which laid such fertile ground for rampant – and ultimately toxic – risk taking. Alas, they did not. Barely four years after the collapse of Lehman Brothers, JP Morgan was accused of lax supervision and inadequate risk controls after it lost billions of dollars in bad trades involving our old friend the CDS. Former bank employee Bruno Iksil, who was nicknamed the 'London Whale', is at the centre of the debacle after taking bloated positions on credit derivatives markets, and leading a series of bets on whether or not financial instruments or entities would default. Before the extent of the losses was apparent, JP Morgan's CEO Jamie Dimon dismissed the matter as 'a complete tempest in a teapot'. He was forced to back-track when it became evident that the trades had incurred around $6 billion of losses. Dimon could have been speaking at the dawn of the 2008 crisis when he said that the bank's strategy in relation to the portfolio was 'flawed, complex, poorly reviewed, poorly executed, and poorly monitored'.[2] But this occurred four years *later* in a hindsight averse world where volatility and risk continued to prance about unchecked.

The fines paid to regulatory authorities as a consequence of the Whale trades reached $920 million in September 2013, in the scheme of things actually relatively little given that this figure only represents around 5% of the bank's 2012 record $21.3 billion net profit. Dimon also came away relatively unscathed: although he was given a financial slap across the wrists when his restricted stock options for 2012 decreased 54% to $10 million, that figure soared to $18.5 million for 2013. This is piled atop a fixed salary, which has teetered around the $1.5 million mark over the past few years.

## FIXING

Beyond the excessive risk taking gnawing away at the stability of the global financial system is a number of other practices that have eroded the public's trust in the banking sector, a stand-out case being the rigging of global benchmark rates. On the face of it, you may wonder what this has to do with money laundering and the facilitation of crime, but when we refocus the lens on the circumstances which give rise to these practices, striking family resemblances begin to emerge.

One of the best recent examples of banks rigging key market rates concerns LIBOR, the London Interbank Offered Rate, although its Euro and Tokyo counterparts (Euribor and Tibor) have themselves also become mired in manipulation controversies. LIBOR, which was established in the 1980s, is a benchmark rate of interest calculated through daily submissions of rates by banks with a significant presence in London. The banks are supposed to submit the actual interest rates they are paying, or would expect to pay, for borrowing from other banks by answering the following question daily: 'At what rate could you borrow funds, were you to do so by asking for and then accepting inter-bank offers in a reasonable market size just prior to 11 am?' (Elevenses is considered the 'most active part of the London business day'). The banks' submissions are 'trimmed'; some of the highest and lowest figures are removed and the rest are averaged. Whilst the resulting LIBOR rate – published to the market at 11.45 am – is not the rate at which banks actually lend to one another, it serves as an important bellwether of sentiment in the sense that if the banks feel bullish, they report a low rate and if they feel bearish they report a higher rate. Crucially, LIBOR is often relied upon as a reference rate for mortgages and student loans, and it is referenced by loan and financial contracts worth over $300 trillion. Consequently, any manipulation of the rate contaminates markets and impacts untold millions of consumers.

The LIBOR scandal erupted when it was revealed that banks were falsely inflating or deflating their submitted rates to give the impression that they were more creditworthy than they really were, or to profit from trades. Investigations have revealed significant fraud and collusion by LIBOR member banks connected to the rate submissions. Manipulation was facilitated by the fact that submissions require human judgement and expertise (rather than a sole reliance on automatically generated data) and have been, until recent reforms, largely 'self-policed'. The financial institutions submitting the rates were also inherently conflicted by virtue of their position as contributors to the rate, users of the rate, and participants in the market; a conflict ripe for exploitation.

Barclays was the first bank to settle with the authorities for LIBOR and Euribor rigging. In the US, it entered into an agreement with the Department of Justice to pay $160 million and was ordered to pay $200 million by the Commodity Futures Trading Commission, the US derivatives regulator. The UK's Financial Services Authority (now the Financial Conduct Authority) swung into action and imposed a financial penalty on Barclays of £59.5 million – discounted from £85 million following early settlement – and the scandal very publicly claimed the scalps of Marcus Agius, chairman of Barclays Bank, and Bob Diamond, its chief executive. Among numerous of the FSA's findings was the chummy persuasion of one Barclays trader to an external trader in respect of a three-month US dollar LIBOR: 'duuuude... whats up with ur guys 34.5 3m fix... tell him to get it up!!' The external trader responded: 'ill talk to him right away'.[3] The transcripts were probably not what Barclays had in mind when an independent review of LIBOR recommended that records be kept relating to the submission process, especially those between submitting parties and internal and external traders.

RBS and its subsidiary company RBS Securities Japan (RBSSJ) have also been embroiled in the scandal. The so-called 'Statement of Facts' forming part of the 'deferred prosecution agreement' (DPA) (when a party voluntarily admits to certain facts but does not plead guilty to any charge, nor carry any conviction) entered into by RBS with the US authorities said that between 2006 and 2010, certain RBSSJ derivatives traders had schemed to 'defraud RBS's counterparties by secretly attempting to manipulate and manipulating yen LIBOR'.[4] The traders managed to influence the published yen LIBOR rates 'by acting in concert with RBS's Yen LIBOR submitters to provide false and misleading submissions to Thomson Reuters, which were then incorporated into the calculation of the final published rates'. The assessment of the RBSSJ traders' behaviour in the DPA, serving as a general description of a host of misdemeanours perpetrated within banking walls, simply stated that the traders 'engaged in this conduct in order to benefit their trading positions, and thereby increase their profits and decrease their losses'. The DPA is peppered with astonishing snippets of electronic conversations between traders. In one of these, UBS derivatives trader Tom Hayes asked a RBS yen derivatives trader: 'can you do me a huge favour, can you ask your cash guys to set 1m libor low for the next few days... i'll return the favour as when you need it... as long as it doesn't go against your fixes... have 30m jpy of fixes over the next few days'. Hayes chirpily salutes the trader as he is shutting down: 'off home dreaming of a low 1m libor!'

The penalties keep rolling in. Japanese unit RBSSJ pleaded guilty to a count of wire fraud for its role in manipulating yen LIBOR rates and agreed to pay a $50 million fine. Its parent RBS was fined £87.5 million by the FSA for 'widespread' misconduct comprising 'at least 219 requests for inappropriate submissions' and 'an unquantifiable number of oral requests'.[5] The Commodity Futures Trading Commission hit RBS with a $325 million fine, and the Department of Justice demanded $150 million. RBS was also fined a further €391 million at the end of 2013 following a European Commission investigation into rate rigging.

In 2014 RBS reported its largest loss since the government bailout and set aside £3 billion to cover litigation and consumer claims. As a consequence of RBS' very public dressing downs, the hotly contested question of banker bonuses lingers at the forefront of consumers' scrutiny of the bank.

The LIBOR drama has seen, and will yet see, many twists and turns. In 2013, a 'substantial portion' of the claims made in a highly publicised class action suit filed by the City of Baltimore against a number of banks involved in LIBOR manipulation was dismissed by the US courts, although the law firm representing the city proceeded to test the waters in the UK. Hausfeld LLP had some success in representing the home care operator Guardian Care Homes in a £70 million suit against Barclays linked to LIBOR rigging, which was settled in April 2014. The Serious Fraud Office (SFO), the Financial Conduct Authority (FCA), and US authorities are jointly conducting an ongoing investigation into LIBOR rate manipulation. In the UK, criminal proceedings have been issued against a former UBS and Citigroup trader, as well as ex-employees of Barclays Bank, RP Martin Holdings, and ICAP Plc. Not guilty pleas have so far been entered for the former UBS and Citigroup trader and the two former RP Martin brokers, with trials due to commence in 2015.

It is startling to think that, in the words of the independent Wheatley Review into LIBOR, 'neither submitting to LIBOR, nor administering LIBOR, is a regulated activity under FSMA [Financial Services and Markets Act 2000, which gave the FSA statutory powers]'.[6] The report explains that the FSA actions proceeded 'on the basis of the connection between LIBOR submitting and other regulated activities, and there is no directly applicable specific regulatory regime covering these activities'. In summary, the submissions of key rates in global financial markets, which are referenced in well over $300 trillion of financial instruments worldwide, were not specifically regulated. It is rather perplexing to think that only now, as a finding of the review, is there 'a strong case to support making submitting to LIBOR a regulated activity'. Regulators dragging their heels in enforcing effective oversight in certain corners of the financial industry is but one of the contributing factors to banks forging ahead with their risky and opportunistic approach to doing business.

LIBOR has also not been immune from the pervasive problem of conflicts of interest. As 'the lobby organisation for the same submitting banks that they nominally oversee', the Wheatley Review deemed the British Bankers Association (BBA) critically conflicted and, as a result, the body that formerly administered LIBOR submissions was replaced by bench-mark oversight body ICE Benchmark Association in early 2014 after a public tender.

Andrew Lo, professor of finance at MIT, has said that the LIBOR scandal 'dwarfs by orders of magnitude any financial scams in the history of mar-kets' but a sell-by date is hot on the heels of his proclamation as investigators are now lifting the lid on foreign-exchange benchmarks, where allegations of manipulation are 'every bit as bad as they have been with LIBOR', according to the FCA's CEO speaking in February 2014.[7] In yet a further example of the financial industry's hosting of harmful activities, traders from several banks have been accused of colluding to rig forex market rates in communications via online message groups, where they swaggered about as members of the 'Bandits' Club', 'The Cartel', and 'The Mafia' and exchanged information on each other's client orders.[8] Investment banks have actually been banning certain traders from using these types of chatrooms in an effort to curb the cowboy antics but the extent of redress will only be apparent in the next year or two when regulators establish the degree of the manipulation. Heads have already started to roll – the *Financial Times* reported that more than 18 trad-ers at nine banks had been suspended, placed on leave, or sacked.[9]

The conclusions that one may reach on rate rigging – the conflicts of interest, and the roles of the regulators and central banks – are, of course, not just applicable to this domain of activity. As I proceed, it will become evident that the failures of the financial system in identifying and prevent-ing such large-scale manipulation are caused by lapses which affect every-thing behind industry doors.

## MIS-SELLING

A further recent scandal to erupt with its own distinct flavour is the mis-selling of Payment Protection Insurance (PPI) policies by numerous UK high street banks since 2000 – the latest and most damaging example of banks mis-selling products for many years. PPI mis-selling has involved some of the biggest players in the UK banking sector including Lloyds TSB, Barclays, HSBC, Santander, RBS, and the Nationwide Building Society. The banks have together paid £13.3 billion in compensation since January 2011, with the figure set to double. Despite the *Which?* accolade of the 'biggest financial mis-selling scandal of all time', the PPI affair has been somewhat overshadowed by other City misdemeanours, which John Lanchester attri-butes to there being 'something inherently unsexy about the whole idea of PPI, from the numbing acronym to the fact that the whole idea of a scandal about insurance payments seems dreary and lowscale'.[10] Nonetheless, this and other types of mis-selling vie for the top spots in harmful behaviours in the finance sector, whose roots are entangled with those propping up opportunities to launder money and the industry's facilitation of crime.

The PPI misconduct entailed the sale of insurance policies alongside mortgages, loans, and credit cards that were meant to repay people's borrowings if they suffered a change in circumstances either through loss of income or illness. PPI policies were expensive, ineffective, and inefficient and were mis-sold to people unable to claim on them. The UK independent body Money Advice Service, funded via a levy the FCA raises from regulated financial services firms, enumerates a number of failings on the part of the banks and financial companies touting the policies, including consumers being told the policies were compulsory and firms omitting to question whether the purchaser had other insurance to cover the loan. Pressure tactics were employed by PPI sales staff, one of whom was recorded persuading a potential applicant in the following terms: 'personally, if I'm honest with you, in your circumstances taking out the protection is definitely the right thing to do'.[11] The UK's Financial Ombudsman saw differently and ordered the business to make good.

Lloyds Bank has fared particularly badly throughout the scandal. In May 2011 – after withdrawing from a High Court tussle to avoid paying certain PPI compensation claims – it announced that it would be setting aside £3.2 billion in claim payments. The costs have since spiralled. In February 2014, the bank announced that it would increase its estimate – for the seventh time – for PPI compensation claims to just under £10 billion. Lloyds' woes do not end there. In February 2013, three group entities were fined a total of £4.3 million by the FSA for delaying the payment of PPI claims to 140,000 customers. As a direct result of the PPI debacle it was announced in early 2013 that the bank was clawing back some of the former CEO's bonus: Eric Daniels' £1.45 million in added extras for 2010 was later reduced to £300,000. Adding insult to injury, a *BBC* investigation later claimed that Lloyds had unfairly short changed some of its claimants by applying an 'alternative redress' provision, allowing it to assume that consumers might have bought cheaper policies elsewhere had they not been sold Lloyds' flawed versions.[12]

Again, mis-selling may, on the face of it, seem entirely distinct from the unrestrained trades in risky derivatives, or the ability of a Japan-based trader to nudge a colleague into manipulating benchmark rates. But underlying all of these practices runs a common theme of conflict and poor oversight coupled with a set of shared attitudes which serve to undermine the stability of the whole financial system. Among them the fact that the bigger a bank is, the more able it is to stump up even the very largest of these regulatory fines as their balance sheets can absorb even severe shocks. Criminal redress in all of these cases is glaringly absent. It is precisely these factors, along with many others to be further detailed, that have permitted money laundering, the facilitation of crime, tax evasion, and sanctions busting to take place. As a consequence, flawed methodologies are being applied in the detection and prevention of crime, to lamentable effect. Until these commonalities are fully explored and recognised, and new ways of thinking are promulgated, the criminal abuse of financial services will continue to outrun its pursuers.

## SANCTIONS EVASION

Only ever sporadically reported, as and when a bank is busted for it, a number of household name institutions – UBS, Lloyds Bank, and Credit Suisse among them – have historically provided financial services to people or companies who have been subject to sanctions, particularly targets of the US sanctioning regime. BNP Paribas was most recently exposed for this kind of behaviour, and entered into a multi-billion dollar agreement in June 2014, one the largest settlements of its kind. Whilst not a predicate crime of the same type described in successive chapters (drug trafficking, terrorist financing, and so forth), sanctions evasion warrants elaboration in view of the particularly substantial sums which have been collected in fines and settlements from banks, and the increasingly serious ramifications for banks participating in this activity, highlighted, in particular, in the case of BNP Paribas.

Sanctions have for some time been utilised as a tool by the international community to apply pressure on rogue states or identified organisations and individuals largely as a means of influencing behaviour. The current UN sanctions against Iran and North Korea have as a key objective an attempt to prevent those countries from obtaining or increasing their stocks of nuclear weapons. The 2014 sanctions imposed against close political allies of Vladimir Putin are intended to exert pressure on Russia to reverse its annexation of Crimea. The sanctions programmes against Al Qaeda, the Taliban, Islamic State (IS), and related persons are designed to stem the flow of finances that might otherwise be used for terrorist purposes.

Whilst the bulk of the sanctions imposed by most EU countries (including the UK) are domesticated from UN and EU measures, the US both domesticates UN sanctions and formulates many of its own sanctions unilaterally. Its controversial ongoing sanctions against Cuba and Cuban nationals are examples of the latter. All US sanctions are policed by the Office of

Foreign Assets Control (OFAC), itself a department of the US Treasury that is situated, as if the extent of its power need be emphasised, next door to the White House.

All US legal and natural persons, wherever in the world they find themselves, are required by law to observe US sanctions. All US dollar wire transfers require the involvement of a US person (in the form of a US clearing bank), even if the transfer is between two banks which are not US persons. As the US dollar remains the world's *de facto* reserve currency this poses a significant logistical difficulty for non-US financial institutions wishing to conduct business with countries, organisations, or persons sanctioned by the US. In response, several non-US banks devised methods by which they could continue to transact in dollars on behalf of US-sanctioned customers or counterparties by falsifying the payment messages that were sent to US clearing banks or taking fraudulent steps to conceal transactions. These methods had the effect of preventing the US banks from being able to identify transactions involving US-sanctioned parties so that the transactions proceeded instead of being blocked or frozen.

Identified instances of this type of sanctions evasion date back to at least the 1980s, although US investigations into the activity only really span the past decade or so. UBS was one of the first in what has become a roll call of major international banks to settle with the US authorities over the practice, when it was handed a civil monetary penalty of $100 million by the Federal Reserve Bank of New York in 2004. UBS was accused of 'deceptive conduct' after engaging in dollar transactions with OFAC-sanctioned countries as part of the Reserve's so-called Extended Custodial Inventory (ECI) programme.[13]

The ECI programme was introduced in the mid-1990s to support the introduction and distribution of the newly designed $100 note with its enhanced anti-counterfeiting measures, such as a new watermark and optically variable ink. The programme initially assisted in the distribution of the notes to Europe and former Soviet Union countries, and subsequently evolved into a mechanism whereby banks were granted 'ECI facilities' to promote international dollar circulation. Among other responsibilities, the banks holding the facility were charged with removing old notes from circulation and reporting counterfeit bills.

In his testimony before a House of Representatives committee, the Federal Reserve's general counsel, Thomas Baxter, recounted the trajectory of the UBS investigation. He recalled how *The New York Times* had reported that the US army had stumbled upon a stash of around $650 million in $100 bills in one of Saddam Hussein's palaces in Baghdad. Upon the discovery that some of the cash had originated from the Federal Reserve, an investigation was set in motion to track the movement of some of the notes via serial number. The then Swiss regulator – the EBK – also threw its weight behind the investigation, although this would ultimately only have limited consequences for any malefactors identified given that the EBK had no authority to impose its own monetary penalties (its successor, FINMA, is in the same position today).

The investigation unearthed how UBS had hidden US dollar transactions with OFAC-sanctioned Iran, Cuba, Libya, and the former Yugoslavia (although not directly with Iraq) during its participation in the ECI programme. Before the extent and nature of the concealment became apparent, UBS brushed off the incident citing a mere slip-up; that certain transactions had been 'done by mistake'. The Federal Reserve Bank found differently, reporting that UBS staff had taken 'affirmative steps to conceal these transactions', including 'falsifying the monthly U.S. dollar transaction reports that it was contractually obligated to submit'.

In addition to the $100 million fine levied in the States, the EBK gave UBS a public ticking-off. In the absence of any monetary penalty or legal consequences on home soil, UBS was put on the Swiss naughty step, but none of its toys were confiscated. The Federal Reserve was nonetheless eager to congratulate the EBK on its reproach, saying: 'A Swiss governmental reprimand to the largest bank in Switzerland is, to our knowledge, unprecedented in Swiss history. The EBK took that action, in no small measure, to demonstrate that it would not tolerate deception any more than we would'.

Differing slightly from this type of deception, the practice of specifically falsifying payment messages involving a sanctioned party is referred to as 'stripping'. In recent years, several banks have between them been fined billions of dollars by the US authorities for stripping activity. Various members of the 'Strip club' will be paraded in Chapter 9 to demonstrate, in particular, the extent to which practices such as sanctions evasion can become institutionally acceptable. But, to give a taste, the cases involving Lloyds and Credit Suisse are good introductory examples of this kind of activity.

Lloyds was stung when a US investigation revealed how it had violated OFAC regulations and US law by falsifying SWIFT dollar payment messages that involved OFAC-sanctioned parties (namely entities in Iran, Sudan, and Libya) between the mid-1990s and 2007. These SWIFT (the Society for Worldwide Interbank Financial Telecommunication) messages are used by financial institutions to send and receive payment instructions to one another and are an essential component in the transfer of money from one country to another.

The 2009 DPA entered into by Lloyds described how the bank had admitted to 'serious and systemic misconduct' having removed 'material data from payment messages in order to avoid detection of the involvement of OFAC-sanctioned parties by filters used by U.S. depository institutions'.[14] This behaviour caused Lloyds' US correspondent banks to process payments that may otherwise have been prohibited.

The DPA described in some detail the mechanisms behind the stripping activity, revealing how Lloyds payment processors would 'physically mark up the printed payment instruction to show what information should be changed, including crossing out any reference to Iranian banks or other sanctioned entities and striking a line through Field 52 of the SWIFT payment instruction [identifying the originating bank]'. The behaviour appeared to be fairly routine, even referred to as 'normal' in one internal memo; the investigation found that Lloyds also 'dedicated specific payment processors to focus exclusively on reviewing and amending, if necessary, SWIFT messages pertaining to USD payments for the UK [subsidiaries/branches of] Iranian Banks'.

Amid internal debates over whether Lloyds, as a UK entity, was subject to OFAC regulations, the bank encouraged its Iranian clients to go ahead and pull the wool over Uncle Sam's eyes themselves. Lloyds personnel met with Iranian banks and gave instructions on how to navigate the OFAC filters undetected. Legal filings recount that Iranian banks were taught to populate the relevant SWIFT field for originating bank information with a 'dot, hyphen or another symbol' rather than leave it blank in order to cheat the filters.

The DPA concludes that between 2002 and 2004, Lloyds processed around $300 million on behalf of Iranian banks in London, which were sent to US banks for processing; between 2002 and 2007 it processed $20 million on behalf of Sudanese bank customers through US correspondent banks; and between 2002 and 2004 it processed around $20 million on behalf of a Libyan customer through US financial institutions. Lloyds agreed to forfeit $350 million for the misconduct, at the time the largest ever penalty for violations of US sanctions.

The matter was aired in a House of Commons debate in February 2009. The financial secretary to the UK Treasury, Stephen Timms, responded to questions over why there had been no UK prosecutions in light of the US investigation. As he conveyed his understanding of the case, Timms highlighted the inherent tensions of unilateral sanctions:

we can prosecute only for breaches of UK law, and not for breaches of US law. As I have set out, the US case against Lloyds TSB concerns breaches of US sanctions. I certainly have not seen evidence of breaches of UK law in this case. I have seen no evidence of breaches of international sanctions, money laundering rules or terrorist finance rules. That is consistent with the findings in the US case, which is specific to breaches of US sanctions.[15]

By way of further example, also in 2009, Credit Suisse entered into a $536 million settlement following almost identical allegations of stripping out references to Iran, Sudan, Libya, Burma, Cuba, and Charles Taylor's Liberian regime. These transactions had originated in the UK and Switzerland, rather than the US, but the fact that they involved US banks was all that was needed to bring Credit Suisse under OFAC's remit. Particularly concerning were the allegations that in 1998, Credit Suisse had issued a document to Iranian clients explaining how best to avoid sanctions filters, and that the bank employed a system whereby all payments to Iran were manually reviewed before being sent to the US.[16] It was clear that these steps were not innocent mistakes borne of poor compliance and ignorance but deliberate actions, intended to trick the system and avoid the penalties that OFAC would otherwise impose.

It is no coincidence that most of the banks hauled up for breaching US sanctions regimes also appear on the long list of financial institutions which have been involved in money laundering and the closely related act of facilitating crime. Money laundering and the finance industry's approach to it will be explored in further detail in the next chapter, but at this stage suffice it to say that it is conduct that is treated in most countries as a serious criminal offence, sufficiently serious in fact that it is also usually a criminal offence for financial institutions to fail to have in place adequate measures to forestall it.

## MONEY LAUNDERING

There are numerous definitions of money laundering, most of them unhelpful. Essentially the conduct generally involves financial institutions being engaged in arrangements with customers that have the effect of facilitating the retention or control by the customers of criminal property. Such arrangements frequently have the added benefit (from the customer's perspective) of allowing them to conceal or disguise the criminal origin of property by changing the property from its original form (such as cash) into other forms of financial instruments (loan proceeds for example). Two of the better known laundering scandals of recent years involve Amex and HSBC.

In 2007, American Express Bank International, usually known as Amex, signed a DPA with the US in relation to breaches of anti-money laundering compliance and procedures.[17] It was said that the bank had wilfully violated the anti-money laundering requirements of the Bank Secrecy Act between 1999 and 2004, and approximately $55 million were believed to have passed through Amex accounts – a sum which was understood to have its origin in drug trafficking and laundered via the trade-based money laundering system known as the 'black market peso exchange' (BMPE). It was revealed that undercover agents who had infiltrated Colombian organisations were able to launder money through Amex. Furthermore, Amex operated a number of accounts that were controlled by apparently legitimate accounts of South American businesses but were actually held in the names of offshore shell companies, and used to process high risk 'parallel currency exchange market' transactions. Amex systematically ignored the classic signs of account abuse: the accounts themselves were often held by specific types of third party companies for which there was no lawful rationale; there were numerous wire transfers from persons that did not appear to be related to the holder or the holder's stated business. The risk analysis system was inadequate, particularly given its location in Florida, known as a high-risk area for drug dealing, and insufficient attention had been paid to finding out who really held the accounts and where the money was coming from. Amex had been the subject of a settlement agreement in 1994 with the US Department of Justice and a substantial financial penalty following similar accusations but had failed to fully remedy the weaknesses.

In 2012, the US Senate Permanent Subcommittee on Investigations recounted similarly troubling failures in anti-money laundering procedures at HSBC.[18] The subcommittee's report charted the history of HSBC's Mexican operations, saying that concerns had been raised back in 2004 when an HSBC group compliance officer asked his Mexican colleagues to explain a 'booming business' the unit was doing in travellers cheques. In the first three quarters of that year, HSBC Mexico (HBMX) had sold over $110 million's worth, a figure which represented a third of the entire group's global travellers cheque business. In 2008, Mexico's financial intelligence unit informed HBMX that in the 'majority of the most relevant ML [money laundering] cases' it had investigated in 2007 'many transactions were carried out through HSBC'. In 2008, HSBC's global head of compliance, David Bagley, recorded an exit interview with HBMX's 'anti-money laundering' director, Leopoldo Barroso. Bagley recounted that he had been told by Barroso that 'it was only a matter of time before the bank faced criminal sanctions' and was alerted to allegations that '60% to 70% of laundered proceeds in Mexico went through HBMX'. In October 2010, HSBC was slapped with a cease and desist order by the US regulator, the Office of the Comptroller of the Currency (OCC), who demanded that HSBC improve its anti-money laundering systems. As a Senate subcommittee 'case study', HSBC's internal controls were microscopically dissected, and the bank's failings in Mexico and elsewhere resulted in a settlement of $1.9 billion.

Money laundering is a 'downstream' activity in the sense that it occurs subsequent to the commission of predicate crimes which generate the property that is then laundered. For this reason most banks focus a great deal of attention on the due diligence of where funds derive from and who they belong to in order to avoid handling the proceeds of crime. However, the vulnerability of the finance industry also extends upstream where some of the products and services can be utilised by criminals in the commission of the predicate crimes, generating criminal property at the same time. Where this occurs, financial institutions are in the alarming position of facilitating crimes as well as laundering the resulting proceeds.

## FACILITATION

Unlike money laundering, there is no universally recognisable offence of facilitating crime. Different countries each have discrete offences into which the facts of each act of facilitation may or may not be capable of being shoehorned. Facilitation is certainly not a touchstone issue in the way that money laundering has become since 9/11. This is perverse. If money laundering is simply a symptom or consequence of underlying crimes, then why not place as much or an even greater emphasis on preventing the finance industry from facilitating crime? The anomaly results from a generally poor appreciation of policy-makers on the important role that financial institutions often play in assisting criminals to commit crime. There is a fundamental misconception that the finance industry's involvement post-dates the generation of criminal property. In consequence, little regard is paid to the management of facilitation risk within the industry even though in practice most bankers would likely be more horrified at facilitating a crime than in laundering the proceeds of it.

An excellent recent example of facilitation by a bank was the conduct that led to UBS agreeing in February 2009 to pay a fine of $780 million to the US government and entering into a DPA on a charge of conspiring to defraud the US by impeding the Internal Revenue Service (IRS), which is explored further in Chapter 10.[19] Similarly, in January 2013, Wegelin & Co, Switzerland's oldest private bank, decided to close down after pleading guilty to facilitating US tax evasion. A US district judge ordered Wegelin & Co to pay $57.8 million following allegations that it had allowed clients to hide a total of $1.2 billion from the IRS.[20] It was also alleged that the Swiss bank had actively sought out former UBS clients after a probe into UBS became public in 2008.

Acts of facilitation by financial institutions are not limited purely to tax evasion. Participation in relationships involving the payment of bribes are also common as are the administration of structures utilised in offences such as market manipulation. Occasionally, banks find themselves inadvertently contributing to major frauds such as Ponzi schemes by failing to have in place sufficiently robust controls. The DPA entered into by JP Morgan in January 2014 relating to its involvement in the Bernard Madoff fraud provides a prime example of the latter.[21] For over 30 years Madoff ran a massive Ponzi scheme promising investors that their money would be invested in securities. Contrary to those representations, it was rarely invested and was instead utilised to pay back other investors and to fund Madoff's lavish lifestyle. At the time of its collapse, Madoff Securities maintained over 4,000 investment advisory client accounts with a purported total value of $65 billion when in fact Madoff Securities had just over $300 million in total assets. According to the DPA, between 1986 and 2008 the Madoff Ponzi scheme was conducted 'almost exclusively through a demand deposit account and other linked cash and brokerage accounts held at JPMorgan Chase Bank, N.A.'. The DPA states that the bank suffered from systemic deficiencies which prevented it from adequately guarding against money laundering. The upshot of the bank's failures was an acceptance of responsibility and a stipulated forfeiture in the amount of $1.7 billion.

One of the most striking features of this canter through the banking industry's hall of shame is the involvement of many of the industry's largest players, strongly indicating that each of the different behaviours are symptoms of a common malady. There can surely be no coincidence that many of the banks that have been engaged in money laundering and sanctions stripping activity have also been engaged in fixing and mis-selling and were seriously undermined by the manner in which they exposed their balance sheets because of the excessive risk taking in the run up to 2008. It has been fascinating to observe the way in which the media has reported the issues and the public has calibrated its outrage to each of the different behaviours. Most of the attention has focused on reckless risk taking and a largely misconceived focus on bankers' bonuses. Mis-selling and fixing have attracted a fair degree of publicity though not to the same extent as excessive risk taking. Sanctions evasion, laundering, and facilitation have attracted the least publicity. Put simply, the degree of publicity and resulting opprobrium directed at the finance industry has been inversely proportionate to the toxicity of its conduct. Possibly that results from the notion of bankers as poker players being easier to comprehend than PPI, LIBOR, or laundering. It is true that laundering and facilitation methodologies can be very complex and are not always conducive to selling newspapers, but there is a danger that in the post-2008 crisis analysis, governments have shaped solutions designed to influence the future behaviour of banks without taking adequate account of those excesses that derive from the darkest recesses of the banking industry's psyche. Recognising how and why banks engage in the worst of their conduct, and overhauling the existing industry model for detecting money laundering in particular, have to be the starting point in shaping solutions for a better future for the industry and for the continuing protection of the public interest.

This book is UK and US-centric, largely because London and New York remain the twin epicentres of global financial markets, and Washington DC, much to the chagrin of the EU, is where the tone is set for global efforts to combat financial crime. Therefore, the bodies involved in policing, monitoring, regulating, prosecuting, and sanctioning outside of the UK and US will only be referenced in passing. The sprawling nature of investigations in the UK and US alone are in part due to the involvement of a substantial number of regulatory and legal authorities, with files doing the rounds, and separate but related probes splintering off throughout the process. Investigations can take years, cross borders, and involve the review of millions of documents.

The UK enforcement environment is sanguine by comparison with that of the US. The Treasury is ultimately responsible for the UK's financial system, which has vested regulatory powers in the independent Financial Conduct Authority. The FCA was formed in 2013 as one of two successor organisations to the Financial Services Authority, the other being the Prudential Regulation Authority (PRA), which is part of the Bank of England. The efficacy of regulators and lawmakers will be explored as we go on, but by way of an introductory theme, consider that the FSA was established in 1997 in the shadow of the Barings collapse, and following criticism that the Bank of England had failed to adequately regulate the UK's financial industry. The FCA was instituted following, you guessed it, criticism that the FSA had failed to adequately regulate the UK's financial industry. It was the 'watchdog that didn't bark' in the words of one *Guardian* journalist.[22] The Serious Fraud Office is another organ of state in the UK which is overseen by the UK attorney general and pursues cases of fraud, corruption, and bribery.

Various US national and state enforcement agencies hold the power to investigate and prosecute or impose regulatory censure. The environment is aggressive with distinct agencies often investigating the same facts simultaneously with a view to bringing discrete actions against offending banks. In New York, if a bank behaves badly it is not a question of whether it will be prosecuted but who will beat a path to its door to prosecute it first. As we will see throughout the following chapters, the penalty levels imposed on financial institutions by US agencies are swingeing. They outstrip the penalties imposed by any other country by several multiples. The US can and does apply its laws extraterritorially, much to the confusion and frustration of, among others, would-be sanctions busters. In consequence, the US authorities are unique in the world in having the capability to give major financial institutions pause. It is high time that other major international financial centres followed suit.

# 2

# MONEY LAUNDERING MODELS

In May 2013, the Costa Rican currency business Liberty Reserve was shut down after an investigation, spanning 17 countries, found that the company had laundered an alleged $6 billion of proceeds from an array of criminal activities, including drug trafficking, child pornography, credit card fraud, identity theft, computer hacking, and identity theft. One of Liberty Reserve's founders, Vladimir Kats, pleaded guilty to charges which carry a combined maximum sentence of 75 years. It is thought to be one of the largest ever cases of money laundering.[1]

This is a far cry from the position 30 years ago, when the offence of money laundering did not exist, and criminal property was laundered with impunity by criminals mindful only of their desire to avoid detection. Now, money laundering is universally regarded as an essential component of a successful criminal enterprise and as such is treated as a serious offence in many countries around the world.

Since the attacks on 11 September 2001 money laundering has become closely associated with terrorist financing. The term 'AML/CFT' (anti-money laundering and countering the financing of terrorism) is frequently employed by compliance staff when carrying out checks on customers for the purpose of detecting and preventing both. The two concepts are distinct to the extent that money laundering is concerned with the *origin* of the money, whilst terrorist financing is largely (though not exclusively) about the *destination* of the money.

The approach of the international community to both issues can be seen from the assessments of national legal frameworks on anti-money laundering and counter-terrorism financing conducted by supra-national bodies. These include the Organisation for Economic Co-operation and

Development's (OECD) Financial Action Task Force (FATF) and the Council of Europe body, Moneyval. FATF originally issued 40 'Recommendations' on countering money laundering, which were supplemented by nine Special Recommendations which mainly address terrorist financing; these global standards are endorsed by 36 member nations. Moneyval oversees the compliance of its member states not only with FATF's standards, but also with the terms of various UN conventions. Countries judged to be 'non-cooperative' in the global war on money laundering and terrorist financing are identified and coerced into taking action.

On one level then money laundering appears to be a poster child for international cooperation. However, the issue has also caused tension between those countries that have abided by the spirit of the rules by implementing robust money laundering laws and jurisdictions that have tackled money laundering superficially thereby creating arbitrage opportunities for financial institutions and their customers. The uneven playing field has been fully exploited by criminals.

The origins of money laundering are imprecise but we know that the activity began to develop on an industrial scale in the US in the middle part of the twentieth century as Mafia bosses recognised the need to demonstrate that their enormous pools of wealth had derived from 'legitimate' sources. Meyer Lansky, known as the 'Mob's accountant', developed a significant gambling empire that stretched across the US to Cuba. He was able to successfully utilise casinos and race tracks to place and launder criminal money for the Mob. More sophisticated methods involving financial institutions subsequently evolved as the financial services industry grew and globalised.

The criminalisation of money laundering occurred some decades later, again in the US. In an effort to shore up support from the American middle classes horrified at the devastation caused by drugs in the towns and cities across America, Ronald Reagan sponsored legislation in 1986 that made money laundering a federal crime. Even though the Bank Secrecy Act had since 1970 required the filing of reports designed to create a paper trail for currency transactions, the criminalisation of money laundering was a highly novel concept. The government for the first time effectively press ganged the financial services industry into helping it wage a war on drug trafficking by threatening prosecution and regulatory censure if banks did not play their full part. This was to be the thin end of a very thick wedge.

Given the global interconnectivity of financial services, the criminalisation of money laundering in only the US had limited impact, and in 1988 through the vehicle of the UN Convention against Illicit Traffic in Narcotic Drugs and Psychotropic Substances all signatory states committed to implement a range of measures including the criminalisation of behaviour that came universally to be referred to as 'money laundering'.

Less than a decade after the legislation on drug money laundering was introduced, governments realised the value of expanding the scope of money laundering laws beyond the proceeds of drug trafficking to encompass the proceeds of other crimes. The thinking was that if it was illegal to handle drug money why should it not be illegal to handle the proceeds of a bank robbery and other forms of crime? Countries did this by adapting the existing legal formulations of drug money laundering offences and applied them to wider definitions of criminal conduct. In the US, a long list of predicate crimes was used under the umbrella term 'specified unlawful activities'. Proceeds from any of the long list of crimes – including bribery, embezzlement, kidnapping, illegal gambling, and terrorist financing – became subject to money laundering legislation.

It was at this stage that certain countries formulated money laundering legislation which appeared effective but which in fact framed a narrower definition of criminality than applied in competitor jurisdictions. Some adopted 'dual criminality' models requiring conduct to be illegal both in the country where the laundering took place and in the country where the crime occurred. Switzerland and Singapore introduced euphemistically termed 'all crimes' legislation. This legislation in fact excluded from its ambit the proceeds of foreign tax evasion thereby attracting tax evaders who could no longer risk doing business in jurisdictions such as the UK and the Channel Islands, which had outlawed the laundering of the proceeds of tax evasion in the late 1990s. It was over a decade later that Singapore finally took that step, whilst Switzerland remains to do so. Some countries even formulated a standard of suspicion for reporting that was lower than the standard that applied elsewhere. In Dubai for example, the offence of not reporting is only committed where a person has actual knowledge, whereas in many other countries the offence is committed on the basis of an objective standard of knowledge.

Enhanced legislation has been supplemented by rules requiring financial institutions to obtain and verify identity data from customers. That obligation has also evolved significantly. Industry is now required to adopt a risk-based approach to customer due diligence including in certain circumstances obtaining information on a customer's source of funds and source of wealth. Such an approach ought to account for the risks associated with the services and products a bank offers, as well as the risks inherent in the nature and background of a customer (whether they are politically exposed being one of the most significant risk factors).

The introduction of 'all crimes' money laundering laws seems in retrospect to have been part of a natural evolution in society's efforts to combat crime. In reality however, criminalising the failure of one person to report the suspected wrongdoing of another was a profound innovation. To this day it is not an offence to ignore a suspicion that your neighbour is a serial killer but it is an offence for a banker not to report a suspicion that his customer is a money launderer. This is all the more remarkable given that a banker (unlike the neighbour) owes his customer a fiduciary duty of care. At the time the drug trafficking reporting obligation was introduced, nobody could have foreseen that governments would progress so quickly from penalising drug money laundering to penalising all crimes as money laundering. Financial institutions were, at the same time, required to obtain a steadily increasing amount of data from customers, heightening the likelihood that they might become fixed with information that obliged them to report their customers to the authorities.

The latest development in what has been a relentless erosion of customer confidentiality, and not only of customers suspected of criminality, involves the imposition of an obligation upon financial institutions by the US authorities to share customer data under the provisions of the Foreign Account Tax Compliance Act (FATCA). FATCA will be examined in greater detail in Chapter 10 but suffice it to say at this stage that failure to comply with the terms of FATCA will result in institutions being barred from accessing the US dollar – a form of sanction for failing to share data on customers that 30 years ago was regarded as sacrosanct.

How can this exponential increase in the burden upon the finance industry be explained? Financial intelligence is extremely valuable to the authorities as the notorious mobster Al Capone realised when he was jailed in 1931, not for murder, racketeering, or extortion, but for tax evasion. Power is not just about exercising control over large pools of capital, it is ultimately about being able to access information relating to it. No industry is better placed to conduit that information to the state than the finance industry.

The resulting flood of intelligence material has been a boon for law enforcement agencies as financial institutions started collecting identity documentation on customers that was discoverable by the authorities and to file so-called Suspicious Activity Reports (SARs) on customers they suspected of being up to no good. What became clear very quickly was that whilst individual SARs were not always terribly enlightening, they often proved to be highly revelatory when pieced together with SARs made in other countries. This highlighted the importance of cross-border cooperation between law enforcement agencies which then rapidly developed, posing a major new challenge to international organised crime groups.

The upshot is that today a substantial quantity of intelligence is provided by financial institutions to law enforcement agencies around the world. Speak to any law enforcement official and they will tell you what an enormously valuable role the finance industry now plays in helping them to tackle crime. Whatever failings there have been in the industry (we will look at many more of them in the following chapters) they all need to be viewed against the backdrop of tens of thousands of SARs made every year by financial institutions, many of which take their anti-financial crime responsibilities seriously.

So what exactly *is* money laundering? A good place to start is the original UN Convention that laid the groundwork for the formulation of national anti-money laundering laws relating to drug money.[2] The Convention required the criminalisation of:

1. The conversion or transfer of property derived from criminal offences.
2. The concealment or disguise of the true nature, source, location, disposition, movement, rights with respect to, or ownership of property derived from criminal offences.
3. The acquisition, possession or use of property derived from criminal offences.

Just as many different types of criminal offences that are carefully defined in law come to carry a convenient name tag (human trafficking or piracy being two such examples), so the conduct that the UN Convention sought to prohibit came to be labelled as 'money laundering'. This, as we shall see, was to have a series of unfortunate consequences.

The label 'money laundering' is in fact misleading. It has harmed efforts to prevent the activity it seeks to describe. One of the reasons is that money laundering need not (and frequently does not) involve money either in the form of cash or money in a bank account. Instead it can involve a wide variety of property or asset types (anything from real estate to intellectual property rights), and can make use of various financial instruments and mechanisms for handling money (securities, Bitcoin, credit cards). Another reason is that the active verb 'laundering' suggests that money laundering always involves some form of activity. Just as dirty laundry does not get cleaned unless a washing machine follows a particular cycle, the assumption is that criminal money must also be subjected to some form of laundering cycle to be properly decontaminated. The thinking goes that the more activity the criminal property is subjected to the more effective the process is. In fact as we will see in subsequent chapters, the opposite can be true. Criminal money can be very effectively laundered in relatively passive financial arrangements not identified by financial institutions as suspicious because they do not have the characteristics of a 'typical' money laundering relationship.

The difficulties of perception created by the term 'money laundering' have been compounded by attempts by regulators, law enforcement agencies, and industry trade bodies to help the finance industry identify money laundering activity through the provision of guidance that has in its various iterations attempted to describe what money laundering looks like in practice. Whilst the aim of the guidance is laudable, the execution has generally been lousy because of the reliance placed on a tabloid-like description of money laundering known as the 'three-staged' or 'placement, layering, and integration' model. Regrettably, this mischaracterisation of money laundering is still being perpetuated.

The US Treasury Department's Financial Crimes Enforcement Network (FinCEN) adheres to the model, describing money laundering as: 'the process of making illegally-gained proceeds (i.e., "dirty money") appear legal (i.e., "clean")', typically involving 'three steps: placement, layering and integration'.[3] It explains that: 'First, the illegitimate funds are furtively introduced into the legitimate financial system. Then, the money is moved around to create confusion, sometimes by wiring or transferring through numerous accounts. Finally, it is integrated into the financial system through additional transactions until the "dirty money" appears "clean".' Even FATF, the supra-national body responsible for evaluating country compliance with its globally recognised standards, describes money laundering as a process involving placement, layering, and integration.[4] Relationships in which money is being laundered can exhibit these characteristics, but very often they do not. The difficulty with the model therefore is that it frames money laundering too narrowly by creating a mental picture of money laundering that encourages the possibility that a banking or brokerage relationship in which any or all of placement, layering, or integration activity that is unidentifiable will be above suspicion – even though it may well in fact be toxic. The current model looks like this:

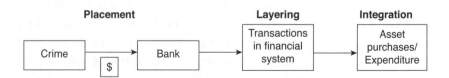

In subsequent chapters dealing with a range of predicate crime types, I examine hypothetical scenarios to illustrate how crimes are facilitated by the finance industry, and the manner in which the proceeds are laundered in practice. But at this stage, the old theoretical model of money laundering bears closer analysis in order for its limitations to be fully understood.

*Placement* – The assumption is that criminal property is 'placed' into the financial system, for example through the use of front companies or structured cash deposits. It ignores the obvious point that many modern day crimes generate forms of benefit that do not need to be placed into the financial system because they are already in it at the moment the crime is committed. The proceeds of insider dealing and bribe payments on arms contracts made by wire transfer are two examples of numerous crime types that generate proceeds which sit directly at the heart of the financial system.

*Layering* – The model assumes that at the layering stage the 'placed' criminal property undergoes some form of transformational process through the medium of financial transactions. The thinking goes that the more complex the transactions, the more effective the metamorphosis of the property from 'dirty' to 'clean'. The expectation of layering activity in all relationships in which customers launder money results in the financial services industry failing to consider the dangers of passive relationships where criminal proceeds do not do the kinds of transactional somersaults typified in this model.

*Integration* – The model assumes that following the layering process, the virgin white property is integrated into the legitimate economy where it is then used by criminals for their benefit and enjoyment, for example, through the purchase of real estate, yachts, private jets, and other luxury items. This has no basis in reality because the so-called integration stage is frequently indistinguishable from the laundering activity that precedes it.

Reliance on this flawed model has led to a disjunction between the activity that the law was designed to prevent and the activity that financial institutions have been attempting to identify and report. Whilst the model suitably applies to the laundering of cash-generative crimes such as drug trafficking, it is positively misleading when it comes to identifying the laundering of non-cash-generative crimes such as bribery, tax evasion, market manipulation, and cyber-crime – crimes which have become much more prevalent since anti-money laundering guidance was first issued over 20 years ago.

A comparison of two examples of money laundering illustrates both the applicability of the old model to the proceeds of street crimes and its irrelevance to the proceeds of non-cash-generative crime.

## EXAMPLE 1

A drug trafficking organisation in the US sells drugs to street dealers in exchange for cash. The cash is accumulated in safe houses where it is collected by associates who variously deposit batches of less than $10,000 in numerous bank accounts (any amount above this sum and the bank is required to file a report to FinCEN), and place it into cash-intensive front businesses (nightclubs, restaurants, taxi companies, and the like). Once in the banking system, the money is wired to the account of an offshore company where it is used to purchase bonds and stocks. The securities are subsequently sold. The money is transferred to the account of another company under cover of a loan, where it is eventually used to pay the credit card bills of the wife of a senior member of the trafficking organisation who has difficulty resisting the temptations of designer boutiques in Paris.

## EXAMPLE 2

A corrupt politician wants to establish a corporate vehicle in which to park a bribe. He sets up a front company in order to disguise his control and beneficial ownership, especially since he does not want his politician status flagged to the bank as it may prompt unwanted scrutiny. The front company's bank account receives a $10 million bribe by way of wire transfer. The money remains in the same bank account and is used as collateral for a loan to purchase a property in Mayfair which he uses during occasional trips to London.

The first example involves easily identifiable cash placement (into banks and businesses), layering (transactions within the banking system), and integration activity (the acquisition of designer clothes). The second example does not. In the second example there is no recognisable placement activity as the bribe money was already in the legitimate financial system before it was wired to the front company; layering is more difficult to identify because the proceeds of the bribe remain passive in the account acting only as collateral; and there is no obvious integration activity because the bribe money does not move. Instead it is used as security for a loan.

The second example of money laundering bears no resemblance to the old model of money laundering upon which so much practical reliance has been placed by the finance industry and law enforcement. Yet, it involves serious criminal money laundering activity to which significant liability attaches, if discovered. How would a financial institution that had designed its internal anti-money laundering defences by relying on the old model (and trained its staff accordingly) have recognised its relationship with the politician as one in which the proceeds of a bribe were being laundered? The uncomfortable reality is that many relationships in which money is being laundered in plain sight are not reported to the authorities because of the expectation gap created by the placement, layering, and integration model.

A new model of money laundering is needed based not on theory but on practice.

## A NEW MODEL OF MONEY LAUNDERING

Designing a new model of money laundering requires trying to place ourselves inside the mind of a criminal. There we will see the desire to:

1. Succeed in perpetrating a crime
2. Avoid detection
3. Benefit from the crime
4. Retain the benefit of crime

In short, criminals want to commit crimes, get away with them, and enjoy the proceeds of them. As Ronnie Biggs, perhaps the most notorious of the British Great Train Robbers of the early 1960s said, 'The flaw from our point of view was that everything was planned up until we divided up the money'.[5]

The key to understanding the new model is to recognise that the finance industry can be exploited to help criminals achieve not just one but all four of the above objectives. The new model looks like this:

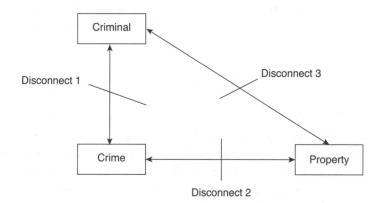

The criminal, the crime and the property are each connected by three axes. Each of the four objectives of the criminal can be met by using financial services along each axis to achieve different 'disconnects'. Consider the following example involving the perpetrator of an advanced fee fraud who is conning naïve victims into advancing money to him in anticipation of a larger return:

## DISCONNECT 1

Instead of committing the fraud in his own name, the fraudster incorporates a company administered and controlled by a law firm on his behalf. The emails are sent to the victims in the name of the company. By utilising a company, the fraudster significantly reduces the chances of being detected because the fraudulent activity is less likely to appear suspicious when transacted by a company than by an individual. It is the financial crime equivalent of a burglar taking the precaution of wearing gloves so as not to leave any fingerprints at the crime scene. Even if the emails are identified as suspicious, his connection to the company needs to be established in order for the involvement in the fraud to be revealed. This is a clear example of the type of facilitation of crime through the provision of a financial service touched upon in Chapter 1.

## DISCONNECT 2

As an alternative to secreting the proceeds of the fraud under the mattress, the fraudster arranges for the company which he controls to open bank and brokerage accounts into which the money is transferred. The fraudster then transforms the proceeds from their original form (cash in a bank account) into a yacht moored lazily in a Mediterranean harbour via a series of share and currency transactions. It becomes very difficult for the yacht to be traced back to the fraud because of the numerous intervening transactions.

## DISCONNECT 3

The fraudster is clever enough to know that he should not risk owning the yacht in his name. Recognising the risk that the frauster could be connected to the fraud through the yacht if it were ever to be traced back to the crime, he instead 'owns' the yacht through a trust administered on his behalf by a private bank-owned trust company. The trustees in turn own a company which acts as the legal registered owner of the yacht. In this way the fraudster's connection with the yacht is disguised but he gets to enjoy roleplaying Aristotle Onassis on board each summer.

I refer to this model as the 'enable, distance, and disguise' model of money laundering. It encompasses a wider range of facilitation and laundering conduct than the old 'placement, layering, and integration' model and is thus much more effective in helping to identify the potential involvement of the financial sector in enabling crime, laundering the proceeds of crime, and disguising the ownership of the proceeds of crime.

The new model allows individual financial products or services to be plotted against it so that the full extent of their criminal vulnerability can be evaluated as a necessary component of product and service risk assessment. It can also be used to assess whether the explanations given by prospective customers of the reasons why they want to buy or use particular products and services are genuine. If a business appreciates that a product is highly susceptible to criminal exploitation, it will be far better placed to both enhance its defences and undertake more effective due diligence on whether the proposed relationship or transaction has a legitimate purpose. This is particularly important because, as countless examples have demonstrated, the most effective question that a financial professional or lawyer can ask in guarding against money laundering and facilitation risk is 'why?' What advantage does this particular product or service confer upon my client?

## PRODUCT & SERVICE VULNERABILITIES

Because every financial service or product has a number of different legitimate uses, it can be very difficult to discern when they are being exploited. Whereas a bank robbery always looks like a bank robbery, the abuse of a product such as a bank account or an investment fund for laundering purposes can appear completely innocuous. Some products and services (and by extension the businesses that offer them) are however inherently at greater danger of abuse by criminals than others because of the extent to which they empower criminals to achieve disconnects. What follows is not an exhaustive list of vulnerable products and services but a selection of those that I have most commonly witnessed during the course of investigations both on and offshore.

The inclusion of each of the product and service types that follow should not be misinterpreted as suggesting that they are illegal or inherently toxic. The opposite is true. They are all frequently used for legitimate commercial objectives. Their inclusion in this chapter is warranted because of their susceptibility to abuse by criminals who are attracted to them because of their legitimacy. Often abuses look just like genuine uses.

### Companies & corporate services

Mention the word 'company' to most people and they will immediately think of offices, employees, assets, and activities. In fact a company is simply a form of legal structure represented by several important pieces of paper – a memorandum of association (a document that governs the relationship between the company and the outside world), articles of association (the rules governing the internal operation of the company), and share certificates (evidencing ownership of the company). Anybody can own and control a company and if you were of a mind to do so you could establish one very easily and have change out of a couple of thousand dollars.

Companies have many legitimate uses, but they are also hugely attractive to criminals for three reasons: (1) they are a form of legal person that can contract, own assets, run bank accounts, and have credit cards in their own right; (2) they can be owned and controlled by criminals either in their own name or through nominees, often cross-border; and (3) they bestow a degree of formality and respectability to activities which if conducted in the name of an individual might appear unusual and thus potentially suspicious.

The degree of attraction that a company holds to a criminal is dictated by a range of factors controlled by the jurisdiction of its incorporation such as the rules governing the disclosure of beneficial ownership, the permissibility of bearer shares (basically a type of instrument whose ownership need not be officially registered and is freely transferrable), the acceptability of corporate directors, and the nature of company disclosure requirements. The more opaque a company is capable of becoming, the more attractive it will be to the wrong type of client. The British Virgin Islands, for example, has significantly more companies registered than other, considerably larger international financial centres. One reason for this is likely to be that the details of a BVI company's beneficial owners, directors, and shareholders are not a matter of public record. In addition, BVI law permits directors and shareholders to be companies, allowing for additional layers of secrecy when those corporate directors and shareholders are registered in, say, Panama or another country with low disclosure requirements. Whilst such characteristics will attract legitimate clients with a genuine desire for confidentiality their magnetism for criminals is patently obvious.

The vulnerability of companies is materially enhanced by the corporate services connected to them. Such services are offered by organisations variously referred to as trust companies, management companies, or corporate service providers (depending on which part of the world you are in). For ease

I shall refer to them as corporate service providers. Every company is constituted of the following actors – directors (responsible for the stewardship and management of the company), shareholders (the owners of the company), and a company secretary (responsible for the administration of the company). It is also necessary for every company to have a registered office in the jurisdiction of its incorporation. Corporate service providers sell the following 'corporate services':

- Company directors – corporate service providers utilise 'in-house' companies to act as directors of client companies. In jurisdictions where corporate directors are prohibited, corporate service provider employees act as directors.
- Registered offices – corporate service providers allow their offices to serve as the registered office of the client companies.
- Company secretaries – corporate service providers utilise a specific 'in-house' company to act as company secretary for client companies.
- Nominee shareholders – corporate service providers utilise further in-house companies to act as registered shareholders of client companies under the terms of a so-called declaration of trust between the nominees and the ultimate beneficial owner.

Once all of the available corporate services are factored in a company goes from looking like this:

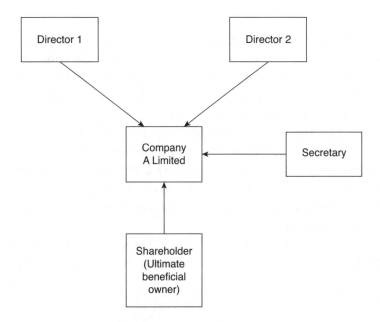

To this:

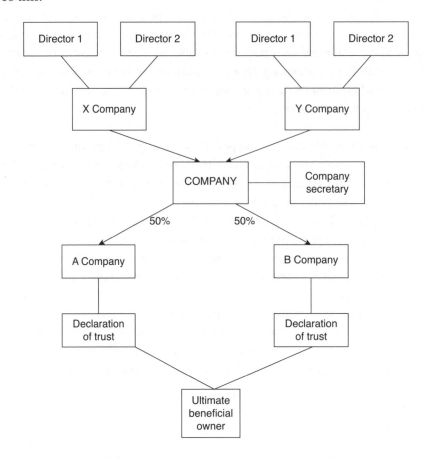

Such corporate services can of course be used for perfectly legitimate purposes but the uncomfortable truth is that they can create disconnects between the ultimate owners and the companies that are either used in the commission of crimes or in the ownership of criminal property. What bribe payer, for example, would choose to pay a bribe personally when he can create a disconnect by using a company to pay it – particularly when that company is legally owned and controlled by a corporate service provider? Similarly, what corrupt politician is going to take the risk of receiving a bribe payment into his personal account when he can utilise a company managed and controlled by a corporate service provider to receive it on his behalf that allows for plausible deniability?

The degree of vulnerability of a particular corporate service provider is ultimately determined by the manner in which it performs its duties, both in the sense of providing services to companies and with respect to properly identifying its clients in the first place. Many corporate service providers operate volume-based businesses in what is after all a highly competitive and price sensitive market. The result is that volume militates against the conscientious performance of duties, gifting to criminals all the benefits of owning and controlling companies that can be very difficult to evidence on paper.

The number of companies administered by corporate service providers can be staggering. The average number administered by a single company administrator varies greatly between jurisdictions. In poorly regulated jurisdictions where 'conveyor belt' corporate service business models are tolerated there is an inevitable absence of 'know your customer' (KYC) information and the rationale for why clients are using the companies is often unknown.

The extent to which a corporate service provider will attract criminals will also be influenced by its location and the nature of the regulatory regime applicable to it. Over the last 10–15 years, many of the better quality financial centres have subjected corporate service providers to fairly rigorous licensing obligations requiring them to follow laws, regulations, and codes of practice. Predictably, this has led to industry contraction as corporate service providers have hunted down arbitrage opportunities and moved to friendlier climes where the regulation of corporate services remains either non-existent or more relaxed. Just as water always flows to the lowest point, so criminals will always identify the weakest spots in the international financial system.

**Trusts**

Unlike companies, trusts are not legal persons. They are instead forms of legal arrangement recognised only in common law jurisdictions but viewed with great scepticism everywhere else. Their existence usually boils down to a single document or deed, although they can also be a matter of verbal agreement. Trusts can exist by operation of law, for example when a financial institution holds the proceeds of political corruption and is deemed by the courts to do so as a trustee for the benefit of the victim country, or more frequently by the express wish of the trust creator.

Several hundred years ago when the trust concept was first recognised in England, it was intended to serve a particular and relatively narrow purpose by ameliorating the strictures of the law which recognised very narrow property ownership rights. Amongst other uses, they were clearly a welcome tool for protecting the interests of women in family homes at a time when they could not legally own property. The concept allowed a registered owner of property (the 'settlor') to transfer it to the legal ownership of another person (the 'trustee') for him to hold for the benefit and enjoyment of one or more others (the 'beneficiaries'). Trustees were usually family members or friends, but as trusts became increasingly professionalised, 'protectors' were introduced to safeguard the interests of the registered owner. A trust structure may look something like this:

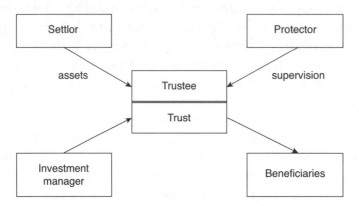

Unfortunately the equitable concept of the trust originally conceived in recognition that the law can truly be an 'ass' has evolved (and many would say exploited) to such an extent that trusts are now used on an industrial scale for purposes that bear little resemblance to the original ideals of equity and fairness.

Trusts have a variety of legitimate uses in tax planning, estate planning, and asset protection but criminals are also attracted to them for the following reasons:

- They are not subject to registration in most jurisdictions. Unlike a company, the existence of a trust is not a matter of public record.
- They can enable criminals to divest themselves of the legal ownership of property in favour of a trustee whilst allowing them to benefit from that property either directly or indirectly through nominees.

The very same corporate service providers that offer the corporate services outlined above also frequently specialise in acting as trustees of trusts. As with companies, the vulnerability of trusts to criminal exploitation depends heavily on the assiduousness with which the corporate service provider discharges the role of trustee. If the responsibilities are discharged with care and attention such that the trustee exercises substantive, not superficial, control the opportunity for criminal exploitation is limited. If, however a trustee is content to act like a puppet on strings controlled by a client, the scope for criminal abuse is substantial. Again, the nature of the regulatory and enforcement environment is key and the differences in quality between competing jurisdictions are stark with many continuing not to regulate the provision of trustee services.

The portability of trusts is particularly alluring to criminals. Consider the following example:

ACME Corporate Services International administers a number of trusts for South African clients through its London office. Many of the clients are in fact evading tax and violating South African capital controls. The UK introduced legislation for all crimes money laundering in 1999 that recognised tax fraud as a predicate crime (i.e., one which would give rise to an offence of money laundering if a financial institution were to handle its proceeds). ACME has, however, contented itself (self-servingly) on the basis of assurances from its clients that they are in fact paying the tax due from them. South Africa then announces a tax amnesty and a number of clients contact ACME alerting the business to the fact that they have actually been evading tax. ACME responds by boxing up the trusts and moving them overnight, lock stock and barrel to ACME's Swiss office in Geneva. By the morning there is no trace that the trusts were ever administered in London. No consent from the UK authorities is required for the transfer because the existence of the trusts is not a matter of public record in the UK.

In recent years various international financial centres specialising in trust administration have developed new forms of trust in their efforts to distinguish themselves from competitor jurisdictions and to attract more business. Such trusts, including the British Virgin Islands VISTA trust and the Cayman STAR trust, have characteristics that make it even easier for clients to benefit from disconnects whilst retaining control of underlying assets.

The subsequent chapters show that trusts are frequently used in concert with underlying companies. It is very rare to observe a stand-alone trust in an illicit structure. Trusts are almost always to be found at the pinnacle of ownership structures with numerous companies and subsidiaries beneath them. In such situations, structures may look something like this:

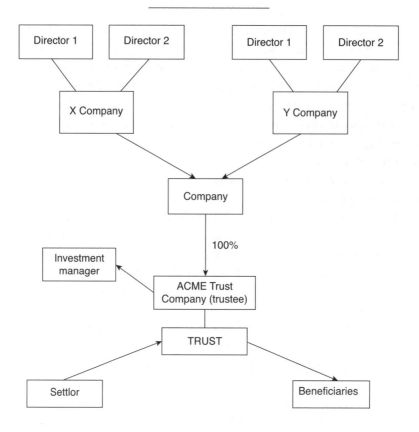

It is unfortunate that those financial centres that have recognised the criminal vulnerability of corporate and trustee services and acted to regulate them properly have not received appropriate recognition for doing so. Such efforts are fundamental to efforts to prevent the disguise and ownership of criminal capital.

**Foundations**

Foundations have until relatively recently been a creature of civil law countries but in a curious development which illustrates the fierce competition that exists between international financial centres, some common law jurisdictions have introduced legislation enabling the establishment of foundations.

Rather like a company, a foundation has the benefit of sounding like something it is not. To many people, a foundation is a structure that exists for benevolent purposes such as the Bill & Melinda Gates Foundation. But in fact a foundation can exist for a purely commercial purpose.

The rules pertaining to foundations differ between jurisdictions but for the purposes of this analysis private law foundations in civil law jurisdictions

such as Lichtenstein and Luxembourg have the greatest degree of susceptibility to criminal abuse because they combine elements of both companies
and trusts. Like trusts, they are not subject to public registration, but like
companies they are legal entities with their own internal organisation. In
effect they have the benefit of legal personality without the inconvenience of
their existence being a matter of public record.

The object of a foundation is to achieve a specific purpose by means of
an endowment made by a person known as the 'founder' or 'donor'. Each
foundation is controlled by a 'foundation council' akin to a company board
or trustee. The endowment (property) within the foundation is applied for
the benefit of 'beneficiaries'. A foundation may be structured as follows:

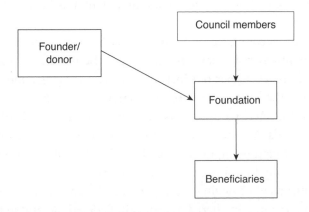

As with trusts and companies, foundations have a wide variety of legitimate
applications, for example in succession planning. But, their vulnerability
to criminal exploitation is obvious because of their potential to be used by
criminals to disguise 'ownership' whilst retaining de facto control.

**Bank accounts**
For reasons of security, convenience, and necessity almost every adult in the
developed world has at least one bank account. Even in developing countries
such as India which is said to have a low level of financial inclusion, the growth
in the number of bank accounts in recent years has been rapid with almost 700
million of the 1.2 billion population having savings accounts. A bank account
may seem harmless enough but it can enable anybody with control of it to
access the global banking and financial system. With a bank account you can
wire money to anybody, anywhere, in a millisecond. Bank accounts are a highly
effective means by which value can be received, stored, and transferred.

Historically of course, bank accounts were operated on a face-to-face
basis allowing bankers ample opportunity to eyeball customers and consider

whether what they saw was lawful. Paradoxically, since the introduction of anti-money laundering legislation the manner in which bank accounts are operated has changed almost beyond recognition. Many bank customers will not have seen the inside of a bank in recent years, preferring instead to manage their accounts on a non-face-to-face basis either by utilising automated teller machines (ATMs) to deposit and withdraw funds or by controlling their accounts through telephone, online, or mobile banking services. The non-face-to-face operation of bank accounts has made them particularly susceptible to manipulation by undisclosed parties. Foreign students who 'sell' their UK bank accounts after they return home having ended their studies do so by handing over their ATM cards and online account log in details to the highest bidders thus enabling potential terrorists to access the global financial system with ease.

Some bank accounts come with optional extras including hold or no mail agreements. A hold mail service obliges the bank not to send correspondence to the customer but instead to hold it for collection. A no mail service obliges the bank not to produce statements. Such services could be of value to a genuinely paranoid customer but they are clearly of enormous value to criminals. A person wishing to create disconnects may not wish to take the risk of mail being intercepted by law enforcement, or indeed anyone else, and being found to be in receipt of mail from overseas banks. An alternative means of achieving the same objective involves the use of numbered accounts routinely offered by banks in Switzerland and in the Middle East. Such an account does not bear the name of the customer but a number and a code word. The customer is able to identify himself to the bank as the customer through the production of the number and the code word. Notwithstanding that Swiss bankers are now obliged to verify the identity of numbered account holders, they are preferred by criminals over regular accounts because of the additional layer of disguise they provide.

### Correspondent accounts

A correspondent account (often also referred to as a vostro or nostro account) is essentially an account maintained by one bank for use by another. They are most commonly used by foreign banks requiring the ability to pay and receive funds denominated in the currency of the country where the correspondent account is located. They allow foreign banks to receive and transfer funds into them and offer customers currency denominated loans and deposits.

Correspondent banking makes use of the SWIFT system, which sends 'messages' to instruct institutions involved in a payment transfer. 'MT103' messages, for instance, instruct a cross-border transfer of a single payment from the originator's bank to the beneficiary's bank. 'MT210' messages are simply a notice to receive funds. The below figure sets out a typical chain of events in correspondent banking, where Customer 1 wishes to pay Customer 2 in dollars, when they, and their local banks, are located outside of the US:

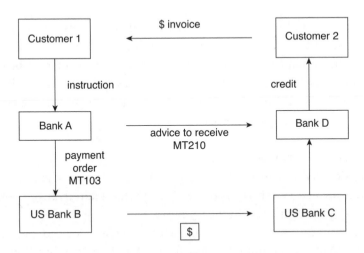

As the US dollar is the world's de facto reserve currency, every bank must have access to it to enable customers to transfer and receive US dollars. Non-US banks do so by maintaining correspondent accounts with US banks. The ability of foreign banks to access the US dollar caused great consternation in the US a decade or so ago with concerns voiced by the Senate that correspondent accounts were a gateway to the US financial system for money launderers.[6] Those concerns have since been compounded by numerous examples of foreign banks transacting in US dollars with enemies of the US sanctioned by OFAC (these abuses will be examined in greater detail in Chapter 9).

Historically, though to a lesser extent today, correspondent accounts were vulnerable to exploitation by shell banks controlled by criminals. Shell banks are entities that hold a banking licence in very poorly regulated centres in which they have no physical presence. They usually have no substance either in the form of facilities or staff. They operate as banks simply by virtue of the correspondent facilities afforded them by real banks. Whilst it remains possible to incorporate and own shell banks registered in jurisdictions such as Antigua, banks in the UK and the US are now prohibited from running correspondent accounts for shell banks, and they are obliged to conduct due diligence on all banks to whom they provide correspondent banking facilities.

The danger remains, however, that shell banks continue to access the global financial system through correspondent accounts they maintain with banks in less well regulated jurisdictions. Those banks in turn provide shell banks with indirect access to the global banking system through their correspondent account relationships with US and European banks.

### Loans

Loans seem at first blush to be harmless but in their simplest form they are a means of value transfer that is susceptible to exploitation. Many different types of business, some more tightly regulated than others, offer a multitude of different types of loans. Credit card companies, payday lenders, banks, leasing, and finance companies all offer loans which may in turn be abused by utilising the following methods:

1. A criminal arranges a loan to purchase property. The loan is repaid over time using the proceeds of crime. In so doing he has transformed criminal property through the loan arrangement into equitable interest in the property.
2. A criminal uses criminal property as collateral for a loan advanced by a bank. In so doing he transforms the criminal money into loan proceeds made by a legitimate financial institution that, handily, provides a 'clean' source of funds.

### Credit & charge cards

Strip away all of the fringe benefits such as Air Miles and free shopping vouchers, and credit cards are simply mechanisms by which holders spend money they often do not have by borrowing it at extortionate rates of interest. Charge cards generally have to be repaid in full each month. Unlike suitcases full of cash, credit and charge cards are mobile. They cross borders without arousing suspicion. They can be utilised anywhere in the world not only in financial institutions but in retail outlets, hotels, restaurants, travel agents, and money service businesses. In short, armed with a credit card you can pretty well go wherever you want and provided the credit limit is high enough, do whatever you please.

Quite apart from their mobility and convenience, credit cards are also vulnerable to criminal exploitation because they can be registered in the name of one person but be utilised by another. Historically, this required the user to fake the cardholder's signature but with the advent of 'Chip and Pin' technology, the user simply needs to be made aware of the four-digit code. Indeed, armed with the credit card number, expiration date, and four-digit security code, the user can transact over the internet or by telephone without even being in possession of the card. As a means of value storage and transfer, credit and charge cards are highly efficient tools that are frequently exploited by criminals.

### Investment funds

Investment funds are large pools of capital contributed by investors and managed by investment professionals on their behalf by following a particular investment strategy as set out in a fund prospectus. Investors put in their hard earned cash, pay a fee (generally calculated as a percentage of the amount invested, plus a performance fee) and pray that they will eventually get more back than they put in. There are tens of thousands of investment funds worldwide invested in a vast array of different asset classes that are managed by thousands of different investment managers. It is a truly enormous industry. According to the Pensions & Investments/Towers Watson World 500 study, the 500 largest fund managers in the world look after some $68 trillion of assets.[7] There are very many different types of investment funds categorised either according to asset types (bond funds, equity funds, property funds, etc.), markets (Europe, Asia, emerging markets, etc.), strategies (long only, hedge funds, fund of funds, etc.), or indeed internal structures (protected cell company, incorporated cell company, etc.).

Each investment fund, which can either take the form of a company, a partnership, or a unit trust, operates through what are known as its functionaries – a custodian (responsible for exercising custody over the fund's assets), an administrator (responsible for administering the fund), a manager (normally responsible for promotion), and an investment manager/adviser (the brains responsible for making investment decisions). Functionaries may stand in relation to a fund in the following manner:

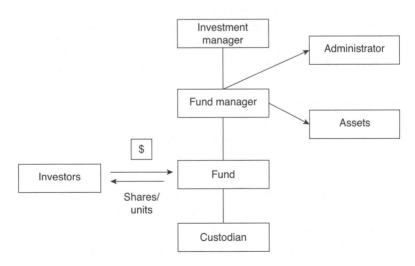

Again perception plays an important part. To most people the term 'investment fund' conjures an image of a monolithic structure managed by one of the big names such as Fidelity or Blackrock, but in reality many investment funds are managed by much smaller players less well equipped to resist the attentions of criminals.

Funds look inoffensive enough particularly when they are jazzed up by glossy prospectuses, but they can be highly susceptible to abuse depending upon the following factors:

- The ease with which they can be established. In certain jurisdictions, the establishment of investment funds can be 'fast tracked'. Indeed many international financial centres compete partially by reference to the speed with which they authorise new investment funds. Many of the same jurisdictions apply a very light touch authorisation process to funds that are essentially self-certified by local fund sponsors. In certain properly risk-assessed scenarios, this can be viewed as sensible, pragmatic regulation, but there is always also a danger that toxic individuals will sneak under the radar and come to enjoy all of the benefits of controlling an investment fund. When that happens, they deflect attention by taking on the guise of institutions.
- Whether they allow bearer securities. Whereas most respectable international financial centres abolished highly risky bearer share companies in the 1990s, there remain investment fund structures managed, for example, in Luxembourg, that issue bearer securities. This means that their ownership is not registered and can be transferred at the drop of a hat.
- The rules governing redemptions of units or shares. If a fund allows an investor to redeem their investment to a third party there is a danger that the redemption may be in favour of a criminal or person who a criminal controls.
- The rules governing the transfer of shares or units. If a fund allows an investor to direct the re-registration of their shares or units to a third party then again the transfer may be in favour of a criminal or his associates.

As subsequent chapters show, the vulnerability of investment funds is largely dictated by the ease with which they can be used as a mechanism for value transfer between two or more parties, thereby allowing criminals to transfer money to their counterparties in exchange for illicit goods and services.

However, they can also be used as vehicles to facilitate predicate financial crimes such as:

1. Front running – an employee or principal of a fund uses his knowledge from pending orders of customers to carry out transactions on the fund for his own personal benefit.
2. Insider dealing – a fund manager and his associates act on his knowledge of price sensitive information.
3. Warehousing – a fund house is involved in a takeover and instead of using its own capital directs its funds to build up substantial stakes in the target company. To conceal the accumulation of shares, the size of the investments will be just below any minimum obligatory disclosure amount.
4. New issues – a fund management company may be offered participation in new issues of shares. They will have the right to allocate them amongst their funds. It is relatively easy for a manager to give an upward boost to the performance of any one fund by allocating new issues to it at the expense of other eligible funds, thereby potentially artificially inflating their performance fee.

**Letters of credit**
A letter of credit is essentially a document issued by a bank which guarantees that a vendor will be paid for their goods, subject to certain conditions having been met. The risk that the buyer will fail to pay is transferred from the seller to the bank issuing the letter of credit. Letters of credit are frequently relied upon to grease the wheels of international trade. They appear on their face completely innocuous but they regularly feature in trade-based money laundering schemes in which criminal property is transferred upon the satisfaction of the terms of a letter of credit in circumstances where no actual trade takes place. Because an issuer of a letter of credit is several steps away from the supposed trading activity, they place reliance on documentary evidence that can be easily falsified. Money laundering through trade finance, often involving letters of credit can be achieved in the following ways:

1. Over invoicing: overstating the price of the goods as a means of transferring funds to the seller under cover of trade. A similar result can be achieved by shipping less goods than are stated in the trade documentation.
2. Under invoicing: understating the price of the goods as a means of allowing the buyer to gain value under cover of trade. A similar

result can be achieved by shipping more goods than are stated in the trade documentation.

3. Ghost shipping: this occurs when no goods are transported and all trade contract documentation is falsified but relied upon by a bank in transferring funds on the back of a letter of credit.

### Lawyers

Lawyers are well placed to facilitate crime and money laundering. They have the expertise to draft and put in place complex financial transactions. They operate client accounts through which large sums of money flow and which can effectively enable lawyers to offer clients a banking service. They are respected by financial services providers and viewed as being above suspicion. For these reasons they have been described as potential 'gatekeepers' for illicit financial arrangements.

Investigations have illustrated the involvement of lawyers in money laundering in at least four ways:

1. The crooked lawyer who allows his client account to be used to harbour or channel illicit funds;
2. The lawyer who acts as adviser to criminals by drafting documents and setting up structures without concerning himself with the fact that what he is helping to achieve is illegal;
3. The lawyer who does not facilitate but whose advice is sought on matters such as banking secrecy whilst turning a blind eye to the blatant criminal ambition of his client;
4. The lawyer who owns and is a director of a corporate service provider business associated with his law firm.

The degree of 'privilege' (that is non-disclosability, even to law enforcement agencies) that attaches to communications between a lawyer and his client differs significantly between jurisdictions. In most common law jurisdictions, communications between a lawyer and client designed to further a criminal enterprise are not privileged. In other jurisdictions, the rules are much tighter.

In many jurisdictions, anti-money laundering rules for lawyers apply only to certain areas of their practice such as conveyancing and handling client assets. Such limitations, the reasons for which are predicated upon the old model of laundering, can make it very difficult for the authorities to get a firm handle on the activities of lawyers.

**Private banking relationships**
Private banks as distinct from retail and investment banks cater to 'high net worth individuals' (HNWIs) through customer service usually delivered by a dedicated relationship manager and the provision of a vast array of services and products designed to cater to the various needs of HNWIs. These include not only banking, but investment management, insurance, and the cross-border management and administration of wealth management structures (usually in the form of companies, trusts, and foundations). Minimum requirements are usually one or a combination of a client's net worth, minimum opening deposit, and minimum average balance, ranging from the tens of thousands to the millions.

Having made a pile of money, most HNWIs spend most of their time worrying about how not to lose it. Private banks are geared towards helping them to hang on to it and grow it. Traditionally and to a large extent it remains the case that private banks also offer the allure (if not always the reality) of confidentiality and discretion. Private banks in Switzerland benefitting from a history of Swiss banking secrecy have long traded on this, but private banks in many EU member states have also sought to emphasise the discretion with which they are willing to handle their client's affairs.

The vulnerability of private banking stems from two sources: firstly the nature of the clients that the sector attracts as a result of the emphasis it places on service and discretion; and secondly the willingness of private bankers to accommodate their client's desires because of the heavy emphasis on customer service. HNWIs come in all shapes and sizes but the most problematic are Politically Exposed Persons (PEPs) such as politicians, their family members and associates, as well as other wealthy individuals at risk of involvement in bribery and corruption, including senior military figures, members of the judiciary, and high ranking civil servants. In Chapter 5, I examine examples of bribe facilitation and money laundering by private banks for PEPs.

All private bankers are under pressure to maintain lucrative relationships and that does not always sit comfortably with the need to conduct due diligence on valued clients to ensure probity. Few relationship managers with an eye to career progression are oblivious to the danger of damaging highly valued HNWI relationships by scrutinising their client's affairs and creating an atmosphere of distrust. Questions such as 'where are the funds coming from?', 'what do they represent?', 'where are the funds going to?', 'why are they being transferred?' risk undermining the relationship between a private banker and his client. This can be particularly problematic in certain cultures where posing such questions can be tantamount to accusing a client of impropriety. The result is that the degree of due diligence that some private banks conduct is inversely proportionate to the degree of risk posed by money laundering clients. After all, what private banker wants to be responsible for jeopardising his employer's multi-million dollar relationship with the nephew of the ruler of an oil rich African country for the sake of asking one or two additional due diligence questions about where the funds have come from and what they represent?

**Securities**
Securities come in all shapes and sizes: equities, bonds, certificates of deposit, bills of exchange, investment trusts, mutual funds, options, futures, credit default swaps, to name but a few. They collectively present a veritable sweet shop of sugar-coated opportunity for money launderers for two reasons: (1) the securities market is enormous, thus creating the opportunity to conduct transactions that are virtually impossible to identify amongst the billions of securities transactions that take place on a daily basis in the primary and secondary markets throughout the world; and (2) the market is incredibly diverse, involving dozens of different securities types that can be bought and sold with ease internationally thereby creating an audit trail that can be virtually impossible to follow with the result that securities can be very difficult to link back to criminality.

The securities market can be used both for the purposes of committing predicate crimes (e.g., market manipulation, fraud, and insider dealing) and for laundering the proceeds of other crimes. Examples of securities being used to either of those ends are as follows:

1. Penny stocks: Chapter 10 shows that penny stocks destined for stock exchange listing represent a type of low-value security vulnerable to criminal abuse. The scenario in that chapter presents just one example of how the manipulation of the value of publicly listed penny stocks facilitates tax evasion. These sorts of securities are also used for the purpose of laundering funds: a criminal may acquire penny stocks with the proceeds of crime, then sell the stock once it has been listed on an exchange, giving the criminal's funds a newly acquired air of legitimacy.

2. Bearer securities: Bearer securities pose a threat to the financial system due to their anonymity and ease of transfer. The proceeds of crime can be introduced into the financial system via the acquisition of these types of securities and may be transferred

to another party without the need for a financial institution to request 'know your customer' information.

3. Insurance contracts: a criminal may invest a lump-sum into a range of securities, such as a mutual fund or a unit investment trust, via products touted by insurance companies. The 'cooling off' period attached to these products offers an opportunity for criminals to purchase a contract with illicit funds, and a few days later demand a refund from the insurer, thereby quickly generating 'clean' money.

4. Internet traded securities: the trade of securities over the internet is a growth industry, and the decreasing costs associated with obtaining a licence for a trading platform are broadening the field of applicants. There have been reported cases of criminals posing as securities dealers, defrauding investors by establishing an online trading platform by using a company incorporated in a poorly regulated jurisdiction. Risks are also heightened due to the difficulties of gathering comprehensive and legitimate KYC information for those involved in trades which require so little face-to-face interaction.

5. Securities trading: the general activity of buying and selling securities is vulnerable to the predicate crime of insider trading. When a person holds non-public information which he knows will affect the value of shares and proceeds to trade on the basis of this knowledge, there are significant illegal gains to be made.

An important figure in the securities market is the securities broker or dealer. The very nature of this role carries with it a handful of vulnerabilities, and not necessarily because of a willingness or advantageous position to engage with any criminality, but because of misguided assumptions by the broker/dealer. Key amongst these is related to KYC checks, which many a broker/dealer will assume have been satisfactorily completed by a financial institution which has already opened an account on behalf of its client.

### Digital currencies

The emergence over the past 20 years of the internet and rapid connectivity has catalysed the development of digital currencies (sometimes also referred to as electronic money or virtual currencies). Just like conventional currencies, digital currencies are mediums of exchange that can be utilised to purchase goods or services. The relative simplicity of digital currencies enhances their attractiveness to criminals – unlike conventional currencies they do not leave a paper trail for law enforcement to follow and in the case of decentralised digital currencies, records of transactions are not maintained by an intermediary again making effective investigations into their abuse very challenging. One particular decentralised digital currency, Bitcoin, has recently gained widespread notoriety. Bitcoins are digital coins that can be sent from one person to another without the need to deal through a financial institution such as a bank or credit card company thereby reducing transaction costs for users. This makes Bitcoins very attractive to online traders who typically have to absorb 2–3% in credit card transaction fees.

Whilst all digital currencies are inherently vulnerable to criminal exploitation simply because they are virtually anonymous mediums of exchange – you give me drugs and I give you digital currency that you can spend – historically there has been limited cross-over between digital and conventional currencies making cashing out of digital currencies into conventional currencies tricky and thus less than ideal from a laundering perspective. However, because Bitcoins can be – and are – widely exchanged for conventional currencies such as US dollars and British sterling they are regarded in certain quarters as having a particular vulnerability not only to exploitation in illicit online activities but also in facilitating non-web based crimes. Such concerns are well founded – Bitcoin has a very low barrier to entry and allows any user to transfer value in nanoseconds whilst remaining anonymous. Obfuscation is easy through the transfer of a myriad number of different Bitcoin addresses before cashing out for goods, services, or conventional currencies. The world of electronic money is a paradise for money launderers.

**Informal transfer system**
Hawala or hundi are ancient and widely used value transfer systems that originated in the Middle East. They enable the transfer of value without the physical or electronic movement of money by the existence of two brokers (hawaladar), one in the origin and one in the destination country. The person sending the funds hands them to the hawaladar, who in turn contacts a fellow hawaladar in the destination country. Details and a code are agreed, and then the recipient approaches the second hawaladar and is given the sum of money. Value has been transferred but no money has crossed borders. Periodically, the two hawaladars balance out each other's accounts with transactions in the opposite direction, or with occasional cash transfers.

Hawala systems are operated worldwide by companies such as Al Barakat and Dahabshiil, and they are particularly prevalent in countries where there is no other way of moving money, such as Somalia. The 750,000 Somalis living in North America, Europe, Australia, New Zealand, and the Gulf states are said to send around $1.3 billion to Somalia through these kinds of transfer companies.[8] This figure represents around a quarter of the country's income.

Offices of such perfectly legitimate companies are common on British high streets where there is a large community of immigrants who make use of them. Although regulation of such transfer systems is increasing (in 2010 Dahabshiil received FSA authorisation in the UK), and technically all hawalas are required to be registered, the transfer of funds in this manner is still much less likely to attract scrutiny than doing so by a normal bank. In Chapter 6, I examine a scenario involving the criminal exploitation of hawala to move funds from Somalia to the US. Whilst the example provided in that chapter is entirely hypothetical, Chapter 8 will demonstrate how the compliance risks posed by the hawala transfer system have made certain banks very nervous in maintaining relationships with hawala businesses.

# 3

# ONSHORE/OFFSHORE DICHOTOMY

Because jurisdictions colloquially referred to as offshore centres are frequently accused of attracting more criminal capital than onshore centres, the similarities and differences between them requires some consideration. Is the criticism that offshore centres are essentially Treasure Islands controlled by modern day pirates with or without foundation?

One of the fundamental challenges is to look beyond the enormous volume of politically motivated rhetoric that the debate generates. It is unquestionably a polarising argument with both sides completely entrenched. On the one hand, we find much of the mainstream media and NGOs denouncing offshore jurisdictions as toxic. At the time of the 2008 financial collapse, prominent economist Joseph Stiglitz penned an article in the *Guardian* in which he criticised offshore banks, 'whose raison d'être is', he said, 'for the most part, regulatory and tax evasion, facilitating terrorism, drugs and corruption'.[1] On the other hand, we see offshore centres claiming that they play a valuable role in international capital markets. The Cayman Islands' promotional website, which champions the 'innovative' legislation offered alongside crystal clear waters, says that offshore centres offer the opportunity for 'an environment in which complex financial deals which might not otherwise happen in onshore jurisdictions'.[2] Offshore centres also accuse onshore centres of hypocrisy because they judge against standards which they do not themselves follow, for example, in areas such as the regulation of corporate and trustee services. The debate is made more curious by the fact that many onshore centres offer the same or very similar products and services as offshore centres, rendering the distinction between 'on' and 'off' shore jurisdictions almost meaningless.

Offshore has become a misnomer for what is, in reality, a set of activities and services which present favourable (to the offshore customer) opportunities in the areas of tax optimisation, confidentiality, local laws, and regulation. The term 'offshore' has come to have pejorative connotations to the extent that many offshore financial centres now prefer to call themselves 'international financial centres'. It is undeniable that in the minds of many casual observers 'offshore' sparks ideas about profit-obsessed corporate giants, gangsters sipping cocktails beneath palm trees, lax to non-existent regulations, and piffling rates of tax. John Grisham's best-selling novel *The Firm* did a great deal to cement the perception that if you want to launder criminal money, then a Caribbean island is a good place to start. However, the term offshore can apply equally to jurisdictions that do not fit that image, and there is a wider story to tell than that which involves crooks, cloaks, and daggers.

'Offshore' in a financial sense simply means somewhere other than where a customer's assets or activities are located (regardless of whether the customer in question is a legal or a natural person). So if a person is a resident of Spain but chooses to bank in Luxembourg, then Luxembourg for that purpose is offshore to that person's place of residence. Similarly, if a US company bases certain of its subsidiaries in Ireland, then Ireland is offshore to the US. Neither Ireland nor Luxembourg is palm fringed. Still less so the United Kingdom which is, in fact, one of the world's leading offshore centres as a result of the beneficial treatment it provides to UK resident non-domiciliaries. Foreigners who choose to live in the UK obtain the privilege of not paying any tax on income arising outside of the UK in return for paying a relatively modest annual fee (for the 2012–2013 tax year, this was £50,000 for those who had lived in the UK for at least 12 years[3]). As home grown UK entrepreneurs move offshore to escape paying 45% capital gains tax, the UK actively encourages foreign entrepreneurs to reduce their tax burden and invest their savings in the vacated penthouses of Knightsbridge and Belgravia.

The offshore/onshore debate is inextricably intertwined with equally highly charged discussions around tax optimisation. Since tax avoiders are perceived as using offshore centres in order to deprive the taxman, the argument goes that tax avoidance is bad, therefore offshore centres must be harmful. But, very many countries create tax arbitrage opportunities to attract foreigners because their economic well-being depends on attracting as much capital and business activity as possible. Strange as it may seem, the world is one big group of country-sized supermarkets each competing, often fiercely, for as much capital as possible. For example, 'high net worth individuals' (HNWIs) have a smorgasbord full of tax optimisation opportunities open to them upon obtaining citizenship of sovereign states like Malta available for $891,000 in cash, and up to $685,000 in property and investments.[4] With 700,000 unsold homes, Spain is currently offering residency permits to applicants investing more than €500,000 in Spanish property. In Mauritius, the necessary investment level is only $500,000. Once you invest the stipulated amount and demonstrate residency for the required period (generally anything from one to five years) you can enjoy worldwide (non-domestic) tax-free income. As the search for capital has become a zero-sum tax game, other jurisdictional features have become pivotal including whether the airport runways are long enough to accommodate certain types of private jets, and trivia such as the quarantine duration for imported pets. One jurisdiction where the six-month quarantine period was proving to be a barrier to entry for some HNWIs who could not bear to be parted from their pooches for that length of time reduced the period to only two weeks for investors over a certain value. In the effort to attract capital seeking more advantageous tax treatment, almost anything can be made possible.

For corporate tax efficiency hunters, the Netherlands allows businesses to reduce taxes on capital gains and dividends from subsidiaries. It also has an extensive network of tax treaties that enable businesses and HNWIs to reduce their tax bills. In consequence, the Netherlands attracts a great deal of capital that might otherwise have no obvious reason to be there. For example, members of the music group U2 are said to have shifted their music publishing company from Ireland to the Netherlands following a change to the tax rules in Ireland applicable to music royalties. U2 has always rigorously defended its accounting practices. Band member Bono described Ireland's own tax competitiveness as having been hugely beneficial to the country's economy, with policy-makers accepting that 'some people are going to go out, and some people are coming in'. Given his country's approach to tax affairs, he has said that the band is in 'total harmony with our government's philosophy'.[5]

Consider the following wholly legitimate scheme and variants thereof utilised by several of America's largest corporations. Known as the 'Double Irish', the scheme works by exploiting the differences between the US and Irish tax regimes:

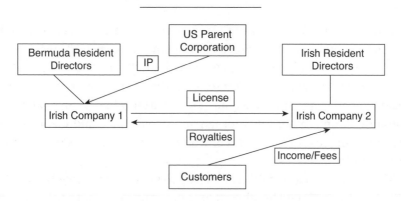

A US corporation is required to pay tax on all profits arising in the US. The opportunity therefore exists with respect to its non-US activities for it to maintain profits outside of the US in jurisdictions that levy lower rates of corporate taxation. The corporation arranges for its intellectual property rights to be held in an offshore subsidiary company thereby allowing that company to receive all of the income arising from the exploitation of those rights. Provided the profits are not remitted to the US they will not be taxed there. In the Double Irish scheme, Irish Company 1 owns the rights and will be tax resident (through the location of its management and control) in a jurisdiction with an even lower rate of corporate tax than Ireland, such as Bermuda. Irish Company 1 then licences the rights that it owns to Irish Company 2. Income arising from the use of the intellectual property rights outside of the US flow into Irish Company 2. Much of that income is then paid by Irish Company 2 to Irish Company 1 as royalties. What remains in profit in Irish Company 2 is taxed in Ireland at 12.5% but the bulk of the profits have flowed into Irish Company 1 which pays either no or very little tax in the jurisdiction where it is tax resident.

You may well question the sustainability of this scheme. After all if a US corporation continues to accumulate all of its non-US generated profits outside of the country how will it be able to pay dividends to shareholders without first repatriating the profits and paying 35% tax? With ease. Instead of repatriating the profits to the US the corporation borrows what it needs and to add insult to injury, then claims a tax deduction on the loan which it offsets against its US-based profits.

How can the role of Ireland in this scheme be explained? How else, indeed, can the toleration of the use of the scheme by US companies be justified by the US Internal Revenue Service? The answers lie in recognising both that jurisdictions compete with each other and that large corporations hold the whip hand when dealing with governments acutely aware that capital and jobs are highly mobile. For the US, being in receipt of say 3% of tax on a company's worldwide profits is more desirable than receiving nothing at all if the company is seduced into relocating its headquarters to another jurisdiction offering a more advantageous tax deal. What tax official is going to proudly claim responsibility for having encouraged a multinational business employing tens of thousands of workers to relocate overseas because he would not play ball?

There is of course a legitimate debate to be had about whether HNWIs and corporations should be allowed to transact offshore and pay less tax, but until such time as a global consensus emerges that tax optimisation should be outlawed (a very remote prospect) capital will flow to where it is treated most efficiently. It is highly opportunistic. Recognising this fundamental economic reality, small offshore centres with little other business activity to sustain them beyond sugar or potato crops have since the end of the era of exchange controls attracted foreign capital through the formulation of low or zero tax regimes. Financial services industries, often highly specialised, have developed in order to service the attracted clients.

Despite or perhaps because of the ardent protestations of offshore critics, it is important to recognise that criminal activity and tax avoidance are not the only motivations for customers to utilise offshore structures and services. Customers can also be attracted by what they perceive (sometimes incorrectly) as the enhanced confidentiality on offer offshore for perfectly legitimate reasons. Consider the following example: a wealthy Mexican industrialist resident in Mexico City with his wife and two young children is fearful of the risk that one or both of his children may be kidnapped and ransomed. Aware that an extortive kidnap takes place in Mexico tens of thousands of times a year, he knows that the risk is very real. With this in mind, he decides to disguise the full extent of his wealth by placing the ownership of certain assets in the name of offshore companies in turn owned by an overlying trust. He stresses the importance of confidentiality to the corporate service provider. Viewed through the optic of an offshore sceptic such a relationship, in particular with a customer from Mexico, can mean only one thing – money laundering – but in fact the relationship is perfectly legitimate, driven simply by the customer's understandable desire to protect his family. As kidnapping has become a cottage industry in many parts of the world, it should come as no surprise to anyone that HNWIs at risk from it are increasingly looking to shelter their assets offshore. What would the position be for the Mexican industrialist if the concept of offshore did not exist?

Offshore centres have been very successful in attracting HNWIs and corporations. A quick glance at the CIA World Factbook list of the world's richest jurisdictions by GDP per capita confirms just how successful. The following centres feature in the top 20 – Lichtenstein, Bermuda, Luxembourg, Monaco, Singapore, Jersey, Isle of Man, Hong Kong, Switzerland, Guernsey, Cayman Islands, and Gibraltar.[6]

Whilst most of the leading names offer a full range of services, each offshore centre has a reputation for specialising in a particular product or service type: Luxembourg for funds, Bermuda for captive insurance, the British Virgin Islands for company registration, the Marshall Islands for ship registration, the Cayman Islands for funds and securitisations, Jersey for banking and structured finance, and increasingly Mauritius for company management and administration. And so it goes on.

The value and volume of business conducted in and through the offshore centres is staggering. Nobody knows with any accuracy the value of funds deposited in and property held through structures managed and controlled in each centre but according to a study by James Henry and commissioned by the Tax Justice Network (a pressure group that campaigns against tax havens) the figure at the end of 2010 was $21–32 trillion, equivalent to the combined economies of the US and Japan.[7] In the Cayman Islands alone as of June 2013 total international assets and liabilities (cross-border positions in all currency, and domestic positions in foreign currency) were reported as $1.503 trillion and $1.524 trillion, respectively, ranking the jurisdiction sixth internationally based on the value of cross-border assets.[8]

In addition to tax arbitrage opportunities, there are other areas of competition between offshore centres and onshore jurisdictions that blur the distinction between 'on' and 'off' shore still further. Company registration and corporate services are one such example. Delaware, Nevada, and Wyoming – all states in the US (which has been at the forefront of efforts to clamp down on offshore centres outside of the US) – have successful offshore industries largely because of the opaqueness of the companies that can be incorporated within their borders. The vulnerability of US companies to criminal abuse was baldly emphasized by US Senator Carl Levin when he said:

> The United States has been a leading advocate for transparency and openness. We have criticized offshore tax havens for their secrecy and lack of transparency, and pressed them to change their ways. But look what's going on in our own backyard. The irony is that we don't suffer from lack of transparency - there is just no information to disclose. And when other countries ask us for company owners

and we have to stand red-faced and empty-handed, it undermines our credibility and our ability to go after offshore tax havens that help rob honest U.S. taxpayers.[9]

Delaware is the largest of the three states, with company registration fees contributing approximately one quarter of the state's annual budget. There are more active companies than people in Delaware, and the state authorities report that over half the Fortune 500 companies are registered there. To name but two: Google is registered at 1209 Orange Street in Wilmington, and Facebook is around six miles west at 2711 Centerville Road. Their respective registration agents – CT Corporation and The Company Corporation – have thousands of clients for whom they provide registrant agent services.

The so-called 'Delaware loophole' is a boon to companies which incorporate there, but whose operations take place elsewhere. Tax-free royalties and other revenues migrate onto the accounts of Delaware entities and tax-free items on the books in Delaware can be tax-deductible elsewhere. This heady concoction is a magnet for non-resident owners.

The disclosure rules in Delaware are lamentable. Unlike many of the world's leading small offshore jurisdictions, the identity of the flesh-and-blood ultimate beneficial owners is not disclosed to the authorities at the time of registration. Couple this with the patina of respectability that a criminal obtains from using a US corporation (as opposed to a company registered in a small offshore tax haven), and the appeal of US corporations to the criminal fraternity becomes very clear.

The uncomfortable truth then is that many 'on' shore countries are playing the same game as small offshore island jurisdictions. Labelling the small centres as pariahs because they give onshore jurisdictions a run for their money (literally) does not advance the cause of preventing the movement of criminal capital.

In view of the increasingly tenuous distinction between on and offshore centres and the business they seek to attract, what then is the nature of the objection to small offshore centres? The onshore community claims the game is rigged for two reasons. Firstly, onshore centres are not as nimble and thus they cannot compete. With large, ageing populations and bloated bureaucracies how can they possibly contend with islands in the Caribbean that do not levy any form of taxation? And so, the argument goes that their economic interests are prejudiced. Secondly, the offshore centres play by a different set of rules – regulation of financial services is too lax which means that as a by-product of attracting some legitimate business they attract significant amounts of criminal money which is harmful to international efforts to prevent tax evasion, money laundering, and terrorist financing.

Much to the delight of the better regulated small offshore centres it is this latter objection which has framed the debate about their role in recent years. Shifting the discussion away from the flawed 'onshore good, offshore bad' dialogue to a higher plain on which offshore centres are judged not by their label but by whether they are well or poorly regulated (in comparison with onshore jurisdictions) has been to the advantage of many of them, much one suspects to the chagrin of their critics.

The 2008 financial crisis gave onshore governments an opportunity to shine the spotlight on offshore centres and examine the role they had played in the run up to it. In 2009, the then UK prime minister, Gordon Brown, called for action against tax havens, saying they had 'escaped the regulatory attention they need'.[10] The difficulty from his and the G8's perspective was that the offshore centres had already been subjected to a decade of intense scrutiny from a range of supranational agencies and some of them had passed muster. Alleging that offshore centres like Jersey had facilitated systemic instability was very difficult to reconcile with the Financial Stability Forum's earlier assessment of the island as a Group 1 jurisdiction.[11] How could a charge that Jersey did not adequately tackle money laundering stick, when in 2008 it was deemed to adhere to the equivalent of the requirements of the Third EU Money Laundering Directive; a feat that 17 EU member states had still not achieved three years later?

Having recognised that offshore centres per se are neither inherently bad nor poorly regulated, the debate it seems has now matured beyond the indiscriminate to a point at which they are being judged on a level playing field with their onshore counterparts. This is highly beneficial to global efforts to combat financial crime. Focusing so much, often unwarranted, attention on offshore centres because of stereotyping has allowed bigger centres such as the US, Dubai, Singapore, Ireland, Luxembourg, and the Netherlands (the latter three all being full member states of the EU) to escape the scrutiny they deserve. Taking Dubai as an example, this tiny Middle Eastern emirate has emerged as a very important international financial centre and is universally recognised as an important entrepot for international trade and investment. Almost every major financial institution in the world has a presence there. The use of cash is common and culturally acceptable. It is geographically proximate to several very high-risk jurisdictions associated with both drug trafficking and terrorism. Yet by 2008 (nine years after the introduction of legislation on all crimes money laundering in many small offshore centres), a FATF Mutual Evaluation report on the UAE revealed that despite the size and systemic importance of its domestic and free-zone finance sector, it had not even created an offence for money laundering that was predicated on the following crimes: participation in an organised criminal group and racketeering; human trafficking and migrant smuggling; sexual exploitation, including of children; illicit trafficking in stolen and other goods; currency counterfeiting; counterfeiting and piracy of products; kidnapping, illegal restraint, and hostage taking; robbery or theft; smuggling; extortion; forgery; or insider dealing and market manipulation.[12] Equally worryingly, the report also remarked that Dubai's anti-money laundering law did not define what constitutes a suspicious transaction or the basis upon which a suspicion should be judged. Little wonder then that the report also concluded that the level of SARs was low relative to the size of country's finance sector. Altogether the report was a shocking indictment of one of the world's leading international financial centres. The report garnered next to no attention from the international media and virtually no comment from the usual critics of small offshore centres.

How then can we identify the financial centres that offer criminals the greatest opportunities? There are, I think, some fairly obvious criteria that should be used:

1. *Does the jurisdiction have statutory bank secrecy in place?*
   Bank secrecy jurisdictions are those with laws that criminalise the disclosure of customer details unless certain conditions apply. Most bank secrecy jurisdictions also allow numbered or coded bank accounts – accounts to which a customer name is not attached for additional privacy reasons. The world's leading bank secrecy jurisdictions are Switzerland, Singapore, Luxembourg, and Lebanon.
2. *Has the jurisdiction enacted money laundering legislation that criminalises the laundering of the proceeds of foreign tax evasion?*
   This is particularly important not least because criminals do not like paying tax. Representing to a bank or corporate service provider that the rationale for doing business with them is to evade tax is a very convenient cover story that can disguise a plethora of more egregious forms of underlying criminal activity. The world's leading international financial centres that do not criminalise the laundering of foreign tax evasion are Switzerland, Dubai, and Luxembourg. Singapore amended its law to include foreign tax evasion as a predicate crime in

2013, 14 years after the British Crown Dependencies. During the intervening period Singapore and Switzerland in particular were the net beneficiaries of significant outflows of business from the Crown Dependencies.

3. *Is the legislation effective?*

Whether or not an offshore service provider operates in an environment where anti-money laundering and counter-terrorist financing legislation is enforced is critical to the detection of financial crime.

An illuminating study, published in 2012 by Findley, Nielson and Sharman, tested whether providers of shell companies complied with international standards set by FATF on collecting identity information from customers. Those rules would require that enhanced screening was conducted for high-risk customers, and that identity documentation was certified by a third-party (e.g., a notary). Contrary to popular belief, the study found that 'it is more than three times harder to obtain an untraceable shell company in tax havens than in developed countries'.[13]

The authors made a total of 7,466 anonymous approaches to 3,773 corporate service providers in 182 countries via email. 1,785 of the corporate service providers were from the US, 444 from other OECD countries, 505 from tax havens, and 1,039 from non-tax haven developing countries. Their findings were collated into a 'Dodgy Shopping Count', enumerating the average number of approaches a customer would need to make before being offered an untraceable shell company.

The study reported that the Dodgy Shopping Count for tax havens was 25.2, while rich, developed countries scored 7.8. In the US, Wyoming, Delaware, and Nevada were among the most likely to offer untraceable shell companies. Some of the best faring jurisdictions were offshore islands such as the Seychelles, the Cayman Islands, and the Bahamas.

4. *Does the jurisdiction regulate the provision of trust and corporate services?*

Having considered the inherent vulnerability of offshore companies and trusts, and the associated businesses that administer them in Chapter 2, it is imperative that corporate service providers and professional trustees are licensed and appropriately supervised to ensure that they obtain and hold information on

ultimate beneficial owners of companies and settlors and beneficiaries of trusts in accordance with 'know your customer'
principles. The study cited above found that nearly half of the
replies from shell company providers did not ask for proper
identification, and 22% did not ask for any identity documents
at all. One respondent gleefully responded to one anonymised
solicitation contributing to the study: 'Regarding confidentiality, no information is taken, so none can be given. It's that
simple!'.

The idea that anybody, without reference to a regulatory authority should be able to set up a corporate service provider to offer
access to such inherently vulnerable products and services is a
cause for very serious concern. Regrettably it remains possible
in some financial centres such as the UK and Switzerland where
corporate service providers are not licensed per se though they
are subjected to anti-money laundering requirements.

5. *Does the law of the jurisdiction require the disclosure of the identity of the beneficial owners of companies?*

Insisting that the identity of the ultimate beneficial owners of
companies incorporated in a given jurisdiction is disclosed
to the relevant authorities is a major disincentive for criminals, including tax evaders. Neither the UK nor the US has yet
introduced this requirement, although plans are afoot in the
UK to go from zero to a hundred miles an hour by introducing
a publicly available company ownership register, and pressure
is being placed upon the Crown Dependencies to follow suit.
This initiative is well intentioned but wholly misconceived
because it is likely to drive legitimate customers who have a
reasonable desire for confidentiality (as well as illegitimate
customers) to jurisdictions with lower standards than those
already followed in the Crown Dependencies where disclosure
of ownership has been required for 35 years. This will prove
economically harmful to those centres (effectively punishing them for having had higher standards than competitor
jurisdictions in the Middle East and Asia), but make the fight
against criminal capital more difficult to win by driving it further underground.

Given the clear differences between the standards observed in many of the
world's leading small offshore centres in contrast with their large onshore

competitors, the debate about the role of the former begins then to look sus-
piciously less about regulation and more about tax competition.

The OECD first issued a list of 'tax havens' in 2000, defining them as
jurisdictions with no or low taxes, lack of effective exchange of information, lack of transparency, and no requirement for substantial activity. The
list was comprised almost entirely of only small offshore centres but since
then it has evolved substantially as the OECD has been forced to concede
that there are larger countries that display the same characteristics, such
as Switzerland and Luxembourg. Regrettably, the OECD has not been bold
enough to include countries such as the UK, the US, the Netherlands, or
Ireland on the list. Their absence has no basis in logic. Dancing on the head
of a needle the OECD now has three lists: a white list of jurisdictions that
follow a certain standard; a grey list of jurisdictions that have committed
to the standard; and a black list of jurisdictions that are yet to commit to
the standard. Predictably, the grey list features countries that are not identified by the OECD as tax havens but which are recognised as 'other financial
centres' rendering the exercise somewhat farcical. Nevertheless, many of the
small offshore centres have scrambled to meet the standard and gain a place
on the white list by entering as many Tax Information Exchange Agreements
(TIEAs) as possible, thus rendering themselves white-listed tax havens!
Whether their efforts have been in vain will depend on where the OECD
shifts the goalposts to next.

Small jurisdictions exercising their sovereign right to apply low or zero
tax rates in a global free market is all well and good but in using their sovereignty as a commodity in this way is more harm being caused than good?
Critics, of course, say yes claiming that the arbitrage created by state sovereignty is detrimental to the interests of a far greater number of people than
it benefits. Offshore tax schemes responsible for lost tax revenues in the US
have been estimated at a total of $150 billion each year.[14] But supporters
of offshore centres say that they are beneficial for a variety of reasons, not
least because they enable the efficient pooling of capital thereby encouraging onshore investment. They also maintain that they help to keep onshore
tax rates low, and thus stimulate economic growth. There is undoubtedly a
symbiosis that exists between centres such as the Crown Dependencies and
the City of London and Cayman and New York. The offshore centres are
frequently part of a transaction train together with their larger neighbours.
For example, many companies that list on the London Stock Exchange are
held by tax neutral offshore entities. In 2013, the Lord Mayor of London said
of Jersey that it was 'a fantastic adjunct' to the UK economy adding 'They
gather funds in a tax-efficient way and send them on to London. That's a

great advantage to the UK'.[15] Whether he is right about that is beyond the remit of this book, but one cannot help but reflect on the obvious, which is that small offshore centres, despite the pressure that has been brought to bear upon them, continue to be tolerated. One suspects that if their existence was deemed to be too detrimental to the interests of the UK and the US, then more draconian measures would have been adopted making it impossible for onshore banks, corporations, and HNWIs to use them. As such steps have not been taken since 2008 – in what after all has been a period of almost unprecedented onshore austerity – one suspects that the offshore centres are beginning to feel more secure than they have for many years.

In part they have China to thank for that. Hong Kong and Macau (both large financial centres with tax haven characteristics) are conspicuous in their absence from the OECD grey list. Why? Because of pressure from China. It is undoubtedly true that the Chinese leadership recognises the value to the Chinese economy of the capital conduit that flows through its offshore satellite jurisdictions. In consequence, China will not countenance any moves by the international community to prejudice the continuing operation of those two centres. If the UK and the US were to effectively shut down their offshore satellite centres, the large pools of development capital residing therein would head east bolstering yet further the emerging economic dominance of Asia. Were that to happen, a greater proportion of global capital would reside in centres, which by the nature of their orbits, would be much more difficult to influence and police. Critics of the Caribbean and Crown Dependency centres need to be careful what they wish for. Pertinent to this are the revelations from *Offshore Secrets*, a two-year investigation led by the International Consortium of Investigative Journalists, which obtained more than 200 gigabytes of leaked data from companies in the British Virgin Islands.[16] It found that numerous members of China's political elite have, with the assistance of accountancy practices and private banks, also sought to secrete and protect their wealth behind offshore structures. Viewed through the prism of a Chinese apparatchik, offshore centres must appear like a very handy capitalist innovation indeed. Turkeys do not tend to vote for Christmas and the prospect of China lending a sympathetic ear to G8 histrionics about offshore centres is remote indeed. For now at least 'offshore' – whether located in London, Ireland, Delaware, or on a palm fringed island – looks set to remain in the toolkit of corporations, HNWIs, and crooks.

# 4

# DRUG TRAFFICKING

In 2010, 3,111 murders were reported in Ciudad Juárez, the Mexican border city to the south of El Paso, Texas. To put this into perspective, London's population is eight times the size of that of Ciudad Juárez, but in the same year the city's Metropolitan Police handled 124 murder cases.[1] It is estimated that in the whole of Mexico, around 25,000 people are murdered each year, and there are regular group killings. The bodies of the victims are frequently dismembered or disfigured in some way, and groups of corpses left on display in public places are not unusual; an indicator of the power of the drug cartels and the consequences for those who oppose or betray them. On one single day in May 2012, 49 decapitated bodies were found dumped by a roadside near the north eastern city of Monterrey, with evidence suggesting that one of the largest criminal syndicates in Mexico, *Los Zetas* ('The Zs'), was behind the massacre. A few days previously, 18 dismembered bodies had been found in abandoned vehicles to the west of the country, and earlier in the month 23 bodies were found in another border city, Nuevo Laredo.[2] For cartel leaders, the lives lost mean nothing in comparison to the riches to be gained from controlling the drug routes. Execution-style killings play a powerful role in reminding the Mexican population of cartel power.

The blame for the grim death tolls in Mexico in recent years lies with the drug cartels who jostle for supremacy in the territory straddling the US–Mexico frontier. The border, which measures 3,145 kilometres in length (around three times the length of the UK), runs along the US states of California, Arizona, New Mexico and Texas, and the Mexican states of Baja Mexico, Sonora, Chihuahua, Coahuila, Nuevo León, and Tamaulipas. Domination of the drug supply routes north into the US is the aim for criminal groups such as the Juárez, Tijuana, Zetas, Gulf, and Sinaloa cartels. The murder rate rose exponentially with the start of the latest 'Drug War', triggered in 2006 by the new government of Felipe Calderon, which declared war on the drug gangs and resulted in a crack down on their territories.

The World Health Organization estimated in 2004 that illegal drugs are responsible for the deaths of around 250,000 people each year worldwide.[3] The annual retail market for illicit drugs was estimated at $320 billion by the UN's Vienna-headquartered Office of Drugs and Crime (UNODC) in its 2005 *World Drug Report* – a figure which, the report notes, was 'larger than the individual GDPs of nearly 90% of the countries of the world'.[4] The sum was at that point almost 1% of global GDP. This figure can only ever be an estimate, and it may actually be conservative: by nature, the market is secretive and people are reluctant to admit to the sums involved.

Sadly, the countries with the highest rates of drug production have some of the highest levels of poverty and the lowest levels of law enforcement and security in the world. The reliance of certain economies on drugs forces them into a vicious circle where attempts to restore law and order simply cause more chaos. Drugs are incontrovertibly linked to development issues, crime, terrorism, and political instability: opium production accounts for around one fifth of the Afghan economy and earns the Taliban millions of illicit dollars used to fund their activities; and drug trafficking is a major contributor to the coffers of the Colombian FARC guerrilla organisation. The 2011 indictment of the Lebanese-Colombian Ayman Joumaa on charges of distributing drugs for the Zetas cartel, laundering up to $200 million a month, suggested that members of the Joumaa network donated proceeds to Hezbollah. This is an illuminative example of the interlinked nature of drug trafficking and terrorism.[5]

Four key categories of illicit drugs are produced around the world: cocaine, opium, cannabis, and amphetamines.

Cocaine is manufactured mostly in South America, with the majority of the crop of coca leaves being produced in Colombia, Peru, and Bolivia. It is then processed, generally in Colombia, in secret laboratories deep in the jungle before being distributed across the world through a network of traffickers. The vast majority of cocaine destined for the US market travels via Mexico; it enters the US either across the border by land or by sea. To cross the border by sea, it is transported in boats or one of a number of increasingly sophisticated and long-range submarines owned by the cartels. The methods used to pass drugs over the border by land are numerous and in recent years have included ladders, tunnels and a catapult to fire packages over a fence. The portions intended for the European market sometimes travel via the US but, since the disruption of routes across the Caribbean, the trade increasingly occurs via West Africa where coastal authorities and border patrols are less able to interdict it.

Afghanistan is the world's primary producer of opium, representing 74% of the global production in 2012, whilst other smaller producers include Laos, Burma, and Mexico.[6] Once opium has been converted into heroin (usually in the country of origination or close by), it is sent down a variety of routes to its eventual end user. From Afghanistan, the drug commonly makes it way to Europe via the Balkans and Turkey, whilst US consumers are mainly supplied by producers in Colombia and Mexico. Trading routes evolve, as has been seen in East Africa; countries in this region are becoming a hotspot for opiate distribution.

Cannabis resin and cannabis herb are the two main products of the cannabis plant. Herbal cannabis is grown worldwide, with an emphasis on South America and Asia, but smaller-scale localised production is prevalent in all countries. It is an important source of revenue for Central American cartels and elaborate smuggling methods are used to move it across the border. Cannabis resin is mainly sourced from Afghanistan and Morocco. UNODC data suggests that Spain is the European entry point for Moroccan resin, whilst Afghanistan-sourced resin is distributed to neighbouring countries and northwards into Russia. Resin seized in the US is mainly sourced from Morocco, whilst that seized in Canada originates principally from Afghanistan.

In addition to naturally derived substances, there has been an increase in the quantity of synthetic drugs (MDMA, amphetamines) many of which are also produced in South America using chemicals imported from Asia and which follow similar supply routes to cocaine and opium. The UN has also recently identified a concerning pattern in the increase of so-called 'new psychoactive substances' (NPSs), also referred to as 'legal highs', yet to be controlled in a legislative framework. At the end of 2009, UN member states reported a total of 166 distinct NPSs in circulation; by mid-2012 this figure had rocketed to 251.

The mark up on drugs for every step they take towards the paying customer is huge. A quantity of cocaine may have cost a few dollars to grow and process in Colombia, but with each move down the supply chain – to the cartel distributors, over the border, into a US city, out to a main dealer, onto the street, to the user in the club – the drug's value increases exponentially. The drug does not improve in quality or become more effective such that the increase in value is justified (quite the reverse: it probably has been cut with a potentially dangerous agent to make it go further). The UNODC published a report in 2011 entitled *Estimating Illicit Financial Flows Resulting from Drug Trafficking and Other Transnational Organized Crimes* in which it was estimated that, despite the fact that profits from cocaine sales in 2009 were collectively $84 billion, farmers of the coca leaves from which the drug is derived only earned about $1 billion that year.[7] Each dollar's worth of raw coca leaves had its value multiplied 84 times by the time it reached the consumer in the US or Europe. The profits accruing to the individuals who mastermind drug trafficking are massive.

The costs of the drug trade to society cannot be underestimated. Not only does it cause havoc in the countries where the products originate, it also causes severe environmental damage from the processing chemicals. Further, in the countries of consumption, there is the societal cost of the abuse of illicit substances: crimes committed to obtain money to pay for the drugs, murders committed to protect the drugs, and health and social budgets to deal with the physical and emotional fallout of addiction. The US government estimated that in 2007 the cost of illicit drug use was over $193 billion, whilst the cost to the UK was calculated at approximately £15 billion for the same year. These figures include health services, prisons, legal costs, loss of productivity, deterrents, and welfare, and equalled around 1% of the GDP of both countries.[8]

An astonishing level of corruption also accompanies drug production. It is no coincidence that Afghanistan ranks 175 out of 177 countries on the 2013 Transparency International index of perceived corruption and on a scale of 1 ('highly corrupt') to 100 ('very clean'), it scores 8; Mexico and Colombia, countries with vastly superior wealth and infrastructure, score only 34 and 36 out of 100 respectively. An ability to pay off those who might disrupt their trade and to threaten their lives (and those of their families) if they do not play ball gives the cartels extraordinary powers, to the extent that large swathes of Central America are effectively run by drug organisations who pay sums of money to the law enforcement authorities and politicians. Guatemala and Honduras, two countries that are important in the trans-shipment of South American drugs, are beset by a constant tension between corrupted police and military forces and US-backed government forces attempting to regain control.

In some cases, the overlap between the forces of law and order and the forces of violence and threat is absolutely explicit. The Zetas cartel was itself formed from a Mexican Special Forces unit formerly employed to resist the traffickers. This unit broke away from the army and joined the Gulf cartel, bringing arms and military expertise. It soon split into its own, extremely efficient and brutal organisation, now considered responsible for some of the most vicious murders in Mexico. It covers the largest geographical area of any cartel in the country.

Across the main cocaine trading zone, high-ranking officials are regularly arrested for alleged corruption, with fears that it is of such endemic proportions that it can never be stamped out. In 2010, Maria Ernesto Villanueva Madrid, the former governor of the Quintana Roo state in Mexico, was extradited to the US on charges of corruption. He faced allegations that he had been paid large sums of money by the Juárez cartel to prevent law enforcement agencies from taking steps to intercept shipments of drugs into territory under his jurisdiction. According to the indictment against Villanueva, bribe money had been laundered through a representative of the now-defunct bank Lehman Brothers. He pleaded guilty to money laundering charges in early 2012 and was sentenced to 11 years in prison.[9]

Hundreds of policemen, politicians, lawyers, judges, and other people employed in facilitative jobs such as customs officers and prison and border guards are also in the pay of the cartels. Joaquin Guzman, head of the Sinaloa cartel, escaped prison in 2001, reportedly by hiding in a laundry cart after paying a substantial sum to the prison guards to assist him. During his years as a fugitive, *Forbes* magazine ranked Guzman number 1,153 on its 2012 List of Billionaires and 67 on its 2013 list of the World's Most Powerful People.[10] Allegedly footing the bill for entire restaurants full of people to buy their silence, Guzman was finally tracked down to a location in Maztlán in early 2014.

The Central American drug cartels have highly sophisticated and well-organised networks that rely on expert legal and financial advisers, effective weaponry, and modern communications technology in their management of what are, in effect, multinational business structures. They have extremely imaginative and constantly evolving money laundering techniques and are adept at using many aspects of international finance to their advantage. As a result, it is unsurprising that financial institutions so frequently discover that they have been exploited by drug traffickers. What is sometimes surprising is the failure of certain of those institutions to take more effective preventative action.

Little is known about the methods used by opium traffickers. The fact that its main producers are failed states with little or no access to formalised financial networks means that producers and traffickers rely much less on conventional banking methods and are much more likely to receive their share of profits through alternative remittance systems such as hawala, the informal payment system structured around a network of brokers. The

UNODC estimated that around 90% of the transactions in Afghanistan move by hawala and that in 2005, over $1 billion dollars of heroin cash was moved via hawala in the Helmand and Herat provinces alone.[11] For this reason, infiltration of standardised financial products by the original distributors is rarer, although the groups who deal on a smaller scale in their own countries may well make use of them. This was recently illustrated in the UK when the standard and hawala banking systems were both used in a drug-related money laundering case cracked by the Manchester police. A UK court heard how drug proceeds were handed to a hawala money lender overseas, who, in turn, 'transferred' the equivalent value to a hawala broker in the UK. One of those prosecuted in the case collected the funds from the lender using a password, typical of hawala transactions, and then deposited the cash into bank accounts in Manchester.[12]

The overwhelming majority of the drug trade takes place in cash. From the user purchasing a small quantity for a few dollars on a street corner to the local distributor selling on significant stocks to his dealers, and the cartel boss buying raw products from his producers, the sales take place in cash in order to avoid detection. However, cash alone is of little use to the sellers; it is increasingly hard to use it to make large purchases or to pay into bank accounts without suspicions being raised. The majority of the cash profit is not made in the country or the currency of production, and in order for the cartel heads to get their hands on the money, it has to be moved into the financial system and transferred cross border. A cartel head in Mexico or Colombia might be collecting millions of US dollars every month. Some of it will be used for cash pay offs and bribes, some for transactions in the black economy; but in order to be mobile, the remainder will need to enter the financial system and be converted into pesos.

Drug dealers therefore use a variety of methods to launder their takings. Traditional methods have included combining tainted funds with the genuine profits of businesses that historically dealt heavily in cash: casinos, taxi firms, bars, and small shops. However, as banks and governments gradually crack down on large cash deposits, launderers have found other ways in which to secrete their funds.

A favoured and economically important method of laundering money, which is often used by Colombian drugs cartels, is the black market peso exchange. This is a trade-based financial exchange system which provides mutual satisfaction for all involved: cartel heads offload large quantities of US dollars in return for local currency, middlemen exchange dollars for pesos on the black market to earn a commission, and (otherwise) legitimate businessmen can easily acquire dollars to import goods to sell locally.

In a typical scenario the money originates in the US with consumers handing over cash in exchange for their piece of nirvana. With millions of such transactions taking place on a daily basis the cash soon piles up – usually in dedicated 'stash houses' – creating a logistical difficulty for the cartels. Often the physical quantity of the cash on US soil is far greater than the physical quantity of the drugs that generates it. The cartels want the money back home, and in pesos, but depositing bulk cash into US bank accounts is impossible without detection, and transporting and converting dollars into pesos in Colombia also carries the risk of interdiction and confiscation.

A typical scenario unfolds with five main actors: a drug dealer, a broker, a Colombian resident in the US, a Free Trade Zone company, and a Colombian businessman. Essential additions to the plot are: a US stash house, a US bank account, and several blank cheques. There are four main acts: Colombian opens US account; dealer sells dollars for pesos; businessman buys dollars, pays in pesos; and businessman purchases luxury goods. The action typically takes place across three locations: Colombia, the US, and a Free Trade Zone in a country such as Panama.

The first part is straightforward and hinges on the participation of individual Colombians residing in or visiting the US. These Colombians open cheque accounts in the US on behalf of a black market peso broker in exchange for a few hundred dollars. A handful of small deposits are made into the account – just enough to maintain a veneer of legitimate activity. The account holder signs each of the cheques issued to him, but the amount and beneficiary he leaves blank. The account holder then hands over his chequebook to the broker, and so the following relationships begin to emerge:

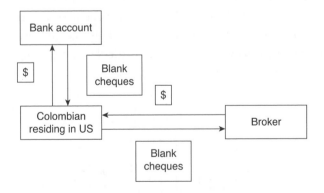

The dealer now wants his drug money in Colombia, in pesos, and the broker is just the person he needs. The broker will relieve the dealer of his US dollars in exchange for pesos. The rate they agree on is probably less than the official one, but the dealer takes the hit so everything remains beneath the radar. With the rate agreed, the broker transfers the pesos from one of his accounts in Colombia to the drug dealer's account, also in Colombia. The drug dealer now has his pesos, and directs the broker to the US stash house to collect the dollars. The dealer can now exit the scene. The broker has his 'smurfs' descend on the stash house to collect the dollars he has just paid for, and this is deposited into the US 'shell' accounts the broker has purchased.

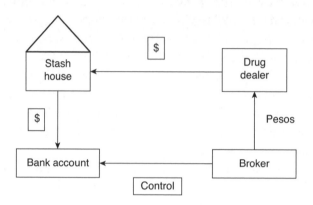

A third party now enters the scene: the Colombian businessman who wishes to buy dollars in order to engage in international trade. Let's say he wishes to import $30,000 worth of gold from a business based in the Colón Free Trade Zone in Panama. The businessman and broker agree to an exchange rate for $30,000 worth of cheques: the businessman pays in pesos and is handed a cheque filled out for $30,000. Thus the businessman has the means to pay the Colón business in dollars, evading both official scrutiny and the necessity of paying high customs or formalised bank exchange fees, and the broker has just replenished his stock of pesos (depleted after he had paid the dealer for his stash house dollars).

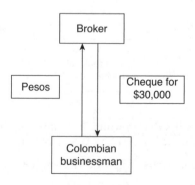

Finally, the businessman inserts the Colón company name into the payee field. This wings its way to the gold company, which deposits the cheque (perhaps locally or in a US bank account) and sends the gold. The businessman sells the gold in Colombia.

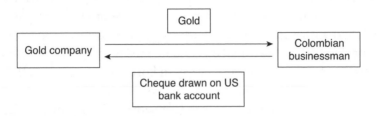

In this way, the drug dealer has received his pesos in Colombia; the businessman has imported goods from Colón using dollars; the US cheques have served as an instrument to buy the gold; the Colón company, which may well be complicit in this crooked cycle, gets paid in dollars; and the broker tidies up with a commission and fees.

A similar set-up has existed in Venezuela ever since the availability of US dollars was restricted in an attempt to limit drug money laundering. It did not have the desired effect; it simply forced the dealers to think up a more creative scheme for transferring the funds across the border disguised as trade debt payments, eluding customs in the process. Another scam included the purchase of racehorses by front companies acting for the Zetas cartel, whereby cash proceeds were laundered by selling horses at over-market value to others in the scheme.

Another popular method of obtaining access to the normal banking system is the use of exchange houses – *casas de cambio* (CDCs) – where drug dollars smuggled into Mexico can be converted into pesos. Smugglers have statistics on their side – less than 1% of the total cash believed to cross the border is seized according to government estimates.[13] Tightly bundled notes have been found shoved into every conceivable nook and cranny of the vehicles ferreting cash over the border. On the same day in January 2014, for instance, police discovered $301,000 in cash hidden in a wheel-well of a car crossing the Arizona border at Nogales and $108,000 hidden in the centre console of another car crossing the border 100 miles east.[14]

When the vehicles pull up on the other side of the border, the dealers get their hands on the cash but probably want much of it converted into local currency. *Casas de cambio* have been known to provide just such a service. Both parties stand to benefit from the exchange: the drug dealer shifts the dollars and obtains local currency, and the dollar hungry CDCs obtain a source of discounted US currency. The worry from the US viewpoint is that the US correspondent accounts for CDCs are a gateway for the drug money to enter the US financial system.

Whilst some of the annual profit generated by the drug trade is re-invested back into the business by buying more product and paying the smugglers, distributors, dealers, guards, corrupt policemen, and politicians, it is estimated that well over half of it is laundered through standard banking products. Far from it being stored away in boxes at the homes of the cartel heads, it enters the international financial system.

Despite the international and condemnatory publicity surrounding the collapse of the Bank of Credit and Commerce International in the early 1990s, after the bank was found to be knowingly and deliberately laundering money for Pablo Escobar's Medellin cartel, the last decade has illustrated the continuing vulnerability of the banking industry. Some financial institutions have failed to embed the types of checks required to prevent money being laundered by drug traffickers, thus enabling them to move significant sums cross border with relative impunity.

One notable example was the case of Wachovia, which was, at the height of its operations, one of America's largest banks (it was acquired by Wells Fargo in 2008). Wachovia came under the spotlight after a wider investigation was launched into the financing of aircraft that delivered drugs into the US.[15] Pursuing the course of drug-dusted paper trails, investigators were led down to the vaults of the North Carolina bank. It turned out that Wachovia's lax anti–money laundering controls had allowed certain customers to launder drug money through the bank.

The CDCs sat at the heart of the enquiry. In the September 2005 to December 2007 timeframe examined by investigators, Wachovia provided correspondent banking services to 22 of these currency businesses. Official documents recount that US investigators found 'readily identifiable evidence' and 'red flags' of large-scale money laundering in its probe of the CDC banking activity at Wachovia. Examples of that conduct related to three services offered to CDCs by the bank.

Firstly, Wachovia provided wire transfer services to CDCs. The CDCs could thereby wire money from their Mexican customers to recipients in various locations across the globe. The investigation unearthed various abuses of this service. In one instance, a set of ten wire transfers were processed through Wachovia in the space of two days, all in nice round numbers and all destined for an aircraft broker's escrow account. It later turned out that the identities of the individuals who sent the money were false, and the business involved in the transfer was a shell company. The aircraft was later seized with 2,000 kilograms of cocaine on board.

Secondly, various CDCs signed up for Wachovia's bulk cash service that sent stacks of dollars deposited at the CDCs back to the US, ultimately destined for the Federal Reserve. In less than three years, nearly $14 billion in cash was repatriated from Mexico for high risk CDCs and other foreign correspondent bulk cash customers. If this money was sent in $20 notes, that is the equivalent of 780 tons of cash making its way from Mexico to the US. It is staggering that this – coupled with the fact several of the CDCs exceeded their expected monthly activity by at least 50% – did not trigger urgent reviews of the provenance of these funds. Startlingly, the bank had no written, formal anti–money laundering policies to ensure that any suspicious activity relating to this service was reported.

The third point of entry into the US system was via 'pouch' deposit services. The CDCs bundled together batches of customer cheques and travellers cheques (drawn on US banks), dropped them into a 'pouch', and sent them to Wachovia for depositing. A transaction review undertaken by Wachovia found that the majority of $20 million's worth of sequentially numbered travellers cheques that were processed by 13 Mexican CDCs through Wachovia between April 2005 and May 2007 did not contain a legible name, and 64% of them had 'unusual' markings. These factors were described in the Factual Statement to the DPA as 'readily identifiable patterns of money laundering activity'.

Although all of Wachovia's CDC relationships had ended by the close of 2007, the bank appeared to previously welcome the CDC business, despite the glaring risks: Miami is known to be a high intensity drug trafficking area and the risks posed by *casas de cambio* correspondent accounts were hardly a secret. Despite warning bells sounding, Wachovia ramped up its exchange house business and even 'purchased the right to solicit the international correspondent banking customers of Union Bank of California' in 2005, according to official records. Wachovia apparently knew that Union Bank of California had decided to exit the exchange house business because of anti–money laundering problems. Union Bank of California's exit from the business would correlate to a sharp increase in Wachovia's own CDC business.

A veritable *Who's Who* of authorities hopped aboard the investigation: the Drug Enforcement Agency, the US Attorney's Office for the Southern District of Florida, the IRS, FinCEN, and the OCC. Throughout the course of the investigation – in which, it is noted, Wachovia fully cooperated and made eight million pages of documents available to the authorities – at least $110 million in drug proceeds channelled through CDC accounts at Wachovia were identified. Whilst there was no suggestion that Wachovia knowingly facilitated any money laundering via its provision of services to the CDCs, the bank's failures in monitoring the flows connected to CDCs were deemed 'serious and systemic'. Among the conclusions listed in the Factual Statement were: inadequate monitoring of $14 billion received from bulk cash customers; inadequate monitoring of over $40 billion in monetary instruments passing through correspondent accounts at Wachovia in a two-year period; and a failure to promptly detect and report suspicious activity on the $373 billion in wire transfers processed for the CDCs. A member of Wachovia's staff – who later became a whistleblower recounting his experiences to the *Guardian* – said that he had been raising the alarm about these type of transactions for some time and had been ignored by his superiors.[16]

Following the investigation, in 2010 Wachovia signed a DPA with the Department of Justice to resolve charges including that it wilfully failed to establish an anti–money laundering programme and failed to report suspicious transactions. It forfeited $110 million and agreed to pay a fine of $50 million. To what must have been the utter dismay of campaigners in the 'War on Drugs', US federal prosecutor Jeffrey H. Sloman referred to Wachovia's compliance failures as giving 'cartels a virtual carte blanche to finance their operations'.[17]

The activities of HSBC in Mexico have also been scrutinised by various official bodies over the past decade. In their respective assessments of the bank's anti–money laundering practices in Mexico and the US, the Senate's Permanent Subcommittee on Investigations and various organs of the US justice system recounted a litany of systemic failures that enabled drug money to wheedle its way through the chinks in the bank's armour and permeate the US financial system.[18] In the DPA entered into by HSBC in 2012, HSBC admitted that it had wilfully failed to establish and maintain an effective AML programme, and had similarly failed to establish due diligence for foreign correspondent accounts. The DPA determined that *at least* $881 million in drug money, including drug proceeds from the Sinaloa cartel in Mexico and the Norte del Valle cartel in Colombia, was laundered through the US as a consequence of these failures. The final settlement, for these and other failures, involved a fine of $1.9 billion, or around 10% of the bank's pre-tax profit that year. Among a number of other steps the bank has since taken, HSBC in the US (HBUS) has spent $290 million on remedial measures.

HSBC's woes in Mexico date back to 2002 when the bank purchased Mexico's fifth largest bank, Grupo Financiero Bital, and absorbed millions of local customers and thousands of staff members. The problems that HSBC in Mexico (HBMX) would encounter over the following decade were in no small part rooted in that acquisition and fears over a possibly damaging legacy were raised before the deal even went ahead. A pre-acquisition audit undertaken by HSBC found that its target 'does not, in reality, have a Compliance Department', and HSBC group's head of compliance, David Bagley, similarly acknowledged in an email around that time that anti–money laundering and compliance functions were 'virtually non-existent'. A senior member of HSBC's compliance function also reported to colleagues that a Mexican regulator had serious concerns about Bital's controls and conveyed that the bank's legal department was 'not guilty of bad faith but extreme mediocrity'. Despite these concerns HSBC went ahead and purchased Bital for $1.1 billion in November 2002.

The issues inherited from HSBC's purchase of Bital were both a cause and catalyst for ensuing failures at HBMX. Existing problems took root and flourished in an environment friendly to Mexico's underworld, which regulators claimed had been evidenced in a tape recording 'of a drug lord recommending HBMX as the place to bank', and where drug traffickers 'designed specially shaped boxes that fit the precise dimensions of the [HBMX] teller windows'. A lack of communication between HSBC headquarters in London, HBUS and HBMX on money laundering related issues only aggravated the situation and was further compounded by HBMX's lax approach to training identified in the bank's own audits.

The US perspective starts with a concern that foreign or domestic proceeds of crime are being laundered through the US financial system and that US currency is being used in the process. These risks are supposedly factored into the way that banks treat overseas customers and transactions, and HSBC affiliates attached a specific level of risk to different jurisdictions, determined by the potential money laundering risks represented by entering into a banking relationship in that country. Curiously, and despite many indicators to the contrary, HBUS assigned Mexico its lowest risk rating (the risk rating was, more appropriately, ramped up three grades to its highest level in 2009). One of the consequences of its prior risk rating was that $670 billion in wire transfers from Mexico were found to have been excluded from the bank's monitoring system.

HBUS' neglect in properly monitoring its correspondent banking services proved a critical failure. HBMX, for instance, used its correspondent relationship with the US to process the funds deposited in its customers' Cayman Islands accounts.. A number of the Cayman accounts that HBMX opened for its clients were highly dubious in nature due to a complete absence of KYC information (one particular sampling showed that '15% of the customers did not even have a file'). Some Cayman accounts, in the words of one HBMX compliance officer, were subject to 'massive misuse [...] by organized crime'. In 2008 the Cayman accounts jointly held nearly

$2.1 billion in assets spread over 60,000 accounts for nearly 50,000 customers. The risks associated with the accounts were only 'brought into sharp focus' at the group level in mid-2008, seemingly partly prompted by the discovery that certain HBMX Cayman customers had been making significant payments to a US company 'alleged to be involved in the supply of aircraft to drug cartels'. After measures were enforced to remediate the KYC deficiencies in the Cayman accounts, HBMX was said to have 20,000 accounts and $657 million deposited in the accounts. In view of the risks inherent in an offshore jurisdiction like the Cayman Islands, the Senate subcommittee warned that it was up to HBUS to 'evaluate the risk and determine whether to continue to process Cayman account transactions through the HBMX correspondent account'.

HBMX also rendered the US financial system vulnerable to money laundering via the banknotes relationship it held with HBUS. In 2007 and 2008, HBMX sold a total of $7 billion to HBUS in banknotes, an amount which authorities believed could only be reached if it included drug money. Between January and September 2008, the sum of money repatriated by HBMX to the US represented 36% of the market 'and double what the biggest bank in Mexico, Banamax, had repatriated, even though HBMX was only the fifth largest bank in the country'. Between 2006 and 2009, HBUS failed to adequately monitor its banknotes business with HSBC affiliates and, as such, was apparently unaware of the tide of dollars washing through the HBMX account. In a two-year timeframe, HBMX exported $1.1 billion from the Sinaloa state alone; this was amid the bank's discovery of a 'massive money laundering scheme' involving HBMX employees at branches throughout the same state.

The banknotes business was, in particular, open to abuse by the highly risky CDCs that provided transfer services to US bank accounts. The most prominent of these CDCs in respect to HBMX was Casa de Cambio Puebla. Puebla started banking with Bital in the 1980s, and in 2004 it opened a banknotes account with HBUS. Year-on-year growth in banknotes business was explained away without considering 'whether Puebla might be accepting illegal drug proceeds that drug cartels were then smuggling into Mexico from the United States'. The bank could no longer claim ignorance after $11 million of Puebla funds were seized in 23 Wachovia Bank accounts in London and Miami in May 2007. Upon discovering the news, HBUS immediately suspended its relationship with Puebla but HBMX failed to do the same until the Mexican attorney general demanded they do so some six months later.

Another example suggesting failures in monitoring and anti–money laundering oversight involved the wealthy Mexican-Chinese citizen Zhenly Ye Gon. Ye Gon was allegedly linked to the Sinaloa cartel and was arrested on drugs charges in July 2007. Besides the fact that Ye Gon was found to have laundered funds through Puebla, HBMX actually held its own accounts for Ye Gon and his companies, one of which was called Unimed. Unimed had attracted the attention of regulators several years previously, and HBMX rejected advice to close its account, arguing that Unimed was 'fine, properly documented and known by the business'. The Mexican Ministry of Finance and Public Credit eventually found that from 2003 to 2006 Ye Gon and his companies had used four Mexican banks, including HBMX, and several CDCs, including Puebla, to move funds of $90 million in 450 transactions.

Wachovia and HBMX are but two of very many large financial institutions whose inadequate anti–money laundering controls enabled drug traffickers to abuse banking facilities to launder the proceeds of crime. In both cases, and in many others, weaknesses in monitoring systems are exploited by criminals determined to shift money through the legitimate financial system. With so many billions generated by drug trafficking there is, sadly, an inevitability that most major financial institutions will handle drug tainted funds.

In the course of my career, I have been exposed to a wide variety of methods by which financial institutions have been contaminated by drug money but one particular kind of structure stands out in my mind as being particularly effective because of its simplicity.

## SCENARIO

A UK nightclub owner replete with a gold medallion and an expensive drug habit allows drugs to be sold in his nightclubs by a particular organisation in return for a slice of the action paid to him in cash on a weekly basis. Business waxes and wanes but his cut ranges from £10,000 to £25,000 each week. He infuses some of the cash into the nightclub bank accounts representing it as legitimate takings, and some he uses to pay unofficial staff members in cash. He spends some himself but still finds that he is left each week with a fairly sizeable amount of cash which represents both a logistical difficulty and a risk. The drug dealer he does business with knows that he receives the cash each week, so he is a sitting target. He is also acutely aware that if he is investigated by the police and is found to have tens of thousands of drug tainted bank notes at his home or office he will face a long stretch in jail. He needs a solution that both enables him to offload the cash without arousing suspicion and allows him to enjoy the money without attracting the unwelcome attention of the authorities. With reference to the new enable, distance, and disguise model of money laundering examined in Chapter 2, he wants to achieve the following disconnects:

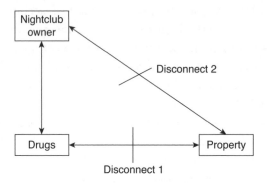

The nightclub owner is introduced by a friend to a UK high street solicitor who in turn effects an introduction for him to an offshore corporate service provider, which is conveniently located in a jurisdiction that has not criminalised the laundering of the proceeds of foreign tax evasion. He explains his predicament at length to a director of the corporate service provider over dinner at one of his clubs. Drug money is not explicitly mentioned by the nightclub owner, but instead he says that the excess cash represents nightclub revenue that he wants to keep away from the 'thieving hands' of the taxman. The director sympathises and says that he is happy to help, suggesting that a trust and an underlying company be utilised for the purpose. He explains that his business already has existing 'on the shelf' charitable trusts and companies which can be used, thereby avoiding the need to involve the authorities by incorporating a new company at this early stage of the relationship.

The director arranges for an employee of his business to meet the nightclub owner every month to collect the cash. The cash, he explains, will then be 'settled' into a wider structure he has at the ready, whereupon it can be used for a variety of purposes from paying off the nightclub owner's credit card bills to the purchase of foreign properties, boats, private jet fractional ownership hours, and so on. He assures the nightclub owner that his business utilises tried and tested methods of transporting cash and dropping it into a structure he has crafted. A fee is agreed on, and the director arranges for the first cash pick up to take place the following week.

Elsewhere in London reside two existing customers of the same corporate service provider, who have been provided with similar structures comprising trusts and underlying companies. The first is a professional man who consulted around the world on large engineering contracts. He too has suffered from an allergy to paying tax on his income and to avoid having to do so, some (though not all) of his clients have settled his fees historically by transferring funds to an employment company owned under a trust administered for him by the corporate service provider. The engineer is now retired and he would like to benefit from some of the money in the structure but he cannot afford to rouse the attention of the UK authorities lest they investigate his past use of the structure. For that reason, wiring the money from the structure to his UK bank account is not an option.

The second customer is a UK politician with close connections to the pharmaceutical industry and one pharmaceutical company in particular. For many years, prior to the emergence of much greater parliamentary transparency and in return for payments made into a structure administered on his behalf by the corporate service provider, he lobbied on behalf of the pharmaceutical company with a view to certain of their drugs either being approved or being purchased by the UK's National Health Service. On one or two occasions he even tabled formal debates in parliament designed to promote the interests of the company and its sector more generally. Like the engineer, he wants to extract some value from the offshore structure so that he can enjoy it; but again, and particularly given his position, he cannot afford to expose any links to an offshore trust and company structure.

The final piece of the puzzle is a 'pooled bank account' administered by the corporate service provider into which the engineer's and politician's money has been deposited. The corporate service provider now has all the structures in place, he just needs to dispatch the courier. The first cash pick up from the nightclub owner in the amount of £42,000 goes as planned. The courier then travels directly, first to the engineer to whom he gives £21,000 and then on to the politician to whom he gives the remaining £21,000. Both are delighted. How though does £42,000 enter the nightclub owner's structure? The corporate service provider is to be found behind every layer of the following structure.

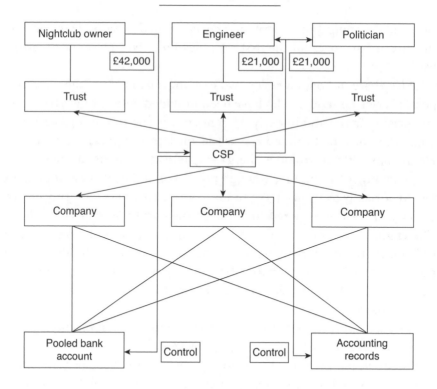

Without any of the cash collected from the nightclub owner entering the banking system, the corporate service provider successfully settles £42,000 into his structure by manipulating the bookkeeping records of the three structures such as to increase the entitlement of the nightclub owner's structure in the pooled account by £42,000. There are corresponding entries in the books of the engineer and politician's structures reducing their share of the pooled account by £21,000 a piece, but there is no trace of the movement in the banking system as the structure has avoided the need to wire transfer the funds. Using this method, the nightclub owner goes on to secrete over £2 million into his structure over a two-year period.

Under his direction the corporate service provider arranges for a loan secured by the cash in the structure to purchase a large villa in Ibiza owned in the name of the company within the structure. The nightclub owner opens an account with a Spanish bank in Ibiza and applies for a credit card. He rents the villa out for 20 weeks of the year. The rental proceeds totalling in excess of £100,000 per annum are paid into the bank account. As far as the bank is concerned the income represents the proceeds of a completely legitimate activity. The funds are then used to settle the nightclub owner's profligacy with the credit card which he uses to sustain his lifestyle in the UK and Ibiza.

The authorities in the UK, the offshore centre, and Ibiza are oblivious to the existence of the nightclub owner's connection with the offshore structure. The director of the corporate service provider contents himself that tax evasion is not a reportable offence in his jurisdiction and fails to address his mind to the possibility that the nightclub owner and the politician may in fact be engaged in even more serious forms of reportable criminal activity.

This form of abuse of trustee and corporate services, bank accounts, and a credit card relies upon the connivance of a dangerous unlicensed corporate service provider through which the nightclub owner is able to achieve a disconnect between the crime and the benefit and a further disconnect between himself and the criminal property. You may have recognised, I hope, that this example does not feature any discernible placement, layering, or integration activity and as such the old model of money laundering is completely incapable of being used to identify it. It would no doubt come as a nasty surprise to the bank with which the corporate service provider had maintained the pooled account that it was being used to launder drug money in circumstances where no activity took place between the three structures. The first time the funds in the account were 'activated', they were not transferred, but just used as collateral for a loan to purchase a foreign property. What could possibly be wrong with that?

You may be wondering what the engineer and the politician were each doing with £1 million in cash? The answer of course is that they would not have received anywhere near that amount because the corporate service provider had several hundred other clients in a similar situation to them all wanting to extract value from their offshore structures without being in receipt of wire transfers into their UK bank accounts from offshore. Just like the engineer and the politician, they were handed cash that had been collected from the nightclub owner by the bagman.

This method of laundering can be used across colluding corporate service providers that match customers with a need to dispense with cash, with customers that need cash. Transactions between structures justifying adjustments in the entitlement to assets are 'legitimised' by loan or service agreements which appear to be completely above board and which ironically lend an aura of formality to activity from which bankers derive comfort.

# 5

# BRIBERY AND CORRUPTION

One white, crystal-covered 'Bad Tour' glove; a fedora worn by Michael Jackson onstage; a Ferrari 599 GTO; two Cape Town properties; three Piaget baguette diamond-studded watches; an André Charles Boulle antique cabinet; works by Degas, Renoir, Gauguin, Matisse and Bonnard; 1,403 bottles of high-end wine; 109 items acquired at the auction of the Yves Saint Laurent estate; a 12-acre Malibu estate; a six-storey luxury property in Paris; and a Gulfstream G-V private jet. These are among the assets listed in official documents as belonging to Teodoro Nguema Obiang Mangue, the 40-something international jet setting son of Equatorial Guinea's longstanding president, Teodoro Nguema Obiang Mbasogo, who wrestled power from a family member in a coup d'état in 1979.[1] Teodoro Nguema Obiang Mangue's penchant for the high life coincides with a career as Equatorial Guinea's minister of forestry and agriculture for 14 years, and his subsequent appointment to the post of second vice president May 2012.

The glitz and glamour lifestyle enjoyed by the president's son, also known by his diminutive nickname 'Teodorin', is starkly different from that of the vast majority of his fellow countrymen (not to mention incongruent with his reported $6,799 monthly stipend he collected as minister) and has earned him a description as 'the poster child of Africa's kleptocratic political elites' by *Time* magazine.[2] A high proportion of Equatorial Guinea's population lives on a dollar a day; the country is ranked 136 on the UN's Human Development Index, with a life expectancy of 51; and it has an unemployment rate of 22%. Ten percent of Equatorial Guinea's children are underweight and the country has the 14th worst infant mortality rate in the world. However, since the discovery of oil in 1996, this tiny West African country with a population of around 736,000 has ranked on paper as one of the wealthiest countries in Africa with a GDP per capita of approximately \$24,000.[3] This figure is over ten times that of Nigeria and on a par with Portugal and Saudi Arabia. Consider that the country scores 19 out of 100 and sits in 163rd place on Transparency International's 2013 Corruption Perception Index, and it comes as no surprise that US officials have attributed the extraordinary good fortune of Teodorin Obiang to extortion, bribery, and the embezzlement of public funds. The country appears subject to a destructive domination of its economy by the profits from its oil and timber that make it potentially such a success.

This type of corruption, known as 'grand corruption', is one among many that range from an official demanding money to perform a basic and free service, to a senior politician contracting deals and pocketing millions as a fee. It is often a cross-border phenomenon: wealthy Western countries will pay immense bribes to gain contracts in developing nations, knowing that there is a ready supply of politicians who will accept the free cash in return for a business relationship. One only need look at the scandals involving two global corporations to comprehend the importance corruption has on the international business stage.

In 2007 the Securities and Exchange Commission (SEC) announced a settled enforcement action, charging US oil company Baker Hughes with violations of US anti-bribery legislation (the Foreign Corrupt Practices Act).[4] Without admitting or denying the SEC's allegations, the company agreed to pay \$23 million in disgorgement and prejudgment interest, and paid a civil penalty of \$10 million. The complaint alleged, among other things, that Baker Hughes had failed to adequately reassure itself that payments made in Indonesia, Nigeria, and Angola were not being used to bribe officials in those countries. The company did, however, agree to plead guilty to three criminal counts relating to corrupt payments in Kazakhstan, and paid a criminal fine of \$11 million.

The total sum of those fines was dwarfed by the \$1.6 billion that German engineering giant Siemens parted with a year later to settle bribery charges brought by US and German authorities. A US acting assistant attorney general said that an investigation into its activities had revealed that, for much of Siemens' global operations, 'bribery was nothing less than standard operating procedure.' Despite systemic failings, the company was credited by the US attorney for the District of Columbia with having taken 'extraordinary steps' to recognise and rectify the criminal conduct (which included the appointment of a former German finance minister as compliance monitor); the company CEO spoke of 'regret', but gave a reassurance that 'appropriate measures' had been taken.[5]

But it remains the poorest countries which are most susceptible to corruption, and which can least afford the diversion of large sums of public money into the hands of a small group of businessmen and politicians. It sets up a vicious circle by which even if a state is massively wealthy in terms of mineral deposits and fuel resources that wealth is never spent on human development and infrastructure, which discourages investment and entrenches poverty still further – a phenomenon referred to as 'the resource curse'. It inhibits business growth and is instrumental in allowing drug traffickers and other organised criminal gangs to prosper without the fear of involvement by law enforcement agencies. Furthermore, it has a serious effect on international aid efforts, often discouraging them: at the end of 2012 a number of donors suspended aid to Uganda amid public corruption fears.[6]

Corruption's evil flows not just from the fact that some individuals are able to become very rich by dishonest means; it causes untold damage to the state itself from the diminution of public funds, the barriers to business and fair competition, the wastage of international development aid, and also from the pillage of natural resource wealth. When a politician steals, he does so from the people on whom that money should be spent and thereby deprives them of schools, hospitals, roads, and water.

However, it is not just the existence of corruption that is the problem. An essential participant in either the corrupt transaction itself or the retention of the money accrued through bribery or theft is the international financial system. Banks play a fundamental role by providing accounts and corporate structures which enable illegal deals to take place by disguising the origin or destination of the money and by permitting the corrupt money to be retained and then accessed when desired by its recipient. Corporate service providers, particularly those in jurisdictions that have the least stringent requirements concerning the identity or purpose of a vehicle, play a vital role in the storing of corrupt wealth in locations often far removed from its country of origin. Poor levels of compliance with regulatory standards, including substandard customer due diligence and the incorrect risk rating of clients and account activity, bear a substantial amount of blame for the facilitation of international corruption. Particularly problematic and widespread are the failures of financial institutions to correctly identify customers as Politically Exposed Persons (PEPs) – holders of public office and their close family and associates – or to identify corporate clients as companies which, by the nature or location of their business activities, are more likely to pay bribes. The identification of a client as a PEP should automatically trigger enhanced due diligence procedures and corruption risk assessments: failure in this process can have devastating consequences. Also problematic are jurisdictions that willingly furnish parties with complex trust and corporate structures that may have little rationale other than deception, and the banks or service providers that set them up.

Corruption is usually defined as the abuse of public power for private gain. Common scenarios see an illicit transfer of public funds made to a private company or individual, or a state sector employee demanding an unwarranted payment from a private individual or private sector company. At its lowest level, it manifests itself in a culture where petty officials make unjustified demands for money to perform, or not perform, basic and, usually, free services that are ordinary functions of their role. At a medium level, state employees demand 'facilitation fees' for business start-ups or accept money for concluding contracts with particular firms of suppliers or contractors. These firms may not offer the best value for public money, but the state employee is personally enriched at no cost to himself. At the highest level, so-called 'grand corruption' concerns the highest-ranking government officials and consists of awarding contracts either to other firms in return for vast sums of money or to firms owned by the politician himself; the partisan control of state resources such as gold or oil; and simple theft, with huge sums of money removed from government or state funds and expended on personal lifestyle enhancements.

Estimates of the sums involved in corruption are notoriously hard to come by due to its secretive nature. The European Commission estimates that corruption costs the European economy €120 billion per year.[7] The World Bank estimates that, worldwide, the bribery and business-facilitation sector of corruption involving private firms interacting with the public sector alone amounts to about $1 trillion annually.[8] This latter figure is based on surveys of businesses which are asked about facilitation fees and bribe payments for procurement services and does not include the sums lost by embezzlement or from the exploitation or theft of public assets or reserves. We only need look at the sums attributed to some of the most notorious examples of grand corruption as listed in one Transparency International study (such as former Philippine presidents Joseph Estrada and Ferdinand Marcos, former Nigerian president Sani Abacha, and former president of Peru Alberto Fujimori, whose personal gains, TI reports, stretched from the millions to the billions) to see that the type of figures that exist in this category are immense and in the contexts of the poverty of the associated countries, almost unimaginable.[9] A study by the Global Financial Integrity group, based on IMF and World Bank data, rated the top ten countries from which illicit money flowed: China is by far the highest, with an estimated $2.18 trillion between 2000 and 2008; Russia was next at $427 billion in the same period; the ninth and tenth were Qatar and Nigeria, $138 and $130 billion respectively.[10]

Corruption is frequently closely linked with a range of other political and economic issues. It is no coincidence that many of the most corrupt countries have a high degree of mineral wealth, in particular gas and oil, fuelling the 'resource curse'. The most corrupt countries often suffer from extreme authority gradients in their political systems that are caused either by the dominance of a ruling family, by sudden regime change such as the Soviet collapse, or by power-grabs in post-colonial Africa. An example of the inter-linkage of these problems was provided by a case in South Africa in which Teodorin Obiang swore in an affidavit that it was normal in his country for government ministers (many belonging to his family) to own companies that could win state contracts and thereby pocket a large percentage of the profits, stating explicitly that 'a cabinet minister ends up with a sizeable part of the contract price' – a type of blatant conflict of interest that is illegal in most other countries.[11]

Economic corruption rarely exists on its own and is generally accompanied by problems in the press and police. The corruption of police forces is particularly problematic because it becomes effectively impossible to address the corruption of higher ranking officials or to fight many other sorts of crime. As Chapter 4 shows, the purchase of the goodwill of members of the police force, military, and border forces in Central and South America by drug cartels is instrumental in ensuring that drug traffickers are able to carry on their trade and impedes attempts to fight either the traffickers or the corrupt officials. The low wages of such officials in many developing countries make them particularly susceptible to bribery, laying fertile ground for other types of crime.

However, it is a mistake to think that all instances of corruption are clear cut and can be easily remedied by simple legislation and punishment. In some countries, persistent petty corruption is deeply enmeshed in the culture of both commercial and municipal transactions, and may be beyond the reach of a police force which itself is likely to be compromised and reliant on its own hierarchical bribery. In others, the personal enrichment of the top officials who squirrel away millions in foreign banks and property investments whilst the rest of the country's population suffers is linked to the pervasive power of those few officials, who make investigations into their conduct and finances impossible. In some of the most subtle cases, national interests are traded between states, often with financial incentives; cases of corruption on paper, but arguably justified by the pragmatic demands of national security and public safety. The harder it is to prevent corruption internally, the more important it is to take steps to prevent it being profitable externally.

There are many societies where petty bribery in all aspects of public life is normal. The Indian website *www.ipaidabribe.com* was set up as a result of increasing public intolerance to the country's all-pervasive low-level bribe culture. Its aim is to encourage people to report when they were made to pay money to access a public service. A quick glance provides a fascinating insight into a world where cash is regularly demanded to facilitate or evade the performance of simple tasks. Reports include a fire service that insisted on payment once they had put out a fire; a victim of theft who was asked to pay in order to get their property back at court; and a motorcyclist who was pulled over and forced to pay a traffic officer to avoid his bike being impounded for an offence he suspected did not exist (he watched the officer do the same with several other bikers in the next half hour). Versions of the website have been rolled out in other countries with reports of similar municipal bribes. These are small-scale examples, but they are symptomatic of national cultures where bribery is part of the fabric of commerce, where public officials participate widely, and where, by analogy, commercial and corporate bribery is able to thrive without the political will to prevent it.

Corruption involving local government contracts is prevalent globally. Concerns also exist in relation to the abuse of power in civilian contracting abroad. In 2006, two US citizens, Philip Bloom and Robert Stein, pleaded guilty to corruption offences concerning the award of government contracts for reconstruction in Iraq. Stein and other US officials who were administering the reconstruction funds and selecting contractors in the area agreed to rig bids in favour of Bloom's company; in return Bloom paid them over $1 million in cash and gifted jewellery, cars, computers and other valuable items. Bloom and Stein were sentenced to 46 months and nine years respectively, and both men were ordered to forfeit $3.6 million.[12]

In 2010, the UK armaments firm BAE Systems avoided corruption allegations and pleaded guilty to false accounting in relation to concealed payments of $12.4 million to a 'middleman' involved in a deal to supply radar equipment to the Tanzanian government. Allegations surfaced that the payment was in fact a bribe (it was over a quarter of the contract price) and that the equipment was more expensive and complex than was needed. BAE would later accept that there was 'a high probability that part of this sum would be used to favour it in the contract negotiations'. A plea was eventually agreed on with the Serious Fraud Office, which led to a fine of £500,000 and a payment of £30 million to the Tanzanian people.[13] The defence/armaments trade is an area of widespread concern: Transparency International stated in a 2011 report that only 13 out of 93 defence budgets surveyed had a high degree of transparency.[14]

Corruption cases also involve national bodies, which are alleged to pay money to foreign national figures in order to maintain lucrative contracts and good relationships between their states. These politically delicate deals are particularly prevalent in Middle Eastern countries where there are precise balances to be struck concerning oil trades and the relationships between pro- and anti-Western interests. In 2000, the Jersey authorities froze £100 million of suspected slush funds found in trusts connected to the Qatari foreign minister, which were alleged to be the proceeds of bribes paid by foreign companies to secure arms deals with the emirate. The Jersey attorney general shelved the investigation in 2002 on the grounds that it threatened good diplomatic links between the countries, and the Qatari minister – who always claimed that his business dealings were legitimate – wrote a £6 million cheque by way of 'voluntary reparation for any damage perceived to have been sustained' and towards the costs of the investigation into his Jersey affairs.[15]

A few years later, BAE Systems was accused of making regular bribe payments amounting to £1 billion to a Saudi prince in order to secure the continuation of a £43 billion contract to supply military equipment. BAE responded to the allegations by stating that the company acted in accordance with 'the relevant contracts' and had the approval of the Saudi Arabian government and the UK's Ministry of Defence. An investigation by the Serious Fraud Office was controversially halted in 2006 on the grounds of national security, apparently after the Saudi authorities informed Britain that if they did not desist, the Saudis would stop supplying intelligence on terrorism.[16] The issues at stake are far more subtle in this type of alleged corruption, which may to a certain extent be beyond the controls of ordinary regulation.

As a rather depressing reality check on what motivates Western companies to engage in bribe payments, regard must be given to the value of some of the contracts they seek to obtain and the fact that Western companies are competing in a global market place with companies based in countries where bribe payments are not only not illegal but are positively encouraged if the resulting contracts stimulate economic activity and domestic employment. The sums involved are often staggering, so large in fact that companies sometimes pay bribes simply to be included in a shortlist of businesses to be considered for the award of a contract. Each shortlisted business is then given an opportunity to pay a further much more substantial bribe to secure the business. In an effort to avoid detection for bribe paying, companies frequently utilise off-balance-sheet vehicles (companies or partnerships often referred to as Special Purpose Vehicles (SPVs) that enter into consultancy or agency type agreements as a means of providing a cover for the transfer of funds. The objective is to dress the bribe up to look like something that it is not, such as a consultancy payment or a charitable donation.

Famous examples of powerful politicians who have become extremely wealthy by corrupt means despite coming from countries with high levels of poverty exist all over the world, but particularly in locations where undemocratic political situations have allowed one person to acquire excessive power or to take control of natural resources such as oil, gold, or timber. The figures cited in Transparency International's 2004 *Global Corruption Report* for the sums believed to have been appropriated by Indonesian president Mohammed Suharto, Philippine president Ferdinand Marcos, Zaire president Mobutu Sese Seko, and Nigerian dictator Sani Abacha each run into billions. The figures for Haitian dictator Jean Claude Duvalier, Peruvian president Alberto Fujimori, and Ukrainian prime minister Pavlo Lazarenko are slightly lower, but only to the extent that they concern hundreds of millions each. Lazarenko, who in 2004 was imprisoned in the US for nine years (reduced to eight on appeal) following his conviction for a variety of crimes related to the financial abuse of his position, was found to have extorted millions from businessmen operating in the area where he was governor and to have laundered the proceeds into the US through a series of corporate vehicles and international bank accounts in Switzerland, Antigua, and the Bahamas. Transparency International estimated that Lazarenko had embezzled somewhere between $114 million and $200 million from Ukraine's public purse. Since his release in 2012, US prosecutors have decided to go after some of Lazarenko's assets, among them a $6.75 million California property and a Picasso lithograph.[17]

In the same ballpark, the fruits of Teodorin Obiang's activities are being pursued by US and European authorities. His combined expenditure from 2004–2011 has been totted up to over $300 million, and he has been investigated in at least three jurisdictions – Spain, the US, and France.

The accusations against Teodorin in France came as a result of the country's wider *biens mal acquis* (ill-gotten gains) investigation that was originally launched after a legal complaint was filed in 2007 by three NGOs, and which accused ruling families in Equatorial Guinea, Republic of the Congo, Angola, Burkina Faso, and Gabon of having swindled public funds and frittering away the money on acquiring French properties.[18] In September 2011, a fleet of Teodorin's luxury cars was impounded, and the following year the French authorities carted off truckloads of luxury goods housed in his €100 million pied-à-terre in the chic 16th arrondissement – a building which was itself also seized. When he subsequently failed to show up for questioning by French magistrates, an international arrest warrant was issued against him in July 2012. Meanwhile, on the other side of the Atlantic, civil forfeiture complaints were filed in 2011 in Washington and California seeking to recover a total of over $70 million of assets held in Teodorin's name in the US. The Americans were themselves spurred into investigating him after a 2004 probe discovered how the now-defunct Riggs Bank had harboured millions of dollars for individuals in Equatorial Guinea's highest echelons of power.

The methods used by Teodorin to accumulate his wealth, as documented in US court filings, are a manual for aspiring students of grand corruption. A number of tactics were revealed; the application of an illegal retroactive 'tax' Teodorin levied personally on foreign timber companies, the misappropriation of funds by receiving millions of dollars 'from fraudulently inflated construction contracts' (by as much as 500%) in the country, the collection of a $27 fee per log for timber-exporting companies, and another 'personal fee' from timber companies seeking concessions. All of this despite the fact that under Equatorial Guinea law, the nation's mineral resources and hydrocarbons belong to the public.

On a slightly smaller scale but no less endemic and damaging to the people whose lands are affected are the numerous Nigerian State governors believed to have pocketed huge sums of money from the oil-rich areas they control, whilst the local inhabitants live with the sort of poverty that proper management of the country's revenues would do so much to reduce. Life expectancy is around 52, and over a quarter of children under the age of five are underweight. One of the politicians to face proper punishment for his crimes is James Ibori, formerly a petty thief at the British DIY shop where he worked, who in 1999 became the governor of Delta State. For the next eight years, Ibori systematically stole from and defrauded the state's coffers, enriching his own personal bank accounts with what the Metropolitan Police estimated to be £157 million of public funds. Despite his official annual salary being £4,000, he lived a life of luxury, owning foreign homes valued in the millions. Arrested and brought to trial in London following a complex international pursuit, in 2012 Ibori pleaded guilty to the theft and laundering of £50 million and was imprisoned for 13 years.[19]

Also charged in the UK was Diepreye Alamieyeseigha, the governor of the oil-rich Bayelsa State, who was arrested in 2005 at London Heathrow Airport. In one of his UK properties (according to one report, he had property assets in the city worth almost £5 million), he had £1 million in cash that was all part of a wealth of over £10 million amassed outside Nigeria and hidden in a range of trusts and bank accounts most of which were in small offshore jurisdictions with his beneficial ownership carefully disguised. His downfall came following the discovery by the Nigerian Economic and Financial Crimes Commission of massive procurement bribes and theft from public development funds. Jumping UK bail – supposedly disguising himself as a woman – Alamieyeseigha returned to Nigeria where he was impeached and pleaded guilty to money laundering offences (on behalf of two companies he controlled). He has since been granted a presidential pardon in Nigeria whilst the British high commissioner of Nigeria has pointed to diplomatic wrangles as the UK tries to extradite the Nigerian to face the charges originally brought against him in 2005.[20]

A common factor in many of these cases of bribery and corruption is the use of the financial system to harbour the proceeds of the illicitly gained funds. Financial institutions assist corruption in two ways. The first is through the provision of banking services to companies or persons that are at a high risk of making or receiving bribe payments and, knowingly or negligently, permitting the transfer of money that is part of a bribe. This may happen when a bank assists a construction or defence company with a presence in a high-risk country to make a payment to a state employee in that country. Not only would the bank potentially have aided the commission of an offence under primary anti-bribery legislation, but it would also likely have occasioned a breach of the regulatory requirements of its home jurisdiction.

Secondly, a bank or institution may assist corruption by opening an account or setting up a structured vehicle ultimately for the benefit of a bribe receiver. When they establish a relationship with a person they either know is a PEP, or in respect of whom their due diligence is insufficiently stringent to leave them unaware that the person is a PEP; or by unquestioningly maintaining an account in the face of suspicious activity and facilitating payments that consist of the expenditure of corrupt money, they encourage the problem.

This kind of behaviour was unearthed by the Permanent Subcommittee on Investigations' enquiry into Riggs Bank and detailed in its 2004 case study report which examined its compliance with the money laundering aspects of the Patriot Act.[21] The subcommittee uncovered serious deficiencies in the way that the bank dealt with its PEP clients. The bank was fined $41 million and shortly afterwards was acquired by PNC Financial Services.

One of its clients was the Chilean dictator Augusto Pinochet. The subcommittee found that whilst Pinochet was under well-publicised arrest in the UK facing serious allegations concerning his conduct in office and whilst his money was subject to a freezing order, Riggs opened a number of accounts and issued certificates of deposit. Despite, or perhaps because of, the numerous allegations of human rights abuses, corruption, and arms trafficking attached to the politician's time in office, Riggs took steps to disguise the ownership of the huge sums (up to $8 million) deposited by Pinochet by opening shell companies and by altering the names on accounts. The bank then made cheques available to be sent to Pinochet or his wife in Chile for cashing. The bank allegedly hid the existence of the Pinochet accounts from the US Office of the Comptroller of the Currency. No references were found in the bank's files of the controversial nature of Pinochet's reputation and no steps appeared to have been taken to ensure that his personal wealth had been acquired by legitimate means.

Riggs also provided accounts and structured vehicles to the Obiang family in the US and in offshore jurisdictions. The bank was found to have largely failed to take into account the high risks that were being run by dealing with PEPs from an oil-rich African state.

From 1995 onwards, Riggs opened accounts for various members of the presidential family and for the oil business without making sufficient enquiries into the obvious risks that were run by doing so. This may not be surprising given that the business Riggs did with Equatorial Guinea was such that by 2003 it was the bank's largest client, with deposits of $400–700 million. Accounts were opened for the government which received huge payments from oil companies operating in the country; other holders, either in name or beneficially, include President Obiang's wife, his eldest son, his brother, and government ministers. In 1999, the bank assisted the president in opening an offshore corporation in the Bahamas, which subsequently received cash deposits totalling over $11 million.

Riggs was by no means the only culprit, nor are banks the only conduits into the US financial system. Teodorin was assisted in this respect by estate agents and lawyers. One estate agent admitted that he was not going to turn away a client who was hoping to make extremely lucrative deals when he himself had no legal obligation to look into his source of wealth. When one escrow agent refused to provide services for the purchase of an aeroplane because Teodorin had failed to provide information about the origin of his money, another was easily found with fewer scruples. Without sufficient probing, Teodorin was able to mislead those dealing with his finances by declaring that his wealth came from sources such as 'family inheritance' or 'trading expensive and custom automobiles'. Offshore shell companies and accounts with benign sounding names such as 'Sweetwater Management, Inc.', 'Sweet Pink, Inc.', and 'Beautiful Vision, Inc.' were opened in banks of major players, such as the Union Bank of California, Bank of America, and Citibank, and money moved despite his clear PEP status. When accounts were closed after the Equatorial Guinea link was eventually discovered, Teodorin merely moved banks and began the process over again.

A 2011 study by the Financial Services Authority entitled *Banks' management of high money-laundering risk situations* considered various banks and how they dealt with PEP clients.[22] A number of concerning deficiencies were discovered and it was found that some banks were unwilling to reject profitable relationships even when the relationship included an 'unacceptable risk' of handling criminal money and that more than a third of institutions examined had failed to put in place adequate PEP controls or manage due diligence records correctly. Significantly, it was noted that despite legal and regulatory changes in the intervening decade, some of the weaknesses were the same as those identified in the FSA's 2001 report into the UK accounts linked to Sani Abacha. Financial institutions fail in their regulatory duties when they do not devote sufficient time to analysing as far as possible the real owner of such structures, or by taking on work without being able to identify the ultimate controllers of the structures concerned. This was evidenced when RBS-owned Coutts Bank was fined £8.75 million in 2012 for inadequately handling its high-risk customers, including PEPs. The FSA found 'systemic' failings in the bank's anti-money laundering procedures between 2007 and 2010, which resulted in 'an unacceptable risk of Coutts handling the proceeds of crime'.[23]

Until relatively recently, there was very little international willpower committed to either criminalising bribe payments or to restricting the provision of banking services to potentially corrupt officials. This led to the perpetuation on an international level of financial structures which have enriched criminal politicians from Africa, Russia, Asia, and South America. Indeed, the UN's Convention against Corruption (UNCAC) only dates back to 2003, making it a far more recent set-up than other similar efforts to deal with other forms of global crime. However, the growing ethical awareness in the last decade of the damage that is being caused by corruption and the role that is being played by unscrupulous financiers has led to a new, more rigorous regulatory approach to providing high-risk services. Increasing pressure from NGOs such as Global Witness and from supranational bodies such as the UN and the OECD, as well as domestic law reform, has raised awareness of the steps banks can take to block access to corrupt money.

There are now two major streams within the anti-corruption framework: the legal and the regulatory, which, whilst distinct, also share characteristics and aims. The legal stream penalises the making of a bribe or corrupt payment and includes within its remit individuals, companies, and also, potentially, financial organisations which knowingly facilitate corruption. The regulatory stream provides guidance that must be followed by banks and other financial institutions as to what steps should be taken in terms of due diligence to identify PEPs, how they should be risk-rated, how their account activity should be monitored, and what to do if a suspicious transaction occurs. Failures to adhere to this guidance constitute regulatory offences which can result in heavy fines from the local regulator. However, there are still significant deficiencies in the manner in which these are applied.

In terms of the legality of corruption itself, many Western countries have instituted legislation which unequivocally criminalises such activity. The US led the way with the Foreign Corrupt Practices Act of 1977 which outlawed the making of payments by US persons to foreign officials for the purposes of gaining favourable business outcomes. The 2001 Patriot Act also contained measures intended to prevent money laundering and terrorist financing. In the UK, it was not until 2001 that the Anti-terrorism, Crime and Security Act outlawed bribery overseas in the UK. The creation of the 2010 Bribery Act, a far more comprehensive piece of legislation which enacts a range of personal and corporate offences at home and abroad, was a clear indication of the intolerance towards corruption and the change of political will. In an effort to see more prosecutions, a small but significant tweak to the act is now being tabled which would give the Serious Fraud Office wider ranging powers to pursue financial crime. However, corruption is not illegal everywhere in the world, and a significant problem arises when an official demands a 'facilitation fee' in a country in which the payment of a bribe does not constitute a criminal offence under domestic law.

In terms of regulation, the international Financial Action Task Force (FATF) has led the field in making recommendations concerning the steps that institutions should take to ensure the least possibility of exploitation by those involved in bribery or corruption. FATF's original 40 Recommendations have since been supplemented by a further nine 'Special' Recommendations that relate more closely to terrorist financing. Many of the original 40 are particularly relevant to anti-corruption controls, particularly those which deal with PEPs, the beneficial ownership of trusts, transparency, and customer due diligence; and it is these Recommendations that banks and other institutions should be following in a bid to ensure that they minimise their risk exposure to corrupt clients. However, analysis by the World Bank's Stolen Asset Recovery Initiative (StAR) reveals that compliance with these standards is poor: for example, only 6% of the surveyed countries were 'largely' compliant with Recommendation 5 (customer due diligence) with 53% rated as 'partially' compliant and the remaining 41% non-compliant. Even among FATF member states, only 12% were 'largely' compliant.

In regulatory terms the most essential criteria which should establish immediately whether a potential customer is a corruption risk is whether he is a PEP, which automatically triggers enhanced due diligence procedures. Herein lies a difficulty because jurisdictions define PEPs slightly differently: in some, a PEP loses this status a certain number of years after leaving office; in others, he remains a PEP for life. Some risk-rate family members and associates more highly than others; others consider only foreign, and not domestic, officials as PEPs. Such divergence creates laundering arbitrage opportunities for bribe payers, PEPs, and their advisers. For example in countries that employ a definition of predicate criminality for money laundering purposes based on the concept of dual criminality, it can be very difficult to show that the proceeds of a bribe constitute criminal property in circumstances where the PEP is connected to a ruler of a country who says 'I was aware of the inducement and I condone it'. Whilst that may seem extraordinary to many readers, the reality is that there remain numerous economically powerful countries that are run as little more than personal fiefdoms in which the power of the ruler, or his family, is absolute.

Common sense is generally applied when risk rating a client with political connections, and there is nothing intrinsically wrong per se in a bank providing services for a PEP. The salient point is that the PEP relationship should trigger detailed and on-going scrutiny of the client's affairs and account activity, far beyond that of a normal banking client. A bank may decide that the PEP's country of origin and political reputation is simply too much of a risk; they may decide that the risk can be managed by regular reviews and the appropriate steps taken if and when the need arises. A bank should be thinking very carefully before it takes on as a client someone whose ownership of structures is not entirely clear.

Financial institutions must be aware that they can play a very important role in preventing bribery, not only by detecting and stopping possible transactions which may represent the actual bribe payment itself, but by cutting off access to retentive banking structures which enable the corrupt person to benefit. This requires a stringent approach to due diligence and a thorough investigation of all clients so that they can be appropriately risk-rated. Primary legislation will hopefully go some way to discouraging the paying of bribes by Western companies; although with so much competition from companies domiciled elsewhere in the world which appear to be able to pay bribes with relative impunity, it is naïve to assume that outlawing bribery in the US and Europe will prevent it altogether. Furthermore, such attempts in the Western developed world do little to prevent the pervasive problems of corruption which remain in emerging economies and the developing world. Even a country that has anti-corruption laws on its statute book may face real difficulty in bringing home a prosecution of a politician domestically. For example, it is worth noting that Nigeria provides constitutional immunity from prosecution to incumbent officials, which hardly discourages corruption. The ethical considerations raised by the catastrophic problems caused by corruption must play their part too in ensuring that financial institutions recognise the responsibility they have to ensure that they are not exploited by officials who deprive countries and their peoples of a brighter future.

Regrettably, bribery and corruption have featured as one of the most common forms of predicate criminality that I have stumbled across in the conduct of my work. A thread that runs through all of the examples that I have witnessed has been the 'special treatment' afforded to PEPs by financial institutions resulting in them being subjected to a lower standard of due diligence than the average person on the street, proving the old adage that 'it's one rule for them and another set of rules for the rest of us'. I have seen so many different corruption methodologies that choosing just one for this chapter has been very challenging. I have settled on a scenario which exposes the treatment of a $20 million bribe paid by a large European armaments manufacturer to a Middle Eastern government official that illustrates both how bribe payers abuse the financial services industry to pay bribes and how politicians receive and launder their ill-gotten gains.

## SCENARIO

The curtains open to a European arms business, which has a balance sheet running into the billions, learning that a particular Middle Eastern jurisdiction is in the market to update its ageing inventory of military fighter jets. The contract would potentially net the company hundreds of millions and could secure several thousand jobs. Word goes out that there is room at the table for only five bidders, and a place at the table costs $20 million. The arms manufacturer views $20 million as cheap for the economic opportunity of being considered as one of only five bidders for such a substantial contract and is eager to participate. The company knows that this sum is just for openers, and that winning the contract will itself require an even larger inducement. Tapping into its gambling instincts, it thinks the outlay is well worth the potential returns.

The company's participation is brokered through a middleman who represents the Middle Eastern country's defence minister. The middleman demands a $2 million 'fee', equivalent to 10% of the bribe value. Negotiations over, the company has secured a provisional spot in the running, and now turns its mind to transferring the $22 million to the defence minister's representative without being rumbled for breaching the anti-bribery rules in its home country. With reference to the new enable, distance, and disguise model of money laundering, the company's objective is confined simply to using the finance industry to effect the bribe payment. The desired disconnect between the arms manufacturer and the $22 million looks like this:

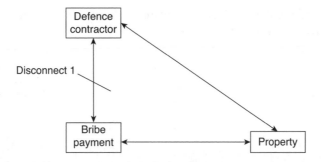

The arms manufacturer conveniently has a tax neutral SPV with holdings of $30 million in a foreign jurisdiction. The SPV was originally set up in anticipation of establishing a joint venture with another arms manufacturer which never came to fruition. The money in the SPV has effectively been written off and sits – legitimately – off balance sheet, away from the prying eyes of accountants and anyone else caring to take a look.

To disguise his receipt of the bribe, the defence minister relies on an army of clever confidantes and advisers who form a trust and underlying company structure on his behalf. The defence minister has a broader set of objectives in abusing the finance industry than the arms manufacturer. He wants to: (1) receive the bribe money without being caught, (2) transform the bribe money so that it cannot be traced back to the crime, and (3) disguise his connection with the laundered property. The disconnects for each of his objectives can be depicted as follows.

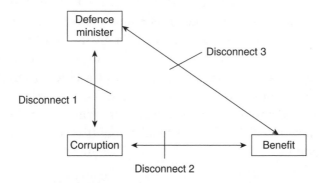

Disconnect 1 for the arms manufacturer and the defence minister is, then, the payment and receipt respectively of the bribe whilst avoiding any scrutiny by law enforcement. The two men are reliant on the participation of the minister's representative, whose structure of choice is a foundation with an underlying company and an associated bank account. The middleman is represented by a Swiss law firm whose partners take their duty of client confidentiality very seriously indeed.

The arms company, defence minister, Swiss law firm, and middleman collude to participate in the following structure.

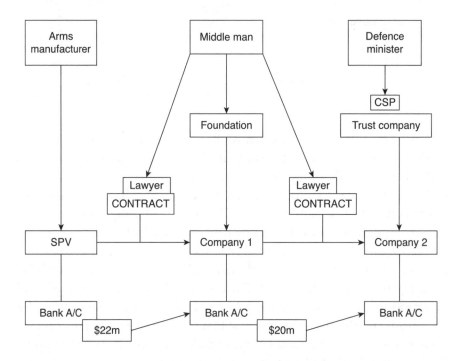

With the structures for each of the protagonists in place, the challenge is to transfer the bribe to the defence minister via the middleman.

The representative first instructs the Swiss law firm to craft some very authentic looking contracts. The arms manufacturer enters into a (fictitious) Master Consultancy Contract with Company 1 for the provision of services to identify potential arms contracts in various parts of the world. The contract states that Company 1 will provide a series of specified services listed in Schedule 1 of the contract, which runs to some 75 pages in length. In consideration for these services the arms manufacturer's SPV will pay Company 1 $22 million in equal amounts of $5.5 million over the next four months.

Company 1 simultaneously enters into a Sub-consultancy Agreement with Company 2, pursuant to which Company 2 takes on the responsibility for acting on Company 1's behalf in a particular region of the world. The provisions of the Sub-consultancy Agreement mirror those of the Master Consultancy Contract between Company 1 and the arms company. In consideration for delivery of these services Company 1 agrees to pay Company 2 $20 million (meaning that the middleman retains $2 million for his efforts). The contracts are signed and the money flows across the bank accounts as envisaged by the paperwork. In the event that any questions are asked about the transfers by an astute banker, the contracts will be produced for the purposes of verification. They will both look and smell right bearing the imprint of the Swiss law firm. The banker draws comfort from the consistency in the scheduled services in both the Master Consultancy Contract and Sub-consultancy Agreement. Taking all of these factors into account the banker is satisfied that the transfers are above board. Four months pass, and as the final payment is deposited into the defence minister's structure, he becomes $20 million the richer.

A blatant bribe has been disguised as a series of payments in exchange for consultancy services. The act of bribing the defence minister has been facilitated by ownership structures and bank accounts without which the bribe could not have been paid. The financial services industry has facilitated an act of grand corruption.

Where is the identifiable placement and layering activity in this scheme? The answer of course is that it does not feature. There is no placement because the money is already sitting in the SPV before it becomes tainted as a bribe; there is no layering because that comes later once the money is in the defence minister's structure as his proceeds of crime. The structure has provided both the arms manufacturer and the minister with the desired disconnect between them and the crime.

Through the structure the minister has distanced himself from the act of receiving a bribe but he remains vulnerable to detection. I turn then to how he handles his ill-gotten gains. He decides to spend half the bribe money on a profitable boutique hotel in Geneva. The profits from the hotel are distributed to trustees as dividends, and the trustees make the money available for the benefit of the minister. The minister is actually never in direct receipt of income from the trustees, but the trustees instead pay for his children's private school fees, fractional jet ownership hours, credit card bills, and certain staff costs. The minister's friends and family members freely come and go from the plush hotel during frequent shopping trips to the watch and clothes emporiums of Geneva and visits to their private bankers. In time, the hotel is used as collateral for a loan which is spent on a ski chalet in Verbier and a 92-foot yacht moored in Monaco. The minister and his family and friends use the chalet in winter and the yacht in summer as and when the fancy takes them.

The minister decides to invest the other half of his bribe money in a successful hedge fund in Switzerland. The returns are spectacular, and proving the old adage that 'money begets money', the $10 million blossoms into $15 million in less than three years. The defence minister has his advisers instruct the Swiss fund manager to pay the $15 million not to the structure from which the initial investment came but to another company held by a trustee acting on the minister's behalf. The $15 million is then invested by that company into a joint venture vehicle which, through the influence of the minister, has been miraculously awarded a contract to develop a large hotel and shopping complex in his home city. As a result of the planning consent, the minister's investment in the development company doubles in value, and so the sorry tale continues.

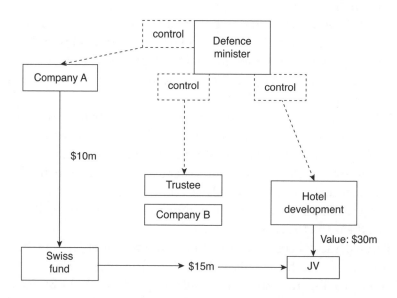

The upshot is that over the course of his term in office, the minister siphons away hundreds of millions in bank accounts and other forms of assets he owns via complex structures overseen by professional intermediaries, private bankers, and corporate service providers. The approach of all of the colluding parties is characterised by sycophancy borne out of a fear of jeopardising a highly remunerative business relationship with a man who has significant political and thus commercial influence in a jurisdiction in which each of the service providers has, or desires, a significant presence.

The scenario begs the question of whether the bank's unwitting facilitation of the crime could have been avoided. There are two instances where the red flags ought to have been raised. Firstly, the banker ought to be in a position to know that consultancy agreements that attach to a standalone trading company present a particularly high risk, and therefore he should have probed the legitimate commercial rationale for the structure. Secondly, the combination of the two contracts for intangible services (and, therefore, difficult to verify), a PEP, and a middleman should set the alarm bells ringing. Had a risk-based analysis been applied to the structure, it is highly likely that these aspects would have been explored further, and ultimately obstructed the course of the illicit funds.

# 6

# PIRACY

In October 2009, in a well-publicised incident, retired British couple Paul and Rachel Chandler were hijacked by pirates as they took a sailing holiday near the Seychelles on their yacht the Lynn Rival. Their boat was boarded by a group of pirates from Somalia who forced them to board a nearby ship, the Kota Wajar, leaving the Lynn Rival adrift. The Kota Wajar herself had been hijacked less than a fortnight earlier, and the pirates had set her to use as a 'mother ship' from which they could launch attacks, extending their operational range by many hundreds of miles from the Somali coastline where they had originated from. The crew of the Kota Wajar, a cargo ship originally sailing from Singapore to Kenya, had been captured, and a ransom payment had been demanded from the ship's owners. Just ten weeks after the initial hijack took place, its crew members were released following the payment of a ransom that was believed to have been $3.3 million. The Chandlers were not so lucky; whilst they were held in Somalia, a ransom demand of $6.5 million was made by the pirates. The demand was clearly impossible; nobody in the Chandler family possessed that kind of money and despite discussions continuing with various brokers and security experts, it was reported that the UK government had prevented the payment of an agreed sum due to its policy of not paying ransoms. Foreign Secretary William Hague was quoted as saying that, after using contacts and attempting to influence the kidnappers, it was 'right that successive British governments have said we don't make concessions to hostage-takers'.[1]

By the summer of 2010, a reported payment of $440,000, raised by the couple's relatives, was airdropped to the pirates, but intent on raising yet more cash the captors hung on to the Chandlers for another few months. After hearing of their plight, it was allegedly an East London Somali former minicab driver who secured the couple's release due to his children urging him to take action after they learnt about the Chandlers' story on television. The pirates told the UK press that a final payment of $300,000 was transferred to Somalia via hawala and after 388 days in captivity the Chandlers were released and their nightmare had ended.

Piracy has a long and often romanticised history but it is very much a modern phenomenon. Contemporary global piracy is characterised by its reliance on hijack and ransom payments that lead to a significant rise in the cost of shipping goods by sea. This type of modern seaborne criminality also raises questions over the purpose and destination of the sizeable sums handed over as ransoms. Exact figures are hard to come by, but to give an idea the estimated average ransom payment in 2005 was $150,000; in 2010 it had risen to $5.2 million. The highest recorded ransom of that year was $9.5 million – the amount paid to release a South Korean vessel that had been captured by Somalis. The World Bank has reported in its *Pirate Trails* study that Somali piracy, such as that endured by the Chandlers, costs the global economy an average of $18 billion a year, equating to a hypothetical 1.1% added 'tax' on shipments travelling through Gulf of Aden.[2] Somali piracy has within its sights access to one of the most crucial strategic shipping zones in the world: the Suez Canal. Although initially mostly shore-based, the increasing use of 'mother ships' has extended their range considerably. The pirates operate as far south as Kenya, north along the entire Gulf of Aden, and east almost as far as Indian coastal waters – a total range estimated to be as much as 2.5 million square nautical miles. Add to that the human cost of captivity and, in some cases, the death of hostages, and the issue assumes an overwhelming importance.

Piracy incidents have increased sharply since the early 1990s. The recent drop in Somali piracy is starting to result in a shift of focus onto the Gulf of Guinea, where pirates formerly operating around the coast of Nigeria have broadened their horizons east and west to waters around the Ivory Coast and Gabon. According to the International Maritime Organization, which compiles annual statistics on global piracy, in 1991 there were no incidents of piracy in Africa, although there were 88 in South East Asia and 14 in the Far East.[3] By 2000, these figures had increased to 68 in Africa, 242 in South East Asia and 20 in the Far East. By 2010, Africa had become by far the dominant piracy location in the world, with 259 incidents; the number of reported incidents also increased in the Far East, to 44, whilst the number in South East Asia dropped to 70. Piracy incidents off the coast of Somalia itself increased exponentially, going from none in 1991 to 139 by 2010, whereas in Indonesia, they declined from a peak of 119 in 2000, to only 40 in 2010, spiking again in 2013 to 106.

The nature of pirate attacks range from short and easily repelled boarding attempts to a full-scale hijacking of a vessel and the capture of its crew, prior to a lengthy and costly ransom negotiation. The ICC International Maritime Bureau found that in 2013, there were 264 reported cases of attempted and actual pirate attacks around the world.[4] A broad range of vessels was targeted: small yachts, dhows, tug boats, trawlers, and huge oil tankers among them. Of those 264 attacks, 12 resulted in vessels being hijacked. A number of the reported piracy incidents were represented by low-level opportunistic robberies in South East Asia, often lasting under an hour, clearly very different in nature to the hostage-taking in other parts of the world.

Whilst Somali pirates accounted for roughly half of all reported attacks between 2009 and 2011, that proportion is dropping rapidly. Only 15 of the 264 attacks (or 5%) in 2013 (just two of which were hijackings) were located in areas cruised by Somali pirates, namely the Gulf of Aden, the Red Sea, Somalia, the Arabian Sea, the Indian Ocean, and Oman. The scale of Somali piracy over the past couple of decades is, in part, the reason for its successful reduction because there has been a concerted and targeted effort to reduce an increasing number of attacks. Navies have upped their patrolling of these areas, and private armed security services are more frequently used aboard ships transiting these waters. Public support for the pirates in their homeland is also said to be waning. These factors have also combined with a relative stabilisation of Somalia's central government to significantly reduce instances of Somali piracy in 2012 and 2013.

Despite the promising outlook, the continuing measures taken by ship owners to deter and deal with Somali pirate attacks, and the economic investment required to do so, demonstrates just how dangerous the waters around the Horn of Africa can still be. Since the 1990s, the pirates operating from the Somali coastline, usually grouped around clan lines, have succeeded in making the Horn of Africa the most dangerous area of sea on earth for commercial shipping. The techniques used by Somali pirates differ from those used elsewhere in the world in one important respect: ransom payments. Pirates in the Far East, and also in West Africa, typically board ships (often whilst the vessel is at anchor) and steal valuables such as cargoes, money, or personal possessions of the crew before leaving again. The typical *modus operandi* of the Somali pirates, by contrast, is the hijacking of ships and crews for ransom. This form of piracy tends to take as its victim ships that are in transit and tends to be considerably more violent than that practised elsewhere. In addition to guns, Somali pirates have been reported to have access to rocket propelled grenade launchers, which add dramatically to the efficacy of their operations. Between April 2005 and December

2012, the World Bank estimates that between $339 million and $413 million was collected in ransoms from pirates operating around the Horn of Africa. These substantial sums raise questions concerning the origin of the backers of the expeditions (including whether or not they are linked to terrorism), and the extent to which the global financial system is used to launder the proceeds of piracy.

Somalia has a population of around ten million and has a GDP per capita of only $248. Two regions to the north, Puntland and Somaliland, broke away in the 1990s to form semi-autonomous regions with greater civil rule, but these are not officially recognised. Until recently, Somali piracy has operated from a country devoid of fully operative government rule or the rule of law. Some pirates and Somali officials have claimed that pirate activities started as a response to illegal fishing and toxic waste dumping by foreign boats in Somali waters, both of which became commonplace when the lack of effective government rendered the Somali coastline an easy target for such activity. Stopping the illegal vessels and demanding money soon became a lucrative trade, which extended itself into the organised hijacking of ships that had nothing to do with either fishing or waste dumping. The lack of a centralised government or organised rule of law in Somalia meant that piracy was able to increase unchecked by internal forces, as governance and legal norms reverted to the old tribal systems in the 1990s.

The country's fortunes appear to be changing with the election of a new federal parliament in 2012. This follows eight years of a transitional authority – the Transitional Federal Government (TFG) – which was formed with a view to re-establishing a basic level of civic control in the country but swiftly found itself rivalled by the Islamic Courts Union (ICU), a group of radical organisations which had taken control of much of the south of Somalia. The TFG succeeded in reclaiming much of the territory that the ICU had overrun, but the ICU then splintered into various other groups which pursued a continuing campaign against the TFG. The most powerful of these splinter groups was Al Shabaab, which was formed in 2006 and believed to have around 8,000 fighters. Al Shabaab's leader 'pledged obedience' to Ayman Al Zawahiri, Al Qaeda's leader, in 2012, and the group claimed responsibility for the Kenya shopping centre attack the following year, apparently in retaliation against the country's military deployment in Somalia. Designated a terrorist group by many countries including the US and UK, Al Shabaab is responsible for large-scale violence, kidnapping, and the imposition of religious militancy across much of the south of the country. Puntland has been active in attempting to drive away Al Shabaab and oppose its activities, and Ethiopian troops have recently joined the

African Union peacekeeping mission in Somalia to suppress Al Shabaab activities. The group's grip on various territories in Somalia may finally be weakening.

Links between Somali pirates and Islamic terrorists are frequently alleged but there is no conclusive evidence to prove that one activity is explicitly supporting the other, and it is difficult to distinguish hearsay from fact. One commentator writing in *The New York Times* recognised 'isolated attempts at cooperation between pirates and terrorists'. This was echoed by FATF's findings, published in its *Organised Maritime Piracy and Related Kidnapping for Ransom* report, that in one particular hijacking scenario, Al Shabaab had advised pirates to sink or burn the ship.[5] A UN adviser has described a 'natural linkage' between Al Shabaab and pirate gangs because of the source of revenue the latter represents to the former.[6] 'Protection money' paid by pirates to insurgents is sometimes suggested, and there have been reports that 20% of the ransom payments was given to Al Shabaab in view of the militia's control of the port at Harardheere, known for its connections to pirate gangs. But the *NYT* commentator ultimately distanced the two groupings by suggesting that, actually, 'Al Shabab has been terrific at stamping out piracy from its ports, due to its harsh interpretation of Shariah and the personal animus between profit-seeking pirates and Islamist militants'. Whatever the case, the scenario set out at the end of this chapter examines the dangers posed by any sort of potential partnership between the two.

Estimating the cost of piracy worldwide is difficult and any attack by pirates results in a number of global costs rising over time. The World Bank's calculation of $18 billion annually is based on various factors: for instance, apart from the ransom payments themselves, shipping companies face higher insurance premiums due to the increased risks they face. Steps taken to evade Somali pirate action include obtaining intelligence, and routing ships by a different course (usually round the Cape of Good Hope) to avoid the area in which Somali pirates are active, adding weeks to voyage times and cutting the number of profitable trips that a vessel can make each year. More popular now are attempts in deterring the pirates by hiring armed guards (previously unusual but, since 2011, permitted by the UK government) or equipping ships with razor wire, water cannons, and foam sprays. Increased security, however, comes at a high cost. It is estimated that the price of patrols by naval forces (the UN, EU, and international taskforces) reaches $2 billion each year. On top of this comes the expense of prosecuting and potentially imprisoning the protagonists who are captured. Quite apart from the costs to the (mainly developed) nations which suffer these expenditures, there are significant losses to the fragile economies of other countries in the piracy zone, which suffer inflated food prices, and a reduction in revenues from tourism.

There is also a difficulty in obtaining reliable information as to exactly how piracy operations are funded. The World Bank proposes that acts of Somali piracy follow three possible business models – *artisanal, cooperative*, and *individualistic*. The perpetrators of the small-scale artisanal schemes usually belong to the same family, their outlay is around $300, and the return on investment is relatively low. In contrast, in the cooperative or 'shareholder' scheme, a collection of financiers pool resources to launch larger scale attacks with upfront costs of perhaps $30,000. This is a far more structured approach in which leaders and committees take on designated roles. The individualistic scheme sees a primary investor controlling the operation and collecting up to 75% of the ransom. In 2009, it was reported by *Reuters* that what was effectively a stock exchange for piracy had been set up in Harardheere. With about 70 companies of pirates on its books, the system apparently allowed for members of the community to assist with money or weaponry in return for a proportion of the eventual profit from the enterprise.[7]

The financing stage is likely, therefore, to involve the movement of substantial amounts of cash (as well as at the ransom distribution stage). Funders may need to access money for the initial outlay either from Somalia or abroad. In the early stages of planning an attack, if a pirate investor needs his money to cross the Somali threshold from an overseas bank account, he may use a trade-based method to do so. For instance, a pirate may collaborate with a legitimate local businessman who wishes to import products from Kenya. The businessman enlists the services of a Kenya-based associate to buy the products there, and then the businessman pays with the pirate's money sitting in a Seychelles bank account. Once the Kenyan products arrive in Somalia, the local businessman repays the pirate funder in local currency; the pirate investor is now ready to spend in the local denomination.

The accuracy of information concerning ransom payments is hard to gauge as there is a strong incentive for ship owners to under-report the ransom payments or in some cases not to report the incident at all. Fears have arisen that by making public the true value that owners are prepared to pay for their ships, pirates may be encouraged in the future to make higher demands and bargain more aggressively. Ship owners can also be keen to avoid publicity and the delay that would result from an investigation, should the hijack become public. From the reported information, ransom demands appear to vary widely, and sometimes appear to depend on the nature of a ship's cargo. The pirates are aware that the human cost of refusal, and the economic cost of the loss of the cargo and the ship itself make it almost impossible for ship owners to refuse to pay up, even though the end sum that they settle for is generally a fraction of what is initially demanded.

In the case of Somali piracy, following a successful hijacking, the ship concerned is typically sailed to Somali waters after which the crew is taken onshore and a ransom demand is lodged with the ship's owners. Negotiations can be protracted, often taking several months. In September 2008, Somali pirates hijacked a Ukrainian ship, the MV Faina, which was carrying a cargo of weapons destined for Kenya. The initial ransom demand was over $35 million. Five months later, following negotiations involving various countries and NATO, a ransom of $3.2 million was paid and the ship and crew released. It is unclear what happened to the millions of dollars' worth of arms on board, although press reports suggest that they remained with the ship after the hijacked vessel was surrounded and blockaded by US warships. In November of the same year, pirates attacked the super-tanker Sirius Star, carrying over $100 million of crude oil, over 450 miles off the Kenyan coast. A ransom demand was made for $25 million, with the hijackers audaciously specifying that it would be counted using machines that could detect counterfeit notes. The final amount was reported to be between $3 million and $8 million. During their escape from the ship, several of the pirates drowned; one of the bodies reportedly washed up with a bag stuffed with $153,000 which suggested that the cash had been divided up immediately after it was dropped.

The negotiations take place with the ship's owners, often via an English-speaking negotiator. The initial ransom offer is usually very high and is negotiated down. When an agreement is reached, the cash is brought to the specified location by a number of methods. Sometimes simple arrangements concerning a person and a suitcase are employed, but the delivery method of choice is an airdrop to a specified location after which the ship and crew are released. In general, the payment of the ransom leads to the release of the ship and crew. However, in some rare cases, crew members are murdered. In February 2011, the SV Quest, a small US yacht with four sailors on board, was hijacked by Somalis. After a ransom was demanded, the US Navy managed to embark on negotiations with the pirates. However, for reasons that remain unclear, the pirates then shot all four of the crew before being themselves captured by the US Navy. At the time of writing, Mohammad Saaili Shibin, an English-speaking Somali, is serving 12 life sentences following his 2012 conviction in Virginia for piracy and hostage-taking for his part in the capture of a German vessel off the Somali coast in 2010 and the negotiations following the capture of the SV Quest the following year. In July 2013, Shibin lost an appeal in which his lawyers argued that because his activities were land-based, he could not be convicted of piracy.[8]

Much remains to be discovered about the distribution, movement, and spending of ransom money, which was investigated in some detail by the World Bank's *Pirate Trails* study. Despite a host of challenges in the collection of reliable data, the report provides a fascinating and useful insight into what has grown into a multi-million dollar industry with cash flowing both inside and outside of Somalia.

The report describes how, once the pirates have secured the ransom, the money is distributed among those involved in the operation. Traders who provide items such as food, fuel, khat, and alcohol for the duration of the hostage period operate on credit and are paid off after the cash drop. Capitalism thrives in this environment and traders attune themselves to their market demands. The World Bank found that khat, a leafy plant which induces stimulation and a mild state of euphoria when chewed, is sold to pirates at around three times the normal market price. Its report comments that 'pirates accept the situation and realise this is the cost and social norm of doing business'. Needless to say, despite these apparent 'opportunities' for local businesses and communities to benefit from an immediate cash injection following a ransom payment, the flow of criminal funds is also a destabilising factor in the country's social, economic, and political landscapes.

Once local debts have been met, the largest proportion of the funds is earmarked for the initial investors; they may receive a figure of between 30% and 70% of the total ransom. A second tier of payment is then allocated to the 'foot soldiers' who hijack the ship and stay with the hostages. They receive something like $30,000–$75,000 each. A 'bonus' might be extended to the first pirate to board a ship in the face of the heightened risk he faces, reportedly up to $10,000.

Smaller amounts of money might be spent on luxuries and prostitution, especially by the 'foot soldiers'. Larger sums have been known to be transferred to Djibouti, Kenya, and the UAE, mainly by cross-border cash smuggling and trade-based money laundering. Belonging to the latter category of money laundering, over-invoicing is one method used to shift cash across borders. Let's say our pirate funder in Somalia wishes to transfer some of his proceeds to a bank account in Kenya. He establishes a 'legitimate' business dealing in white goods, then orders $500 worth of fridges to be imported from a company in Kenya. He asks his associate, perhaps a relative, in Kenya to send the $500 worth of fridges, then sees that the invoice for the goods is bumped up to $700. The pirate funder pays the $500 with legitimate funds, and the surplus is paid from the proceeds of piracy. The person located in Kenya banks the $500, but deposits the extra $200 into the pirate investor's Kenyan account. The money is now deposited abroad and has a hallmark of legitimacy having been processed through an apparently regular business transaction. Money may alternatively be laundered via more traditional methods using cash-heavy businesses, such as hotels and restaurants. Funds from ransoms also seem to flow through other trades, such as real estate, khat, transport, and farming. Whatever the means for laundering the money, it is highly concerning that those involved may be pumping the proceeds of pirate attacks into buying political influence and feeding a cycle of crime by investing in further pirate attacks, human trafficking, migrant smuggling, militias, and military capacities on land in Somalia.

Taking action against the infiltration of pirate money into the global financial system is a complex process. At its core sits the legal situation regarding ransom payments. They are not per se illegal in the UK or in many other countries, but what is problematic is the eventual destination of the money. Most states have legislation that concerns the use of money connected to criminal activity. In the UK, both the Terrorism Act 2000 and the Proceeds of Crime Act 2002 (POCA) contain sections which criminalise the making of payments which assist terrorists, or the assisting of persons to retain the proceeds of crime. There is no dispute that piracy is in itself a criminal activity and that the money it generates constitutes 'criminal property', but there are also the international concerns that acts of piracy may be financially linked to terrorist networks. This means that people who pay ransoms could be liable to increased sanctions under POCA and similar legislation in other countries. As a result, persons who wish to pay a ransom generally must seek consent from their country's law enforcement agencies so that the transactions can be authorised and then monitored. Not making a declaration not only risks criminalising the payer but impedes the ability of financial investigators to follow the money trail.

The UK House of Lords' EU Committee considered the position in a report in 2009 entitled *Money Laundering and the Financing of Terrorism.*[9] The Committee stated clearly that the payment of a ransom is legal in the UK and should remain thus in order to avoid the criminalisation of those seeking to purchase the release of relatives, employees, or possessions. They then proceeded to consider the legal position of a ransom payer. Despite being told that there was no known link between the pirates and terrorists who operate in the same part of the world, the Committee was of the opinion that if a connection were established in the future, a person paying a ransom could commit an offence under the Terrorism Act or POCA. Following criticism of the Home Office's attitudes to the subject, they stated that the government should be in a position to provide guidance as to whether ransoms may assist in financing terrorism. They were critical of the lack of a concrete link between piracy and terrorism and noted what they called the 'sharp contrast' between the large-scale naval efforts being employed internationally to disrupt acts of piracy themselves and the 'lack of any concerted action to inhibit the transfer of the proceeds of these criminal acts or even to establish whether they might be helping to finance terrorism'.

There is also continued debate about whether a UN plan to impose sanctions on piracy would make ransom payments illegal, and the international community's efforts to combat piracy have been hindered by a lack of consensus on such possible measures. The US has proposed that the UN add two alleged pirate organisers, Abshir Abdillahi and Mohamed Abdi Garaad, to its sanctions list, but this was blocked by the UK government in 2010 due to fears as to the consequences of criminalising ransom payments. The US has taken its own stance, and Abdillahi and Garaad are two of the 11 Somalis sanctioned under the OFAC regime. The move has made some in the maritime industry particularly nervous, fearing that the US and others may ban ransom payments altogether.

International agreement and cooperation extends to other aspects of combating piracy that relies on shipping companies, insurers, law enforcements, financial intelligence units, and post-incident investigators. Clearly, the success of this kind of cooperation is underpinned by knowledge of the facts, and this makes reporting the details of hijacking and ransoms and intelligence gathering all the more important. The failure to inform a national police force of a ransom payment has wider ramifications than not guaranteeing immunity from prosecution. In the fight against the abuse of the financial system and organised criminality, a constant supply of accurate data is essential. Without knowledge of a pirate ransom being paid, the international enforcement community is deprived of the chance to investigate the matter further. With a cash-based transaction, the performance of simple tasks such as noting the serial numbers of the banknotes concerned may be vitally important in enabling the notes to be traced if they eventually enter the banking system.

FATF identified several instances where opportunities to trace the cash handed over in ransom payments were lost by poor communication and an insufficiently robust approach. In one case, a 2007 hijacking of a Danish ship, the ransom payment was gathered from an American bank with FBI knowledge. It was said that although US authorities provided their Danish counterparts with the serial numbers of the cash, this information was never received by the Danish financial intelligence unit. The $723,000 in cash was handed over at a hotel in Dubai by a privately hired company, but all trace of the money thereafter disappeared as the Danish financial intelligence unit could not provide the serial numbers to the UAE authorities. Despite the fact that it might appear that an organised meeting in a country with a sophisticated banking system, which was not the country in which the attack happened, presented an unusually good opportunity to investigate the cash flow, the parties evidently did not recognise the importance of providing to each other details that could help in the tracing of the money. A similar case in 2008 also resulted in the Danish FIU not being given the serial numbers of notes totalling $1.7 million and a Suspicious Activity Report not being filed despite the withdrawal of the sums from a Danish bank, again cutting off the normal avenues to information-sharing and investigation.

In some pirate operations, there has been recovery of data potentially useful to investigators, but unfortunately due to the lack of coordination between the relevant authorities, the information has not been utilised in a manner resulting in further evidence being found or money being traced. In one instance, the European Union naval forces discovered details of bank accounts linked to Somali pirates, and passed the information to the Belgian authorities. There appeared to follow a series of communication failures and, ultimately, the leads were not pursued.

FATF identified two further specific factors which increase the vulnerability of the global financial system to the proceeds of piracy: first, that the cash intended for the ransom payment is rarely the subject of a bulk cash disclosure as it crosses borders, making tracing extremely difficult; and secondly, that Suspicious Activity Reports are rarely submitted to the relevant FIUs, who may be unaware that the ransom is being paid.

Besides attempting to follow the money flows, the international community has also invested substantial resources into responding to piracy with armed naval vessels, particularly in the Gulf of Aden. There are three main operations in this area established between 2008-2009 – the EU's Operation Atalanta, NATO's Ocean Shield and the multinational Combined Task Force 151. These have apparently met with success, as can be shown by a significant decrease in the number of pirate attacks in the Gulf of Aden in 2012 and 2013 compared with previous years. However, there have been concerns that due to the nature of their rules of engagement, the forces concerned have been unable to accomplish much beyond patrolling the seas.

However, there has been some success internationally prosecuting pirates that are captured. Piracy is a crime of universal jurisdiction and so does not need to be prosecuted in the country where it occurs. Piracy courts have been established in the Seychelles and in Kenya, both of which have been active in assisting with the legal response to the problem. There are also piracy courts in Mauritius, Tanzania, and Somaliland. Prisons in prosecuting areas are often overcrowded, and the influx of new inmates has put them under increasing pressure. The UN is working on the upgrade and construction of custodial centres in Somalia so that pirates do not take up the resources of the countries that have helped to convict them; a dedicated prison for pirates convicted abroad opened in Hargeisa in Somaliland in 2010. The increased cost of the prosecutors and prison staff required to administer the trial process is a further expense that the community can ill afford.

In Somalia itself, responses to piracy are varied, and the situation is evolving as power bases shift and the new government gradually introduces a level of stability to the country. The process is unlikely to turn things around quickly; the World Bank underlines that, despite progress, Somalia is 'still characterised by ongoing conflict, no legitimate monopoly on the use of force, weak state-society and intrasociety relations, a high dependency on external humanitarian assistance and diaspora remittances, and substantial war economies such as piracy and arms trafficking'. A study complied by Brunel University academic, Anja Shortland, for the UK policy institute Chatham House, analysed detailed data on Somali food prices and wages, measured light emissions, and compared satellite images of important areas between 2006 and 2010.[10] The analysis suggests some inland towns in Puntland had appeared to profit immensely from piracy, whereas small coastal towns did not seem to have gained much. This, and other evidence of increased wealth as a result of piracy, has led to suggestions that the wealth accrued by the pirates dissuades Puntland's authorities from taking the rigorous approach needed to curb the crime because local areas often benefit from investment or expenditure of pirate funds. FATF goes so far as to say that Puntland authorities have been implicated in actually 'supporting or participating' in piracy networks. In contrast, Somaliland has reportedly drawn up agreements with the maritime industry to bolster efforts to combat piracy. There is also a growing recognition that a great deal of potential to stop acts of piracy resides with clan elders, and the new government has extended a partial amnesty to 'foot soldiers' by negotiating with these community leaders. Indeed, despite the widely acknowledged correlation between increased patrolling and a reduction in piracy, the commentator writing in *The New York Times* played down the role of international navies in the decrease of attacks by saying that 'the most likely reason for the decline in piracy is that the Kenyan and Ethiopian war against Al Shabab [...] has disturbed the patronage networks and business conditions along the Somali coast that have enabled pirates to operate'.

When it comes to establishing the efficacy of international and local responses, cause and effect, then, is difficult to establish. Whatever the case, the incentives on dry land are still unknown and little is being done to investigate them. Additionally, and conspicuous by its absence, has been any form of coordinated international response to the challenges posed by the financial flows from piracy. A concerted effort to track the people behind piracy operations and disrupt the money flow is needed, along with a heightened awareness within financial institutions of the role they can unwittingly play in handling the proceeds of piracy.

## SCENARIO

This scenario highlights precisely how money flows can be channelled undetected through the global banking system. Making ransom payments, either partially or wholly, through the financial system makes sense to both the payer and the recipient for two reasons. Firstly, when a ship owner has doubts about the legality of making a ransom payment and does not want to risk law enforcement prohibiting the payment, he may do so covertly utilising offshore structures. Secondly, in the event that a terrorist organisation finances a hijacking, it may want the return on its investment accessible from a bank account in London, rather than sitting in cash in Djibouti. The risk of these kinds of side payments is heightened by the registration of many of the world's commercial vessels in opaque offshore jurisdictions such as Panama and The Cook Islands. This is further compounded by the fact that many vessels are themselves owned by off-shore companies and information relating to these corporate structures can be difficult to obtain.

This scenario proposes a partnership between Al Shabaab and Somali pirates and examines a situation in which ransom payments are used to fund an Al Qaeda attack [Al Shabaab's leader having 'pledged obedience' to Al Qaeda's leader in 2012]. It presents a situation in which a senior operative of Al Shabaab in Somalia orchestrates a ship hijacking in the Gulf of Aden, whilst a Djibouti-based operative links with an Al Qaeda terrorist cell in London, led by a Somali, and whose members include a UAE post-graduate student. Unbeknownst to the ship owner paying the ransom, part of the payment he channels through the banking system is destined to fund an atrocity carried out by Al Qaeda.

Al Shabaab decides to put up the seed money required to finance a hijacking of a very substantial container ship. The hijacking is audacious, and it is targeted at raising funds for its operations in Kenya and, for the first time, in the UK. Al Shabaab has intelligence from a 'sleeper' in Denmark that the ship contains perishables that the ship owner and the exporters of the goods will be keen to recover as quickly as possible.

Directed by the Al Shabaab operative in Djibouti a battle-hardened pirate leader organises a group of experienced pirates to attempt the hijacking, which will be controlled and launched from a mother ship hijacked some weeks earlier. Heavily armed with automatic machine guns and grenade launchers, the pirates jump into four skiffs and speed towards their target. Despite the best efforts of the crew in attempting to repel the pirates with water cannons, they board the ship and take control. In the ensuing scuffle a sailor is shot and killed.

The pirates are in communication with their leader aboard the mother ship who in turn is in radio contact with the Al Shabaab operative on dry land in Djibouti. An experienced ransom negotiator is appointed by the operative to handle the communications with the ship owner. Upon learning that one of the ship's crew has been killed the ship owner is badly shaken. Despite being told by his advisers that he needs to hold his nerve whilst the negotiations are played out, he does not have the stomach for a protracted back and forth because he fears that further lives may be lost. From an initial demand of $10 million the negotiations reach an impasse at $5 million at which point the ship owner caves in and instructs his representatives to make the ransom payment as quickly as possible. A proportion of that sum winds up in the following structure.

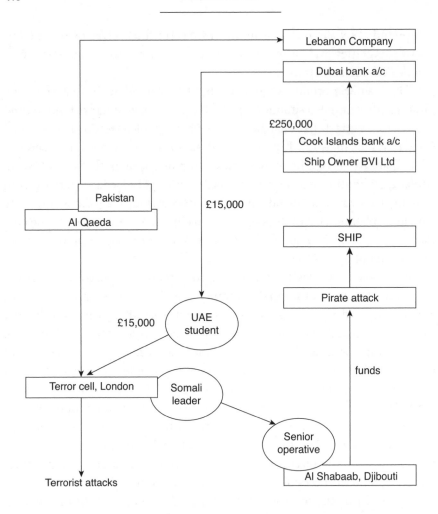

On the instructions of the Al Shabaab operative, the pirate negotiator informs the ship owner's adviser that the ransom is to be paid in two parts: the first in the sum of $4.75 million by way of a cash drop; and the second in the sum of $250,000 by way of a wire transfer to a company with a bank account in Dubai. The hijacked ship is registered in The Cook Islands and owned by a British Virgin Islands company. This BVI company is, in turn, managed and controlled in The Cook Islands where it has a well-stocked bank account used for operational purposes, including the payment of crew, insurances, maintenance, and so on. The $250,000 is wire transferred from The Cook Islands to an account in Dubai. The shipping company's bank requests some information on the purpose of the transfer, and it is satisfied when told that it relates to a payment for essential repairs that were carried out on the ship whilst in Jebel Ali. The bank account in Dubai is in the name of a Lebanese company, ultimately controlled by a senior Al Qaeda operative located in Pakistan. With the $250,000 in the account in Dubai, he converts some of the dollars into £15,000 and wires it to the account of the UAE student member in the London cell. The narrative accompanying the transfer is 'living expenses and tuition fees'. Using this money, the London cell goes on to commit three simultaneous suicide terrorist attacks across London in which several innocent people are killed and badly injured.

Through this method legitimate funds were paid with the intention of securing the release of the hijacked ship, its crew, and its cargo. Funding terrorism was clearly not contemplated by the ship owner or the banks concerned, but a small percentage of the overall ransom within the banking system was diverted to fund a sleeper cell and thus indirectly facilitate three terrorist attacks.

The story however does not end there. Having distributed the ransom cash to the pirates and local elders and funded the purchase of military hardware and vehicles brought across from neighbouring Eritrea, the Al Shabaab operative is instructed by his seniors to transfer $20,000 of the proceeds to an Al Qaeda sympathiser in Minnesota, which is home to approximately one third of the US-based Somalis. As there is no operational banking system in Somalia, he cannot simply wire transfer the money so he instead turns to a hawala money remittance agent in Djibouti. The agent is a member of a large network of Somali hawaladars throughout the Somali diaspora. The agent is keen to obtain cash to fund the collections made from him by native Somalis in receipt of funds that have been transferred to them through the hawala system by family members outside of Somalia. The transfer looks like this:

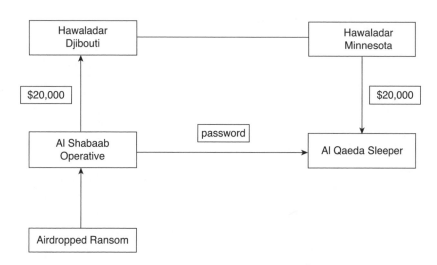

The operative gives the hawaladar $20,000 in cash and in return he is given a password. Not trusting telephonic communications or email, the password is communicated verbally through a chain of Al Shabaab and Al Qaeda operatives until it reaches the sleeper in Minnesota. He visits a local hawaladar, provides him with the password, and is handed $20,000. He utilises the cash for his living expenses and remains below the radar of both the US authorities and the US banking system.

# 7

# TRAFFICKING OF HUMAN BEINGS AND SMUGGLING OF MIGRANTS

In June 2000, customs officials in Dover opened the back of a lorry which had just crossed the North Sea and was apparently carrying a cargo of tomatoes. However, in the darkness they found two barely conscious Chinese men along with the corpses of 58 others who were asphyxiated when the driver had closed the only air vent in order to prevent anyone from spotting them. It is believed that the smuggled migrants had each paid around £20,000 for the journey from their home province to the UK in search of work; a journey organised by Chinese snakehead gang members who had supplied false documentation and plotted the transit through several countries by sea, air, and land, and who stood to make a substantial, almost risk-free profit. Two individuals, who both denied the charges against them, were imprisoned for the deaths: the Dutch lorry driver, Perry Wacker, who was sentenced to 14 years (and whose appeal was rejected), and a Chinese interpreter, Ying Guo, who acted as the UK coordinator for the immigrants and who was sentenced to six.[1] They would have been paid a fraction of the overall sum made from the tragedy, leaving the bulk of the payment in the hands of the Chinese traffickers. For them it was in all likelihood just one in a regular series of such arrangements in which vulnerable and credulous people give their trust and money to criminals motivated by profit alone and without a shred of human compassion.

Criminal activity relating to the smuggling of migrants, as well as the closely associated trafficking of human beings, affects millions of people worldwide. The two activities are amongst the most prevalent and lucrative forms of organised crime in the world and have been linked to other crimes such as conspiracy to commit murder, credit card fraud, mortgage fraud, immigration fraud, and organised prostitution. The prosecutor who brought charges against Perry Wacker deplored the smuggling of humans, saying it had become 'as profitable as drugs';[2] the UN ranks the trafficking of human beings third amongst crimes netting the largest financial benefits after drug and arms trafficking.[3] Despite this, they are almost invisible to the societies in which they operate and comparatively little is known about them. Both crimes rely on the commercial exploitation of usually vulnerable persons for the purpose of financial profit by either charging large sums to make a dangerous and illegal journey in search of a better future or by coercing a person into a situation where they cannot escape and are forced to perform degrading work for minimal pay. Migrant smugglers make money by demanding a fee for the clandestine transport of the person to a new country as well as for accommodation along the way and false paperwork. People traffickers make money from the earnings of victims who are sexually exploited or forced into labour, made to live in locations provided by the traffickers, and have to hand over most of the money that they earn. Victims of trafficking (and smuggled migrants) generally work in extremely poor conditions: illegally in a country where they do not officially exist and are therefore outside its health, social security, and justice systems. Often, they inhabit unsafe or crowded accommodation. Trafficking victims are deprived of the ability to leave when they wish and sometimes have their passports or identity documents confiscated; they are effectively slaves.

People trafficking and smuggling have been subjected to increasing scrutiny since the UN Convention against Transnational Organised Crime entered into force in 2003. The Convention was supplemented by two key protocols: the Protocol to Prevent, Suppress and Punish Trafficking in Persons, Especially Women and Children, and the Protocol against the Smuggling of Migrants by Land, Sea and Air.[4] The protocols, critically, offer agreed definitions on both types of crime within a legally binding global instrument. Whereas in the early 2000s, there were many countries which lacked legislation that criminalised the trafficking of human beings, trafficking is now illegal in most jurisdictions, although there are still significant deficiencies in its enforcement and a lack of international cooperation. The illicit movement of persons remains a rarely detected crime, its victims hidden in a culture of secrecy and fear. Conviction rates remain very low despite extreme profitability and prevalence. In contrast to increased corporate awareness concerning the flows of money resulting from corruption and drug dealing, the awareness concerning the profits of human trafficking and migrant smuggling is poor and ensuring that compliance regimes are active in detecting such activities is not a high priority. Despite recent initiatives, the laundering of funds generated from these particular manifestations of organised crime garners a tiny amount of press coverage and remains dismally low in the public consciousness. That said, Western Union's agreement to pay $94 million in 2010 to settle a legal dispute with Arizona over whether the company was doing enough about the use of its services by Mexican drug cartels and human traffickers to carry out cross-border money laundering is an example of the type of operational and reputational risk associated with a compliance failure in this area and may herald the beginnings of an increased awareness.

The trafficking of human beings and the smuggling of migrants are frequently conflated; however, although they both deal with the illicit relocation of persons for the purposes of work, there are very important differences, some of which affect the manner in which they are policed and the manner in which attempts are made to trace the proceeds. One important difference is that of consent; a person who is trafficked will be relocated and will then work through coercion, either from the outset or as the result of a deceptive situation that they cannot escape. In contrast, a smuggled migrant takes part in a consensual act: wishing to enter a different jurisdiction illegally, the migrant seeks assistance from a professional as to how to do so and will then willingly undertake a journey organised by the smugglers' network. In addition, the trafficking of human beings always involves the exploitation of the victim; whereas although a smuggled migrant may end up, due to their vulnerable and illegal status, in an exploitative labour market or working to repay part of the cost of their journey, this is not a necessary feature of their situation. Further, contrary again to many misconceptions, human trafficking does not have to involve the crossing of a national border, whereas this is the essential feature of migrant smuggling.

There is another important distinction in terms of the manner in which money is actually made, which is relevant to the steps that can be taken to prevent access to financial services. Once the smuggled migrant reaches his destination and pays the balance of the fee, he normally has no further relationship with the smuggler, although there are reports of cases where the smugglers have kidnapped migrants and attempted to extort further money out of them before their release. The migrant then makes his own way, working often in unskilled jobs for a low wage and without suitable employee protection. Trafficked people, however, never leave the control of those who have transported them. Men are often made to work in factories or agricultural, outdoor or construction jobs, and in demanding and dangerous conditions with little concern for health and safety. This is more likely in underdeveloped countries where workplaces are less regulated and where large-scale commercial concerns can operate under the radar. Women too are made to work in factories, but more typically in less visible situations that can exist in both the developed and undeveloped world. Domestic servitude or cleaning work is common, as is being made to work in menial jobs. However, a very high percentage of trafficked women are sexually exploited, often in violent and dangerous circumstances. Children are made to work in factories, forced into armed militias, made to beg in more affluent cities, and can also be sold into domestic and sexual servitude. A very small percentage are trafficked or smuggled for the purpose of organ donation. One such suspected case was flagged by a French bank when a national of that country made payments to a woman abroad citing the reason as 'donation for transplant'; not all instances of trafficking are that easy to detect.

Smuggling and trafficking networks are often globalised groups, with members in a number of transit countries who take responsibility for various aspects of the crimes: accompanying and supervising the travellers, meeting and housing them at stopover points, introducing them to other key members, instructing them in the next form of transport, and meeting them at the destination. In addition, a trafficking network will probably include a wide web of recruiters in the country of origin who spot potential victims and take steps to lure them in, guards to ensure that the contingent of victims is not stolen by another gang, and another wide network in the destination country which will control the accommodation and work of the victim, and also other aspects of everyday life, such as access to medical and banking services. Some gangs appear to have connections to criminal organisations in other countries.

There is now growing and concerning evidence that facilitating smuggling or trafficking is an alluring sideline to other organised crimes such as drugs and arms trafficking. The Zetas drug cartel in Mexico is believed to be involved in such activities, having diversified its portfolio from drug trafficking to a wider range of crimes that include kidnapping and extortion. Drug mules, often vulnerable women who are forced to swallow parcels of narcotics before crossing borders, are in many circumstances victims of trafficking, serving a dual and sometimes fatal purpose for their masters. A spokesperson for a sex-worker NGO in Mexico told *Time*, 'As the drug war has become more intense, the networks that traffic women have made their pacts with cartels'.[5]

The recruitment networks concerned in human trafficking employ different tactics depending on their location. In a classic scenario, young men lure vulnerable women into sex work by promises of romance, generally some distance from their homes. They quickly establish themselves as a trusted person who claims to have the woman's best interests at heart, and then, once dependence is established and she is out of her normal surroundings, he can enslave and exploit her. In South East Asia, reports suggest that it is common for recruiters to be part of the extended family of the victim. This is also the case where the trafficking concerns a forced marriage, or where, in extreme cases, parents have sold their child to traffickers. Whereas the majority of convicted traffickers are men, women are statistically much more likely to be involved in trafficking than in other crimes. In some areas they play an essential part in the recruitment process by gaining the trust of other women and luring them with the promise of well-paid work; in others they are observed to take a key managerial role such as supervising victims and running brothels.

Despite the concept of consent involved in migrant smuggling, the migrant frequently ends up travelling or working in circumstances that are exploitative or dangerous, partially due to his illicit status, and the smuggler can expose his charges to very high risks despite the large sums they have paid. It has been suggested that as the authorities restrict the movement of migrants along certain borders which have historically been easier to cross, the demand for 'specialist' smugglers to navigate the more difficult and more dangerous routes has risen. Estimates suggest that between 1,500–2,000 immigrants and refugees drown in the Mediterranean each year as they make their way in unseaworthy boats from popular smuggling locations on the North African coastline to island destinations such as Sicily, Sardinia, the Canary Islands, and parts of Greece, where remote beaches make a discreet landing more likely. In one journey in 2013 alone, over 360 migrants mainly from Eritrea and Somalia, who were paying around $3,000 each, drowned off the coast of the small Italian island of Lampedusa.[6] Seeking similarly quiet shores, large numbers of asylum seekers and illegal immigrants from the Chinese mainland and South East Asia also drown annually in the waters around Australia.

It is the vulnerability of many illicit migrants that makes them such easy prey to either smugglers or traffickers. Young people who have heard inflated tales of the wages to be made in other countries and who believe (sometimes correctly) that they will be able to make enough money to support their family if they go abroad are often willing participants in smuggling activities. They are, however, unlikely to be aware of the extreme risks that are

run in some of the most dangerous smuggling routes. Trafficking victims
are often chosen because of their desperate personal circumstances: young
women living in poverty, perhaps with a young family; orphans or runaway
teenagers who are susceptible to the attentions of people who befriend them
and pretend to be offering them a better life; and drug addicts and drop-
outs, who are easily lured into circumstances that suit the attackers. The
US Department of State produces an annual *Trafficking in Persons Report*
containing the experiences of victims of trafficking that have come to their
attention. In the 2013 report are the stories of two Burmese 16-year-olds who
were enticed to Thailand with the promise of work as domestic helpers, but
forced to work 19-hour days in a meat-processing factory; an unemployed
El Salvadorian, promised work in the US, only to be sold for sex in Mexico
(and branded by the Zetas cartel with a 'Z' tattoo); and 12 migrants from
Kazakhstan and Uzbekistan who were held captive for a decade in a Russian
supermarket after empty promises of legitimate employment.[7]

The working conditions of smuggled migrants can be equally perilous.
It is believed that the 23 cockle pickers who drowned in 2004 in Morecambe
Bay in the UK were part of an illegal work gang; unsupervised, unsup-
ported, unable to speak English and unaware of the vital safety information
that would have saved their lives. Gangmaster Lin Liang Ren was charged
with 21 counts of manslaughter (two bodies were not recovered), perverting
the course of justice, and facilitating the cockle pickers to break immigration laws, and was given a 14-year prison sentence. Ren, a heavy gambler
and qualified accountant, denied being responsible for the deaths. He was
released after eight years and deported to China in 2012. Although the prosecutions were a victory in one sense, the *Guardian* spoke with some of the
families of the deceased a few years later. The newspaper found that, while
the snakehead gangs bringing the victims to the UK would have been paid
off long ago, the families of the cockle pickers were steeped in debt; one family still owed £19,900 for their relative's passage to Morecambe Bay.[8]

There are certain estimates for migrant smuggling and people trafficking figures, but the raw data for each is patchy and incomplete. For obvious
reasons the subject is hard to research, and the relatively small number of
prosecutions means that there is little solid data.

The International Labour Organisation estimated – by its own admis-
sion, conservatively – that there are at least 2.4 million trafficked persons
at any given point in time.[9] The UNODC has rated people trafficking as
the third most profitable type of organised crime, and the profits are estimated by the ILO to amount to $32 billion each year of which $28 billion is
generated by sexual exploitation. The ILO estimates that a woman who is

being sexually exploited may make $100,000 profit for her captors each year, and Europol estimates that the annual income of a trafficked child can be €160,000: a huge margin, considering that the average price at which a child can be 'bought' is only €20,000.[10]

The UNOCD reports that the income of smugglers who operate on the East/North/West Africa to Europe route amounts to around $150 million annually; for those operating on the South America–US route, it is $6.6 billion.[11] One calculation suggests that migrant smuggling across Europe is a £8 billion industry with around 600,000 migrants entering the EU illegally each year, 80% of them reportedly smuggled by snakehead gangs.[12] Having fled from the US in the mid-1990s, then setting up headquarters in Rotterdam's Chinatown, the endearingly named 'Sister Ping' was one of the industry's biggest earners. By one estimate, she was believed to have earned over £15 million in smuggling over 200,000 people into Europe during her career; the FBI said her earnings were nearer the $40 million mark.[13] She was jailed in the Netherlands in 2003 and two years later given a 35-year prison sentence by a New York court.

The fees for smuggling vary greatly and depend on the destination and the type of work/lifestyle benefits available, the distance travelled, the danger and comfort of the journey, and the type of documentation involved. The most expensive locations are also the most desirable with the US, Canada, and Scandinavia apparently costing the most. Trans-European trips may cost only a few hundred euros; a trip from China to the West may cost over $13,000. The sums demanded for smuggling are often absurdly high given the average incomes in the countries of origin: in some cases, they equate to a decade or two of salary. Clearly even a low-level smuggler stands to make huge sums of money in his home country which makes the role of financial institutions critically important to understand.

Human trafficking and smuggling patterns are very closely influenced by geography and by the economics of a particular region. This has enabled analysts to discern some specific patterns of activity associated with particular areas, which is of assistance both to law enforcement agencies attempting to increase the detection rates and to financial bodies attempting to produce guidance for institutions about how to deal with the flow of money that results from these crimes.

Europe is a major migration destination globally, with people arriving from across Africa and Asia as part of both smuggling and trafficking operations; 55,000 people are estimated to migrate in this way from Africa each year, with Nigeria featuring highly as a country of origin. There are often links between countries of origin and destination that have had a connection to the colonial past, because this may make it easier for trafficking victims and migrants to fit into ethnic and linguistic communities. However, there are also marked patterns of movement within the continent itself. Europol found that the gangs most involved in European trafficking are from the Balkans and former Soviet states: Albania, Bulgaria, Romania, Lithuania, and the former Yugoslavia. They are believed to target persons from their own countries as well as Russia, Moldova, and the Ukraine. The most popular routes involve the Balkans, Eastern Europe, the Eastern Mediterranean, and North Africa/Southern Mediterranean. Brazil and Portugal are also popular destination countries for people from South America possibly because of the linguistic and cultural links. The smuggled or illegal migrants from Africa arrive via the Canary Islands and Spain; from Morocco over sea to Spain, from Libya or Egypt to Southern Italy, and by land or sea to Greece and Turkey.

Within the Americas, migrants, both trafficked and consenting, move northwards from South America to the US and Canada over the border from Mexico. South Americans migrate to a variety of destinations including the Caribbean, the Far East, and Europe. UNODC reports that approximately three million Latin Americans use Mexico as a transit country every year as part of consensual migration and that 90% of Mexican migrants resort to using professional smugglers, also known as 'coyotes'. Hundreds amongst those moving north die every year, mainly from exposure and dehydration. It was precisely this flow of migration which, according to the Statement of Admitted Facts forming part of the 2010 settlement agreement, certain Western Union agents were found to have facilitated between 2003 and 2007 through engaging in a pattern of money laundering violations.[14] Western Union would later sever ties with 7,000 agents in Mexico that fell short of its compliance standards.[15]

Much traffic in Asia constitutes people moving from less developed areas to more prosperous ones; trafficked victims are often moved from the poorer, South East Asian countries to the more wealthy states. However, there is also significant movement to Oceania and also towards Europe. Trafficking in this region is largely overseen by the Japanese Yakuza and Chinese gangs and often occurs in tandem with other crimes, such as drug trafficking and theft.

The sums of money generated by the exploitation of humans, whether by trafficking or smuggling, are enormous. The ILO's $32 billion approximation is concerning enough; a 2011 FATF study showed one Bulgarian sex-trafficking gang earned €10 million in profit in four years (with the organisers paying only 30% of the fees to the women, and only then if they were deemed 'productive'[16]). Both forms of activity are generally regarded as low-risk, high-reward occupations; arrests are relatively rare, and the jurisdictional disconnect between the country of origin and the destination where the trafficked or smuggled person is likely to be detected means that the organiser stands little chance of being traced. It is unsurprising, then, that comparatively little headway has been made in understanding the methods used to launder the proceeds from these activities or that such activities are comparatively rarely discovered. Studies have been undertaken by the Moneyval initiative of the Council of Europe, and by FATF, which have both researched case studies in order to learn about the financial systems used by traffickers and smugglers, but the trends identified are based on relatively few individual examples. No new methods of money laundering or exploitation have been discovered, but many of the financial structures that have been proven vulnerable to abuse by other areas of organised crime are featured.

While smuggling usually involves a one-off fee, trafficking profits are generated on a constant basis, and the types of businesses in which trafficked persons work are often those which generate frequent, low-level cash transactions. A brothel containing five prostitutes in a European capital city can make thousands of euros per day in cash of which only a tiny proportion will be paid to the women. As the businesses which are staffed by trafficked people are often unregistered, illegitimate, and of a compromising nature, they may not operate self-declared business accounts. The money is usually generated in the trafficking destination and will need to be remitted regularly to the organisers of the trafficking gang in their home country, which is often the country of origin of the victims of trafficking.

In terms of laundering techniques, the use of cash and money service businesses to transfer the proceeds is almost universal. However, because trafficking happens within countries as well as between them, a suspicious transaction may not be international. Front companies appear to be prevalent in Europe, with proceeds being spent on real estate and high-value luxury goods such as cars. In America, laundering methods include casinos and import/export businesses as well as universal methods such as money service businesses and cash-based companies. In cases concerning Africa or parts of Asia, the use of traditional remittance businesses such as hawala is common; in Asia, laundering takes place by mixing criminal money with legitimate funds, whereas in Africa studies have shown that money may be invested in clubs and real estate.

Moneyval and FATF undertook a review of a range of cases and distilled these into lists of typologies and indicators of which institutions should be particularly wary. They also considered the methods by which trafficking and smuggling cases were discovered; and although there were some investigations that were triggered by bank monitoring, FATF's 2011 report commented on a survey that showed that trafficking and smuggling generate proportionately fewer Suspicious Activity Reports every year than other comparable predicate crimes. Many investigations were, rather, commenced because of a criminal investigation into the activity which shows that current awareness in the finance industry is somewhat low and that the checks currently undertaken do not always spot the relevant information.

Customer profiling remains high on the list of compliance priorities that may assist in screening out clients who are engaged in human trafficking, either in countries of origin or destination. This is not to say that anybody from Albania or the Ukraine who opens an account in Amsterdam should automatically become suspect, but that banks should be aware of countries with a high risk of smuggling or trafficking activities and ensure that this is a part of screening measures when combined with other factors. Obtaining adequate and credible information about the customer's source of funds and their area of work is also important.

The actual behaviour of persons in bank or money service branches in destination countries can be informative: instances have been found of victims who remit the money themselves to the origin country and the trafficking gang leader. Trafficked females may be made to open accounts which can be used to direct money to their families and to their controllers and may be supervised when they visit banks to make these transfers. Suspicions may therefore legitimately be raised when a woman opens accounts under the supervision of another woman, particularly if she is frequently escorted to the branch to perform other transactions. Also potentially suspicious are accounts which all relate to the same address or the same phone number, and accounts which are opened with letters specifying that the client works in an industry with a risk of forced or menial labour.

The manner in which accounts are used can also be telling. Banks and remittance operators may be alerted by persons who make or receive numerous small cash transfers, particularly involving the same location. Straightforward KYC information may demonstrate that a person's transaction profile and account use does not accord with their lifestyle or income as described on the customer's documentation. Cases have been detected largely because a person received large regular deposits when they were ostensibly unemployed; further enquiries into their background raised suspicions that they were involved in trafficking or smuggling. The company accounts that receive improbably large profits can also indicate criminal activity; again, further research is then sometimes able to suggest a link to migration-related crime.

A situation that was raised in some of the case studies was the exploitation of bank accounts to gain access to credit: the victim's documentation is taken from them on arrival at their destination and bank accounts are opened with it, which are then swiftly used to access loans, overdrafts, and credit and debit cards. Sometimes the same accounts were used to access social security or other loans before the victim was returned home again to evade the banks' efforts to recoup the money.

Remittance businesses are frequently used to launder proceeds because of their less regulated status. An investigation, which was undertaken by Hong Kong and Chinese authorities and referenced in FATF's study, accused one particular remittance agency run by five family members of having transferred around $25.7 million in the proceeds of migrant smuggling. However, increasing awareness is prompting such businesses to take steps relating to compliance, possibly in view of the settlement entered into by Western Union. Numerous remittances to the same, high-risk jurisdiction could be indicative of involvement in trafficking, particularly if they do not fit the normal profile of genuine transactions where someone is sending some of their wages to their family. Other behaviours include remittances that are structured at just below the cash limit or reporting threshold, and the illogical use of more expensive money service businesses in a situation where the person could transfer the same relatively small sum for a much lower fee elsewhere but elects to do so through a particular service provider.

Some behaviours are associated with specific sectors of human trafficking. For example, those involved with commercial sex work may seek to advertise their victims' services in an online directory or in small ads. Someone making small payments to such listings companies on a regular basis may be cause for concern; credit card payments to online escort services for advertising were identified by a US investigation into a human trafficking ring in San Diego.

Financial vehicles that are at risk of exploitation by trafficking and smuggling organisations are similar to those found in other money laundering operations. Front businesses, usually cash-intensive such as restaurants and used car dealerships, and also facilitative businesses such as travel agencies and import/export companies, are popular methods of disguising profits. One large-scale migrant smuggling operation uncovered by UK police, and described by FATF, found that kebab shops, takeaway outlets, and a snooker hall were used to launder their money. Migrants – predominantly Turkish in nationality – were charged €14,500 for the first leg of the journey through

Europe, and an additional £3,500 for a channel crossing. Bearing in mind that the gang arrested in 2005 was believed to have smuggled 20,000 individuals, the resulting confiscation order for £1.2 million was very modest.

As with other forms of money laundering, the same vulnerabilities exist regarding foreign or shell companies, particularly where this assists with the retention of money that has crossed borders to the home of the traffickers and smugglers. Trusts contain the same inherent vulnerabilities to this type of criminality as they do to any other form: their anonymity and secrecy is paramount. One case identified by FATF concerned a South African sex ring which operated by using women trafficked from Eastern Europe and had managed to stash more than £40 million in a trust fund based in Guernsey.

Various initiatives have been established in order to try and encourage financial institutions to include screening for immigration crimes in their compliance procedures. In the US, Project STAMP (Smuggler and Trafficker Assets, Monies and Proceeds) implements strategies to encourage the finance industry to make the most of the tools that can assist with investigating the laundering of money received from immigration crimes. It encourages the use of the Bank Secrecy Act and reminds finance workers about the importance of SARs, currency transaction reports, international currency transportation instruments, and reporting on foreign bank accounts. More complex analyses were proposed in a study by JP Morgan, which looked at the ways in which banks and other risk industries could build into their systems technology that could flag up suspicious client activity on a holistic basis: rather than relying on individual transactions which may not in themselves be suspicious, patterns were detected. One of these patterns indicated customers who had paid for small adverts on internet listings more than 100 times. Amongst FATF's Recommendations are a number that deal with issues raised by immigration crime: an emphasis on implementing Special Recommendations VI (remittances), VII (wire transfers) and IX (cash couriers), as well as a focus on Recommendations concerning beneficial ownership of companies, the role of financial intelligence units, and the benefits of international cooperation. As part of its strategy to eradicate trafficking, Europol is currently undertaking an analysis of the financial investigation of human trafficking, the results of which are expected by 2015.

In recent years, changes have been made to domestic legislation in many countries that have outlawed human trafficking and smuggling, but there remains a lack of information about the laundering of the proceeds of these activities. A problem identified by many of the reports on the subject is that most countries, perhaps unsurprisingly, concentrate on the crime itself, rather than investing effort into following the money trail and attempting to obtain better knowledge of the financial systems used. This is further compounded by the fact that human trafficking often manifests itself in evidence of other criminality such as prostitution, which means that the surface problem is dealt with but not the cause. The obvious unwillingness of victims to admit their situation and testify can be a part of this. Further, in many jurisdictions, legal action for the retrieval and confiscation of the proceeds of these activities is predicated on actually bringing home a criminal conviction. This makes it hard to disrupt a financial network if, for whatever reason, it has not been possible to prove the suspect guilty of the offence. A general lack of cohesion between not only domestic law enforcement agencies and FIUs, but at an international level, means that there is simply not enough effort being invested into analysing the money laundering methods related to this sort of crime. Factoring in the argument that it may not be in the interest of some of the originating countries to pursue these types of crime, and the complex nature of the exercise required to follow the money trail becomes ever more apparent.

Human trafficking and migrant smuggling may be secret crimes; the stories of their victims and the convictions of the perpetrators less publicised and understood than those involved in other types of organised crime. Yet financial services are being used to channel billions of dollars around the globe, often in concert with other forms of criminality which gives a motive and an opportunity to the criminals to continue with their activities. The scenario I have created highlights just this, while juxtaposing the base human suffering of trafficked women from Eastern to Western Europe against the sophistication of an investment fund structure.

## SCENARIO

This particular scenario involves an Albanian criminal gang which ensnares sex workers in Albania and the Baltic states by using gang members to pose as clients. This ruthless and depraved gang traffics enslaved young women to work in the underground sex trade in cities such as London, Paris, Amsterdam, and Frankfurt. They also sell women to work for other gangs in cities where they do not control the sex trade. Once trapped, the women are stripped of their possessions and papers effectively depriving them of their identity and rendering them utterly helpless. In addition to human trafficking, the gang deals in drugs and small arms and munitions. Widespread corruption within the police forces of most former Soviet states allows the gang to conduct their sordid business with relative impunity.

The women are transported by road in lorries. Border guards and customs officials are bribed where necessary, and the vast majority of women are successfully transported without interdiction. When they arrive at their destination they are given a constant supply of addictive drugs to keep them dependent upon their captors. Some of the women are sold to a Northern Italian criminal gang, which also buys drugs and arms from the Albanians. The Italian gang is a highly sophisticated organisation with a long and successful track record in organised crime in Europe and the US. It counts amongst its resources several professional money launderers including ex-bankers and lawyers who engage in financial crimes including telesales fraud and property scams on its behalf. One audacious fraud involves an investment fund set up in a tax neutral jurisdiction, which generates the funds that the Italians use to pay the Albanians for the trafficked women, arms, and drugs.

The Italian gang firstly orchestrates the formation of a private investment fund with a multi-fund structure. It takes advantage of the fast track process for the authorisation of so-called 'Professional Investor Funds', and is assisted by an authorised service provider. The fund is structured with a master fund and three underlying sub-funds that are each invested in a different asset class. One of the sub-funds is described in a glossy investor brochure as an Eastern European property fund which is said to own logistics parks, shopping centres, and undeveloped real estate. This sub-fund is initially seeded with funds diverted from the proceeds of a telesales fraud perpetrated by the Northern Italian gang. At this point, the scenario looks like this:

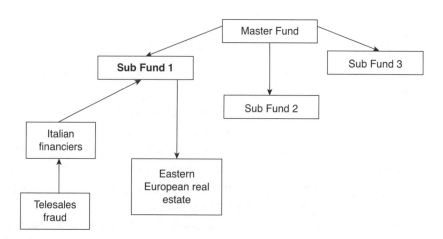

Not uncommon for such a structure, the sub-fund has a 'fund custodian', which has the legal duty of holding the title to the fund's assets (usually a bank) and is administered by a corporate service provider. The latter recently diversified away from administering private wealth management structures to focus on fund administration and was chosen because it is eager for the business, and the Italians feel that its lack of sophistication and experience will reduce the risk of any probing questions. Based on a short track record of positive returns, the sub-fund attracts a small pension fund with a hunch that Eastern European commercial property is the next big thing. The unit price of the fund increases, but unbeknownst to the investor or the administrator, the sub-fund has no assets. A valuation of the sub-fund is calculated by the administrator, who relies upon paper-based property valuations to do so. The administrator understands that the valuations, which are supplied via the fund manager, have been done by property valuation agents in Eastern Europe; little does it know that the valuations are entirely false. The fund custodian believes that it holds copies of property title documents for the fund assets, but such documents that it holds (which it has never had translated) are fake.

All part of the ruse, the money invested in the sub-fund is channelled to wholly owned companies in jurisdictions with double tax treaties with the countries where the properties are said to be located which adds a level of reassurance to the investors. Those companies in turn lend the money to Special Purpose Vehicles (SPVs) ostensibly set up for the purpose of holding each property asset in Eastern Europe. The administrator understands that the SPVs are controlled by representatives of the fund manager; they are, however, controlled by the Italian crime gang's financiers. The funds are not used to purchase the properties but are instead diverted to a third party company in Cyprus, which is ultimately controlled by the Albanian gang. The Albanians proceed to spend the money on weapons; they wire transfer funds from the Cypriot company to the director of an Eastern European arms manufacturer who is selling unlicensed arms.

In this way, the Albanians are paid for the trafficked women, the drugs, and the arms without the risks of transporting relatively substantial sums of cash. The Albanians are very happy to receive 'clean' funds without the need to have to place them into the system. By the time the third party investors and the authorities in the jurisdiction discover that the fund is a scam its purpose from the perspective of the Italians has been fulfilled. The fund sits at the heart of the following structure, which has been used to defraud investors, to finance the Italian gang's criminality, and to transfer criminal value to the Albanians.

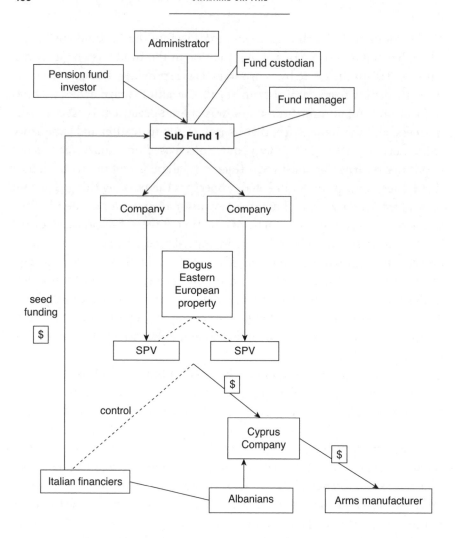

It is worthwhile at this juncture to consider the scam in the context of the enable, distance, and disguise model and to contrast it with the traditional placement, layering, and integration model of money laundering. Beginning with the latter, where in the scheme did placement activity take place? The answer of course is that there was no placement activity because the proceeds of the fraud used to pay for the trafficked women, drugs, and arms were already in the system before it became tainted by criminality. There was no transformational layering activity; the funds were simply diverted through the fund structure to a company controlled by the Albanians. There is no clear-cut stage of integration either, since the Albanians wired funds to the Eastern European arms dealer.

In summary the entire structure was designed to assist the Italians to commit a fraud (Disconnect 1), pay for the enslaved women (Disconnect 2), and to disguise their connection to the Albanians and the property transferred to them (Disconnect 3).

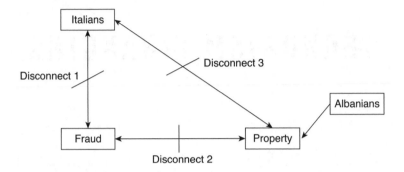

# 8

# TERRORISM FINANCING

In February 2013, three men were convicted at Woolwich Crown Court in London of preparing an act of terrorism. The trio, Islamic extremists from Birmingham, had begun planning and organising an attack which they had hoped would be 'another 9/11'; two of them had attended terrorist training camps in Pakistan, before starting to concoct homemade explosives. They and three others had also managed to raise over 13,500 which they intended to put towards their effort. This money was not obtained by requesting donations from sympathetic allies who wished to support them in planning the atrocity, but through bogus charity collections which exploited the goodwill of ordinary Muslims who believed they were donating to bona fide humanitarian causes. With the group wearing clothing and carrying collection buckets emblazoned with the logo of a genuine charity, Muslim Aid, which had been legitimately obtained when one of their number registered as a fundraiser, the donations were solicited from the local population door-to-door. The group displayed no scruples about duping their fellow Muslims into unwittingly funding terrorism in the name of charity and reportedly even did so during Ramadan when charitable giving is considered an important Islamic obligation. Despite the large sums obtained, only around £1,500 was actually received by Muslim Aid; the group spent some of the remainder on equipment and lost the majority in a fortuitously inept attempt to play the currency markets.[1] The thousands raised by simply posing as a charity collector within a community composed of willing donors points to the ease with which potential terrorists can obtain ample funds to commit atrocities without resorting to overtly criminal acts.

Terrorism is one of the major threats to global security. The Western public's perception of terrorism is often influenced by the large-scale, colossal-impact disasters of the recent decade, such as 9/11; the London, Madrid, and Bali bombings; the Mumbai shootings; and the most prominent 'near misses' such as the Times Square and London limousine bombing attempts. However, as well as massive one-off atrocities, there are many countries where local terrorist or guerrilla networks impose an almost constant reign of fear on the inhabitants and also endanger their often fragile political environment. Countries such as Afghanistan, Pakistan, Somalia, Colombia, Sri Lanka, Indonesia, and Nigeria suffer regular violence as groups seek to impose their own political, ideological, or religious agendas through bombings and shootings.

In the past decade, there has been a growing awareness that the funding of terrorism is taking place through standard financial systems and that not only must radical steps be taken by institutions to identify and disrupt these flows, but that information provided by an active and vigilant institution can be key to investigating and punishing terror participants. Scrutiny is increasing and a variety of new legislative and regulatory frameworks have assisted in raising the awareness of the essential role that banks and other institutions can play. However, there are still very substantial blind spots relating to the manner in which terrorist money is detected and diverted.

Terrorist funding can be much harder to detect than 'normal' money laundering because many of the factors that give rise to suspicious transactions in other areas of financial abuse are absent. The funds are frequently generated by 'clean' money from legitimate sources as well as from criminal activity. Recent research and intelligence has pointed to growing evidence that terrorists are funded not only from donations and state sponsors, but that they are increasingly turning to drug trafficking, arms trading, currency smuggling, and various types of fraud to generate capital. Proper application of anti–money laundering legislation and due diligence therefore becomes all the more important, because people linked to financial crime may have undetected links to terrorism too. While there are examples of transactions at vigilant banks triggering investigations that have revealed vital information, there are also concerning examples of major financial institutions being implicated in the financing of terrorism. It is vitally important that institutions take the threat of terrorist financing seriously, learn about the methods regularly employed, and put in place their own procedures to ensure that any detectable abnormality is scrutinised.

'The different proposed scholarly and legal definitions of terrorism are more numerous than the 150 knights seeking the Grail, and definitional consensus has been at least as elusive as the Grail'.[2] This is the remark of one legal expert and the sentiment has been echoed by numerous other academics, professionals, historians, and politicians. A good place to start in seeking a definition of terrorism is the UN Security Council resolution which frames the activity as:

> ...criminal acts, including against civilians, committed with the intent to cause death or serious bodily injury, or taking of hostages, with the purpose to provoke a state of terror in the general public or in a group of persons or particular persons, intimidate a population or compel a government or an international organisation to do or to abstain from doing any act, which constitute offences within the scope of and as defined in the international conventions and protocols relating to terrorism... [such acts] are under no circumstances justifiable by considerations of a political, philosophical, ideological, racial, ethnic, religious or other similar nature.[3]

The UN may have been able to commit this definition to paper, but UN member states are struggling to achieve unanimity on defining the concept. Oft-cited stumbling blocks strewn in the path to consensus include the issue of government-sanctioned violence against civilians and the rights of those in foreign occupied lands to resist their occupiers.

The arguments are complex, and the topic is emotionally charged. US conflict historian John Bowyer Bell expressed the subjective aspect to defining the notion when he said, 'tell me what you think about terrorism, and I will tell you who you are'.[4] Journalists striving to report 'the facts' are cautious to employ the most neutral language possible when describing potential acts of terrorism. In the Reuters style-guide, journalists are advised against using the term in favour of employing 'more specific terms like "bomber", or "bombing", "hijacker" or "hijacking", "attacker" or "attacks", "gunman" or "gunmen" etc'.[5]

Taking the broadly agreed view that terrorism uses violence to achieve political, ideological, or religious ends, it is hard to deny that terrorists have presented a major international problem for decades. The profile of terrorism has, however, changed significantly in the past ten years. In the 1980s and 1990s, terrorist attacks for political ends were prevalent in several parts of Europe: the IRA's campaign in the UK claimed 1,800 lives. The official number of killings carried out by the Basque separatist organisation ETA since 1968 stands at 829, and the group historically organised frequent kidnappings and extortion rackets. Elsewhere in the world, terrorist networks carried out campaigns in their own countries for political or religious ends: in Colombia, the revolutionary-Marxist group FARC was held responsible for numerous kidnappings and hijackings, executions, attacks, and violence against native American Indians. The Lebanon-based Hezbollah, a militant

Shia Islamic group, initiated attacks and bombings in the Middle East and rocket attacks in the disputed areas of Israel and Palestine remain a regular occurrence. Other groups such as the Kosovo Liberation Army (KLA), Kurdistan Workers' Party (PKK), and Chechnyan separatists also organised violence in response to the prevailing political conditions in their countries.

Since then, these kinds of domestic terrorism have been on the wane, sometimes due to relatively successful ceasefire agreements. At the time of writing, historic progress was being made to secure a peace deal with FARC, and in 2011 ETA called a permanent unilateral ceasefire and has since started disarmament. Attention has increasingly turned to radical Islamic terrorism which operates not just in Muslim countries but in Europe and the US. It is a global phenomenon and has several identifiable strands: events such as 9/11 where the operatives had travelled to the US from their home countries for the purpose of carrying out the attack; localised 'home-grown' cells such as the UK-born London bombers who had appeared relatively integrated into British society; and widespread group attacks by radicals across countries where the general population is Islamic, but often more moderate. Instances of attacks by Islamic fundamentalists in their own countries are common and include Islamic State's (IS) violence in parts of Syria and Iraq, Al Shabaab's campaign in Somalia, Boko Haram's attacks on Christians in Nigeria, Taliban attacks in Afghanistan on politicians and members of the armed forces, and separatist-extremist violence in Indonesia. In 2013, French forces intervened in Mali after a violent uprising by hard-line Islamic rebels. During the same year an attack and hostage situation at a natural gas facility near In Amenas in the Algerian desert was organised by a Muslim group, and ended in siege by Algerian forces and significant loss of life. Kidnappings of Westerners, such as journalists or aid workers, in Muslim countries are also prevalent. Holding hostages for ransom is believed to be a major source of income for jihadist terrorist group IS, which in 2014 demanded a $132 million payment for the return of US journalist James Foley, a payment ultimately refused by the US government. Foley was subsequently beheaded.

Internal ongoing violence in less developed countries may not always attract the international outrage and publicity of attacks on the West, or against citizens of Western countries, but it can imperil both the local population and the political stability of an entire region, which is often parlous in such locations. It also has a discouraging effect on diplomatic relations and on the international development and aid campaigns that these countries so desperately need. There is just as much ethical justification for cutting off the funding sources of people who organise attacks in their own countries as there is in those who organise them abroad.

Terrorist financing is the provision of money which is intended to pay either for a specific terrorist campaign or attack or for the long-term running of a network of people who are working in the promotion and preparation of such campaigns. With the former, funds may be transferred to specific operatives at a specific location with the particular intention that they be used as part of a plot, for example for purchasing weapons or bomb equipment, renting a base, buying cars, and short-term living costs. The latter type of financing supports the running costs of a terrorist organisation which may require funds for: recruitment, communication, and propaganda services (sometimes promoted through television channels, radio stations, social networking sites, and websites owned by the organisation); training operatives; and the social security operations run by some networks, which play a fundamental role in increasing popular local support. Funds are raised in a number of ways including donations, the diversion of charity money, drug trafficking, credit card and other fraud, kidnappings, and state sponsorship. These are more or less susceptible to detection and require greater or lesser interaction with the formal financial system.

One of the most alarming facts about major terrorist events is that the sums of money required to finance them are very small. Estimates suggest that the 9/11 attacks cost less than $500,000 to plan and execute. The London bombings are estimated to have cost under £8,000 and the Madrid train bombings under €10,000. In some ways, the most important factor in the power behind a terror cell is often the mentality of its members rather than sophisticated equipment or significant funding. One determined person with a cheap, homemade bomb can cause huge damage; the biggest risk factors are his commitment and the loyalty and discretion of those around him and his ability to disguise his activities from investigative or monitoring agencies. However, the networks that are often the driving force or inspiration behind such attacks require large sums of cash for their daily running. Although the use of banking systems by terrorists and rebels has been known and understood for decades, it is only in the last decade that global initiatives have been set up to combat the use of the financial services system by terrorist organisations. The *Monograph on Terrorist Financing* written for the National Commission of Terrorist Attacks upon the US, admitted that prior to 2001 'terrorist financing was not a priority for either domestic or foreign intelligence collection'.[6]

Terrorism receives its money in a number of ways, many of which make tracking the financial flows associated with it extremely difficult. Some input comes from legitimate sources, such as donations. Other, illicit, sources include drug trafficking, arms sales, and fraud. IS is understood to raise millions of dollars in funds on a monthly basis through selling oil – sourced from captured oilfields – on the black market. It is also said to regularly extort funds from local businesses and to generate cash through the illicit trade of smuggled antiquities. According to the International Consortium of Investigative Journalists, cigarette smuggling has generated the bulk of funds for Algeria-based Al Qaeda in the Islamic Maghreb whose former leader was known as 'Mr Marlboro'.[7] Estimated figures for the funds yielded by these criminal activities are very hard to come by.

After the 9/11 attacks, the US conducted a lengthy investigation of the funding methods of Al Qaeda. Up until that point, it was generally believed that Osama bin Laden, who came from a prominent and wealthy Saudi family, financed much of the network's operations himself. However, it became plain to the CIA that after his relocation to Afghanistan he did not personally bankroll the organisation. It was discovered that Al Qaeda received about $30 million each year in donations from Islamic charities and from individuals in the Gulf areas; about $20 million of this was spent on supporting the Taliban. The US study found that there was no evidence to support theories that Al Qaeda itself was supported by drug trafficking, diamond sales, securities trading, or state sponsorship.[8]

The 9/11 attacks themselves were funded by a series of small transfers from Germany and the UAE, which did not arouse suspicion and were accessed via cash machines and credit cards. The participants were also given cash donations in Pakistan by the mastermind, Khaled Sheikh Mohammed. Nothing about any of the financial activity linked to the plot would have been spotted by standard bank monitoring patterns, which at that time were more focussed on drug-related crime than terrorism, and the US study states: 'The existing mechanisms to prevent abuse of the financial system did not fail. They were never designed to detect or disrupt transactions of the type that financed 9/11.' According to the House of Commons *Report of the Official Account of the Bombings in London on 7th July 2005*,[9] investigations revealed that the group had been essentially self-funding. They appeared to depend on the personal funds of ringleader Sidique Khan that included a £10,000 loan which more than covered the outlay for the plot. The expenditures included money to pay for travel to training camps abroad. There was little about his account activity that would have raised suspicion: Khan was employed and the loan was not for an inexplicably large sum. The 2004 Madrid bombing, which killed 191 people, appears to have been financed largely by drug deals. Reportedly, the explosives used were purchased from a mining operative in exchange for drugs.

These three examples all show that what makes terrorism financing comparatively difficult to spot and prevent is that the factors that should cause concern with someone involved in, for example, drug dealing, will often be absent. The funds used are often small sums of legitimate money from 'clean' sources that does not need to be laundered in the traditional manner. With issues such as drug dealing, a crude placement transaction or series of blatant layering transactions will often be obviously suspicious to an alert finance worker early on. The origin or amount of the money may be patently suspicious, or there may be a series of identical transactions to the same account. However, for a person making a transfer of a relatively small sum of money which is easily disguised as, for example, a legitimate transfer of wages to support family members, there is a smaller chance of detection. Thousands of such transfers are made every day for genuine reasons, and spotting the one that is destined for a terrorist is very hard.

However, beyond ordinary vigilance, there are two major areas of increasing suspicion in relation to terrorist funding from individuals or groups: the use of alternative remittance systems to transfer money abroad and the abuse of charitable donations. Both of these have been shown to be important conduits of terrorist finance, and there is increasing pressure on these sectors to conform to regulatory norms.

A high proportion of terrorist funding comes under the guise of charitable donation, which offers a convenient and credible justification for money transfers. Many of the areas which either endure high levels of domestic terrorism or are used by terror cells for recruitment and planning are countries with high levels of poverty which by their very nature attract humanitarian intervention and charitable input. The prevalence of trusts in charitable set-ups also assists in anonymising funds and distancing the organisation from the terrorist. Charities and non-profit organisations (NPOs) are of use in three ways: either the collector dishonestly diverts funds which the donor honestly believes are being put to good use; the charity purports to provide humanitarian aid, which it does, but as the charitable wing of a terrorist organisation; or the charity itself is a bogus organisation whose purpose is to mask the real destination of the funds.

The first two lend themselves particularly well to exploitation in areas with a large diaspora population who feel they should donate to a cause connected to their homeland, such as education or healthcare, but is also particularly prevalent in areas with an Islamic presence. *Zakat*, or charitable donation, is a social obligation enjoined on all Muslims as one of the five pillars of Islam, and donations to charities which purport to help Muslim children or establish Muslim schools in areas of conflict are regularly solicited at mosque meetings.

There are numerous examples of the exploitation of *Zakat* in which the charity money ends up in the hands of terrorists. In 2012, London-based 25-year-old twins Shabir and Shafiq Ali pleaded guilty to raising £3,000, claiming that it was to be sent to deserving beneficiaries, when in reality it was sent to their brother who was undergoing terrorist training in Somalia. The judge ruled that they had 'relevant ideological interest' when they transferred the funds and sentenced the twins to three years' imprisonment.[10]

The trial of the Holy Land Foundation for Relief and Development, one of the largest Islamic charities in the US, which purported to provide humanitarian aid to Palestinians, provides an example of the second type of funding. The organisation was placed on the US's Specially Designated Nationals list of sanctioned individuals, groups, and entities in 2001, and a few years later, the foundation and some of its directors were indicted on criminal charges. It was alleged that while some of the foundation's money did indeed to go humanitarian efforts, millions of dollars were diverted to and used by Hamas. In turn, the Palestinian organisation was found to have used some of these funds 'to support schools [...] encouraging children to become suicide bombers and to recruit suicide bombers by offering support to their families'.[11] In the 2008 retrial of the case, five participants were convicted on a total of 108 criminal counts. The verdict was hugely divisive; one spokesman for the foundation lamented the jury's findings, saying that they appeared to have concluded that 'humanitarian aid is a crime', while a US attorney plainly stated that 'US citizens will not tolerate those who provide financial support to terrorist organisations'.[12]

The international financial community is aware of the terrorism risks posed by the exploitation of NPOs. FATF has recognised that the misuse of such organisations is a 'crucial weak point in the global struggle to stop such funding at its source', and guidance is being promulgated to ensure increased vigilance in relation to charities which could be involved in terrorist activity.[13]

In addition to the links between NPOs and terrorists, there have always been ties between terrorist groups and drug traffickers, particularly in areas where drugs are produced: FARC has been strongly connected to the Colombian cocaine trade, exercising considerable control over much of the production in the region; the Taliban took control of much of the Afghan opium trade when it came to power and earned vast sums from it, allegedly hoarding supplies to increase its value and then releasing product at a higher price. Moreover, connections between unprincipled international criminal groups who can mutually benefit from each other's ability to supply drugs, armaments, and cash are nothing new.

Over the past couple of decades it has become increasingly obvious that there is a link between Islamic terror networks and the South American cocaine trade. According to a 2002 report by the US Library of Congress's Federal Research Division entitled *A Global Overview of Narcotics-funded Terrorist and other Extremist Groups*, around six million people of Muslim descent live in Latin America, and there are strong links with fundamentalism, including terrorist attacks in the area throughout the 1990s.[14] More recently it has been claimed that Al Qaeda in the Maghreb has assisted the FARC in the transportation of cocaine to Europe and one estimate suggested that terrorists linked to AQIM had made $130 million from assisting in the drug trade and kidnappings in just a few years.[15] The Lebanese diaspora is prominent in Colombia, and it is believed that major Middle Eastern terrorist organisations such as Hezbollah and Hamas benefit from strategic influence in an area which is highly conducive to the raising of illicit funds. The sophistication of these operations can be grasped from the fact that, according to the sources quoted in the Library of Congress' report, a number of secret global satellite communication devices have been discovered in South America with records of hundreds of telephone calls to the Middle East and Asia which apparently evade the scrutiny of ordinary telephone networks. The challenge of detecting terror links in financial transactions associated with Latin America will require new approaches in the financial communities that deal with both areas.

It is difficult to find reliable estimates of the amount of money raised in the West for the purposes of terrorist networks operating mainly in Africa and Asia. It is, however, plain that large sums do make their way across borders, sometimes through the financial system, sometimes through cash couriers, and sometimes through trade-based systems which allow value to be transferred for ostensibly legitimate purposes. Cash transfers are more prevalent in areas where normal banking is rare and most purchasing takes place in cash, or where border scrutiny is more lax. However, it is believed that much of the money associated with high terrorist financing risk is moved by alternative remittance systems, many of which are insufficiently regulated and operate below the radar of the formalised banking system. Many jurisdictions with a high risk of terrorism are underdeveloped or politically unstable nations where formalised banking is rare, or where a particular community has a link to a traditional money transfer system. Although many countries are moving to increase the regulation of remittance systems, they still represent a significant risk. Alternative remittance systems provide ways of moving money, often without any physical movement of cash. Many of these are based on the principles of hawala.

Although regulation of informal transfer systems is increasing, potential problems still exist: the hawaladar could be unregistered or, for cultural reasons, unaware of, or resistant to, the legislation enacted in a relevant jurisdiction to prevent money laundering and terrorist financing. There may be little that the hawaladar can do to distinguish the motives behind some transactions. Transfers from, for example, the large Somali diaspora in the US usually have entirely legitimate ends such as sending portions of income to family members in the home country. It is therefore easy to disguise sums of money that may be sent for other purposes. In October 2011, two women in Minnesota, home to the US's largest Somali community, which transfers around $100 million annually from the US, were convicted of sending over $8,600 to Somalia to fund Al Shabaab. A few months later, a man from Ohio pleaded guilty to a similar charge. In both cases, it was reported that the funds had been raised under the false pretence that the money was to be donated to charity, but it was instead transferred to Somalia for use by the Al Shabaab militia. Apparently in response to these cases, it was reported that Sunrise Community Banks, the most popular bank to offer facilities to the numerous Somali money transfer businesses in Minnesota, had withdrawn its services due to the risks posed, unfortunately leaving Somalis with no way to send home the money that their families rely upon.[16] A longer-term solution and agreed approach is clearly needed in this respect, as UK banks are following the US lead. In the UK, Dahabshiil won a High Court interim injunction in late 2013 to prevent Barclays shutting down its account. Barclays had attempted to close a number of remittance accounts, including that of Dahabshill, amid fears that they could serve as conduit for laundered money and terrorist financing. Around £100 million per year is sent to Somalia by Somalis living in the UK, and should Barclays win its case, this could have drastic consequences for those in Somalia who rely on the transfers for basic living needs.

The compliance industry is booming and SWIFT has estimated that general compliance costs for financial institutions are set to double every four years and screening on terrorist lists is no small part of this work. In light of this, it may be that many institutions feel that the consequences of allowing small quantities of funds to be passed to terrorists are negligible compared to the cost, in terms of finance and manpower, of trying to eliminate them. In an article discussing the efficacy of compliance systems, one banking industry official even told *The Economist* that enhanced screening was 'hardly worth the effort', given the relatively small chances of uncovering a planned attack via suspect financial transactions.[17] Moreover, in cases such as IS, a group which relies upon the control of local economies and the accumulation of cash, any direct action taken by the financial services industry to choke terrorist funding will only have a very limited impact. However, quite apart from the wider human consequences, recent events have shown that the reputational and financial damage that can be caused from the alleged provision of services to organisations linked to terrorism can be significant.

Three non-US banks are currently facing potentially immense civil compensation claims in the US for their alleged roles in providing banking services to terrorist groups. Under US anti-terrorism legislation, the victims or the families of the victims of terror attacks may bring a claim against those who may have assisted the terrorists by providing 'material assistance', which has been defined to include banking services. In short, this means that US citizens who are victims, or related to victims, of a terror attack, wherever it took place, can sue any institution that comes under US jurisdiction for providing financial services that assisted the terrorists. Currently ongoing are three lawsuits: that of *Weiss v National Westminster Bank*, *Licci v Lebanese Canadian Bank*, and *Wultz v Bank of China*.

The claimants in the first case are people who were wounded, or families of US persons who were killed, in a series of Hamas-led attacks on Israel in 2002–2003. The allegations surround NatWest's provision of British bank accounts to Interpal, a British-based charity which purports to provide humanitarian aid to Palestinians. Several accusations, albeit unsubstantiated following investigation, were made that Interpal was providing financial assistance to Hamas. Interpal was, however, only sanctioned by the US in 2003, some years after the NatWest accounts were opened. The claimants allege that the bank was aware of a link between the charity and terrorism. Through the nexus of NatWest branches in the US, they were granted permission to bring their case in New York, despite the fact that neither the bank accounts nor the attacks were in the US. In 2013, a US district court judge granted NatWest's summary judgement, agreeing that the plaintiffs could not prove that the bank knew or deliberately ignored that Interpal was funding Hamas terrorism. The plaintiffs thereafter appealed.[18]

In the *Licci* case, the families of people killed during Hezbollah rocket attacks in 2006 are claiming that the Lebanese Canadian Bank (LCB) was responsible for organising the transfer of millions of dollars destined for Hezbollah which were eventually used to fund the attacks. In 2009, LCB moved to dismiss all the claims against it for lack of jurisdiction and failure to state a claim; but in late 2012, a judge ruled that the claimants could pursue their case in New York due to the maintenance by LCB of a correspondent bank relationship with Amex in the city, thereby bringing it under New York's jurisdiction.[19]

In the third case the Wultz family is seeking millions in compensation from the Bank of China after the injury of the American Yekutiel Wultz and the death of his 16-year-old son, Daniel Wultz. The plaintiffs allege that the Bank of China – which denies any wrongdoing – was aware that it had facilitated transfers from Iran and Syria to the US-sanctioned militant group Palestine Islamic Jihad. The group claimed responsibility for the 2006 suicide bombing in Tel Aviv which killed Daniel and ten others. Raising the confidence of the plaintiffs, the Wultzes were awarded a $332 million judgement in a landmark legal decision in the US in 2012, which ordered damages against Iran and Syria.[20] It was the first judgement to penalise Syria on terror charges, although both countries are expected to contest payment.

Domestic legislation in much of Europe and the US has succeeded in making the raising of funds for the purpose of terrorism a criminal offence. Once a descriptor applied to drug lords like Pablo Escobar who succeeded in corrupting officials and influencing politics, 'narco-terrorism' has become a catch-all term for the overlap in these two crimes, which has been essentially enshrined in US law. The US Patriot Improvement and Reauthorisation Act, enacted in 2006, creates an offence of trafficking drugs anywhere in the world if the intention is to make a financial gain for terrorism. In 2008, Khan Mohammed, an Afghani, became the first man to be tried for the new offence and, following his conviction for participating in terrorism and trafficking opium, he was sentenced to life imprisonment. The trial uncovered an additional opportunity in drug dealing to meet the trafficker's ideological goals after Mohammed was recorded as saying that the drugs themselves would serve to perform Jihad: '[m]ay God eliminate them right now, and we will eliminate them too. Whether it is by opium or by shooting, this is our common goal'. An appeals court upheld the conviction and at the same time agreed to remand Mohammed's claim of an ineffective counsel to a district court.[21] In June 2012, Haji Bagcho, an Afghan national, was sentenced to life in prison in the US in for supplying heroin and supporting Taliban commanders with the proceeds. The court found that in 2006 alone, Bagcho had conducted heroin transactions valued at over $250 million.[22] He was also ordered to forfeit this amount in drug proceeds along with properties in Afghanistan.

OFAC's 2012 *Terrorist Assets Report* stated that $21 million has been blocked as a result of links to international terrorism or other designated parties. This includes Al Qaida, Hezbollah, and Hamas ($20 million between them) as well as smaller groups such as the Tamil Tigers and the Philippines organisation Rajah Solaiman Movement.[23] The US also claims to have identified $2.4 billion in assets held in the US which belong to 'state sponsors of terrorism' (Iran, Sudan, Cuba, and Syria), most of which has been blocked by economic sanctions. The majority of these blocked assets – $1.9 billion's worth – belong to Iran and are the subject of ongoing legal action. These estimates arise from figures that have been reported to OFAC and probably do not represent the entirety of terror-linked funds held in the US.

International initiatives and groups such as FATF and the UN's International Convention for the Suppression of the Financing of Terrorism provide advice, set standards, develop policies, conduct research, and promote the implementation of regulatory, legal, and operational measures. The international sanctions regime has also allowed states to outlaw payments to particular persons, such as known operatives in terror groups, and regulatory frameworks have considerably tightened their anti–money laundering and counter-terrorist financing requirements that intend for banks to take more seriously the need to make full investigations into the source and destination of funds and the risks that each transaction runs. There is some evidence that enhanced scrutiny and international pressure has decreased the level of state sponsorship of terrorism, but the same must extend to all forms of potentially damaging transactions.

## SCENARIO

The family office of a member of a ruling family in the Persian Gulf maintains a series of corporate and personal bank accounts with two banks in a Gulf state. Despite international efforts to prevent terrorism and the fact that a significant cash economy operates there, the state concerned has not yet criminalised the financing of terrorism. Both banks operate systems of risk control that are in practice rendered redundant by cultural factors that discourage local employees from reporting concerns or suspicions about relationships with members of the state's ruling elite. The family office is controlled on behalf of the ruling family member by a former British banker who is a director of a large energy company which also has significant funds deposited with both banks. Members of both bank's senior management teams are acutely aware that the mis-handling of the family office accounts carries the risk of cross-contamination of the energy company accounts which could be very damaging commercially. The two banks are fierce competitors both recognising the growth potential of the state and its neighbours in the Gulf region.

The ruling family member is a strong supporter (though not a public advocate) for Sunni political Islam. Appalled at the atrocities committed on Sunnis by the Syrian regime of President Assad and believing that Assad's days are numbered he had been channelling financial support to a Sunni Islamic group in Syria, Jaish al Islam, linked to the Al Nusra Front, itself described as the Syrian wing of Al Qaeda. Such financial support had been sourced from one of the family office's corporate accounts out of which hundreds of thousands of dollars worth of local currency had been withdrawn over a period of months ostensibly for the payment of immigrant oil refinery and construction workers from the Indian sub-continent employed across a number of different trading companies owned ultimately by the member of the ruling family. Some of the cash was diverted and delivered into the hands of representatives of Jaish al Islam in Turkey from where the cash was used to purchase weapons and explosives.

With the rise of Islamic State (IS) in Iraq and Syria and an intensification of the sectarian Sunni and Shiite conflict, the bank altered its anti-money laundering policies and tightened controls governing cash withdrawals rendering continuing support in cash from the ruling family member more difficult. The ruling family member is however seduced by the increasingly realistic prospect of a 21st century caliphate and his desire to support its establishment is undiminished by IS's much publicised acts of terror. In consequence a new form of support by the ruling family member for IS commences following the capture by IS of the Qayara and Najma oil fields near the northern Iraqi city of Mosul. IS recognises the huge value of the oilfields hitherto controlled by foreign oil companies that have abandoned them because of security concerns, but it does not have the technical know-how to operate and maintain the fields. Following a meeting with an IS intermediary the ruling family member agrees to assist. He does not do so by direct financing, but he opts to indirectly support IS by paying oil production technicians and engineers to travel to Northern Iraq to operate the captured oil wells. The technicians and engineers (some of whom had previously been engaged by the ruling family member's oil companies) are identified and contracted by a separate company newly established by the family office.

That new company establishes a bank account with the second bank and enters into an employment agency contract for the supply of 'search, select and labour services' to the company banked by the first bank and from which cash was previously withdrawn and transported to Turkey. Funds are thus transferred under cover of what appears to be an arm's length commercial agreement and the money is used to fund the technicians who keep the oil wells pumping. Because of the internal cultural sensitivities surrounding ruling family connected relationships at both banks, and because of the competition that exists between the two banks, neither conducts any due diligence to establish the authenticity of the commercial arrangement between the two companies for fear of jeopardising their relationship with the member of the ruling family and the local energy company.

From Qayara IS transports some of the oil to mobile refineries in Syria where it is converted into low grade gasoline. From there the gasoline is either sold for cash to the Syrian regime of President Assad who because of international sanctions is forced to trade with his enemy, or unrefined crude is smuggled into Turkey where it is sold for cash by traders at significantly below the market price. The oil trade generates approximately $2 million per day for IS none of which would be possible without the technical expertise funded by the ruling family member or the banking and wire transfer facilities provided by the bankers to his family office companies. The way in which the funds are funnelled to IS from the ruling family member can be depicted as follows:

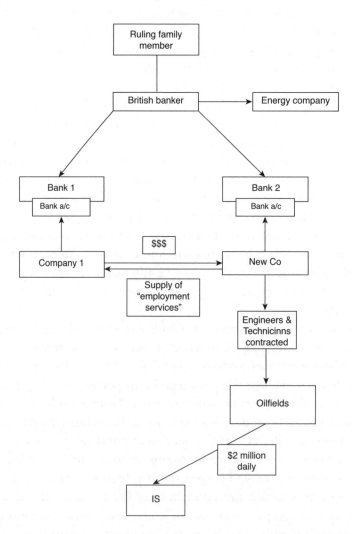

# 9

# SANCTIONS-BUSTING

In the past few years, fines and settlements totalling around $11.5 billion have been paid out by a number of global banks for skirting sanctions regimes. Whilst this activity does not earn the label of money laundering or facilitate crime in the same way that, say, bribery and tax evasion do, the extent of this practice in major financial institutions has been uncovered in a number of large-scale investigations over recent years. As is the case with excessive risk taking and mis-selling of financial products, the sorts of failures in mechanisms to prevent and deter this kind of activity are also common to both money laundering and the facilitation of crime.

The fines for sanctions evasion have been handed over by banks to a variety of US enforcement agencies for alleged systematic breaches of the US economic sanctions regime. In 2014 at least half a dozen US authorities rounded on France's largest bank for breaching US sanctions: the FBI, a Southern District of New York court, the New York State Supreme Court, the Federal Reserve System, the New York Department of Financial Services, and the Treasury's Office of Foreign Assets Control all chipped in. The banks concerned in such cases were not American, and the transactions in question did not for the most part occur in the US: they were caught by the US sanctions regime because they used the US dollar. Huge sums of money continue to be paid over to US agencies in deals that are intended to send a clear message that the US will not tolerate foreign financial institutions breaching its laws. Other nations and supranational bodies (such as the UN and the EU) also impose sanctions, but no state or body is as vigorous in the enforcement of its sanctions regime as the US. Despite the notable sums involved, and the reputational risk that these actions notionally carry, financial institutions have often given the appearance of being essentially unconcerned by the possibility that their names may be in the headlines for facilitating a breach of sanctions. However, there is no sign of the tide of action taken by the US slackening any time soon.

Due in part to its unilateral nature, the US sanctions regime is controversial. Financial institutions not domiciled in the US (termed 'foreign financial institutions' or 'FFIs' in the jargon) resent being restricted in whom they can transact with, and not all nations or corporations agree that states such as Cuba or Burma (both of which are sanctioned by the US) pose such a threat to global security that they are deserving of the financial isolation which the US seeks to impose. However, most nations and corporations recognise that sanctions are legitimate in more extreme cases, current examples of which might include trade with North Korea and the attempted isolation of individual members of Russia's political elite after the country's annexation of Crimea. Notwithstanding this recognition, a surprising number of household name banks have recently been caught in flagrant breach of international sanctions regimes. With the current awareness of the damage that is done by assisting drug laundering, tax evasion, and political corruption, the perception that a bank or institution is also prepared to assist in breaching sanctions is – or should be – immensely damaging to its reputation. Sadly, the one does not always appear to follow the other.

Sanctions are penalties or embargoes that are imposed by one party on another in order to make a political point without having to take military action. Often they are imposed by states on other states, but they can also be imposed on organisations, individuals, and even ships. They generally involve a trade or financial restriction which is designed to impair the sanctioned party's ability to function economically and participate in the global economy. The precise form of individual sanctions measures varies depending on where they are passed and whom they affect; typically, a sanctions measure passed by one jurisdiction will make it an offence for financial institutions or persons domiciled or regulated in that jurisdiction to transact with the country, organisation, or party named in the measure without permission.

Sanctions against countries or governments that are deemed politically dangerous or undesirable are not new, but in recent years their importance and profile has grown considerably on the international financial scene, and breaching sanctions by trade or transaction has become one of the main ways in which banks and financial service providers may fall foul of the law. This development is due in no small part to the aggressive approach adopted by the US to the imposition and enforcement of sanctions measures.

Globally, there are three principal current sources of trade sanctions: the US, the EU, and the UN, although some individual countries also have their own regimes.

UN sanctions, administered by the Security Council, apply to all UN member states. Sanctions were first exercised against the apartheid regimes of South Africa (in 1963) and Southern Rhodesia (in 1965). They were initially voluntary in nature but made mandatory in 1977 and 1968 respectively. The 1990s saw a particularly heavy flow of targeted sanctions, including those against Liberia (1992–2001), Rwanda (1994–2008), and Kosovo (1998–2001). Jurisdictions currently subject to UN sanctions include Afghanistan, Cote d'Ivoire, Iran, Iraq, North Korea, Liberia, Sierra Leone, Somalia, and Sudan.

The UN describes its broad objectives in applying sanctions as 'conflict resolution, non-proliferation, counter-terrorism, democratisation and the protection of civilians (including human rights)'.[1] The sanctions tend to be responsive in nature and concern trading with countries deemed to be a security risk, or trading in commodities that contain elements of risk. Amongst others, UN trade sanctions currently prohibit the import and export to North Korea of certain materials which contribute to the making of weapons and freeze the assets of and impose travel bans on businessmen linked to Charles Taylor's dictatorship in Liberia and known Al Qaeda operatives.

In 2009, the UK engineering firm Mabey & Johnson Limited was fined £2 million and paid £618,000 to the Iraq Construction Fund after it admitted to breaching UN sanctions in relation to Iraq.[2] The Serious Fraud Office had launched its investigation into the business in 2007 on the back of the UN Independent Inquiry Committee's findings (published in the Volcker Report) that the company had paid kickbacks to the Saddam regime to secure a $3.6 million bridge building contract. Criminal proceedings were later brought against three Mabey & Johnson men in the UK: managing director Charles Forsyth was sentenced to 21 months, sales director and major shareholder David Mabey eight months, and sales manager Richard Gledhill eight months suspended. The first two men denied the charges against them, whilst Gledhill pled guilty and gave evidence for the prosecution. Significantly, it was the first time that the Serious Fraud Office had succeeded in obtaining criminal convictions for breaches of UN sanctions measures implemented by UK legislation.

Scotland followed in 2010 with a high profile case in which the Scottish engineering firm Weir Group Plc was fined £3 million by the Edinburgh High Court after the company pleaded guilty to trading with Iraq in breach of UN sanctions in the previous decade. The court judgement read that Weir had illegally paid more than £3 million to secure contracts worth over £35 million. The court also issued a £13.9 million confiscation order, the largest ever made by a Scottish court.[3]

The application of UN sanctions can appear surprisingly wide-ranging. A seemingly more frivolous case, although potentially bearing serious consequences, emerged at the end of 2013 after Irish betting giant Paddy Power hit the headlines over speculation that it may have breached UN sanctions when it gifted various items, supposedly including Jameson whiskey, European crystal, and a Mulberry handbag, to North Korean leader Kim Jong-un. The North Korean dictator was reported to have been presented with the items in December 2013 when Paddy Power sponsored the US former professional basketball player Dennis Rodman's trip to the country. Paddy Power denied that any sanctions had been broken and said that the items were only of 'modest value'. Experts referred to a UN resolution prohibiting the transfer of 'luxury goods' to North Korea, 'including certain kinds of jewellery and precious stones, yachts, luxury automobiles and racing cars'. Paddy Power, which had previously referred to its sponsorship as 'basketball diplomacy', withdrew its support for Rodman and announced that 'circumstances had changed' after reports emerged that Kim had ordered the killing of his uncle.[4]

The EU runs a similar sanctions programme to the UN. The EU version has the power to freeze assets and impose bans on trade with nations, companies, or individuals. Recent targets have included state-owned Iranian oil and gas companies. Revisiting Paddy Power's predicament, the EU's restrictive measures against North Korea are very specific with regard to luxury items banned from export to the country. These include 'high quality ... spirits', 'high quality ... handbags', and 'high quality lead crystal glassware'.[5] The gifts allegedly in Kim Jong-un's goodie pack would no doubt fall foul of these provisions.

Sanctions made by the EU are directly enforceable via the laws of each EU member state. An example is the recent EU regulation 267/2012 which prohibits certain transactions with Iran unless prior consent is sought from the appropriate authority. However, the penalty for breaching such a measure must be brought into effect in the national law of each member state by way of legislation which means that unless the government of a member state passes a law imposing a penalty, breach of an EU sanction remains an offence without a corresponding punishment. Laws of this nature are new in Europe, and there are few examples of breaches leading to fines or other actions being taken.

In the UK, the Foreign and Commonwealth Office is responsible for sanctions policy, whilst the HM Treasury ministerial department maintains the 'consolidated list' of asset freeze targets designated by the UK, UN, and EU under financial sanctions regimes. Banks routinely check names against this list and have been brought to account for not doing so. In 2010, RBS was stung with a £5.6 million civil penalty after the FSA found that the bank had failed to maintain adequate systems to prevent breaches of UK financial sanctions and said that the botches amounted to undermining 'the integrity of the UK financial services sector'.[6] The FSA found that banks belonging to the RBS group (including Coutts and NatWest) had not adhered to UK money laundering regulations as they had demonstrated serious weaknesses with respect to customer due diligence procedures, on-going monitoring and internal controls, and had also failed to screen customers and payments against the HM Treasury consolidated list. The size of the potential risk arising from RBS' activities may be grasped from the following fact: in 2007 the group's payment processing division in London 'dealt with the largest volume of foreign payments of any financial institution in the UK'. The figures are difficult to imagine; inward euro payments processed by the group totalled a mind-boggling £7.6 *trillion* according to the FSA.

These were not complex procedures. The straightforward and easily rectifiable failures were demonstrated, for instance, in the bank's failure to simply consistently record the names of directors and beneficial owners of corporate customers. The FSA had high hopes that 'the financial penalty imposed will promote high standards of regulatory conduct within RSBG [RBS Group] and deter them from committing further breaches'. The reader could be forgiven for wondering whether the FSA had said something similar when they fined RBS £750,000 eight years previously for failing to establish the identity of customers at account opening.[7] In its 2010 decision notice, the FSA bravely hoped that 'the financial penalty will help deter other firms from committing similar breaches as well as demonstrating generally the benefits of a compliant business'.

It is the US that has the sanctions regime with the greatest reach and relevance to banks and financial service providers worldwide. The regime is administered and enforced by the Office of Foreign Assets Control (OFAC), which is part of the US Department of the Treasury. The Treasury's sanctions policy dates back to the early nineteenth century when sanctions were imposed against Great Britain 'for the harassment of American sailors' and its current programme began in 1950 when, on the entry of China into the Korean War, the US blocked North Korean and Chinese assets in the US.

What makes the OFAC regime so important to international businesses and so different from UN and EU systems is that its application is not limited to persons and individuals domiciled or regulated in the US or holding US citizenship: the *de facto* application of the regime is capable of extending to any institution which transacts in dollars. Dollar transactions engage OFAC because they need to be routed via either a US subsidiary or a US correspondent bank. Consequently, if a bank with no US connection makes a dollar transaction in breach of the OFAC regime, the US correspondent bank which assists in it will be involved in the breach, bringing both parties within the scope of the legislation. Causing a US person to breach the sanctions rules is an offence in of itself. US persons are prohibited from taking part in any transactions with US-sanctioned entities, whatever their location at that time and whatever the currency the transaction is made in, unless an exemption has first been granted by OFAC. An American employee of a German firm would commit an offence if he processed a payment from his employer to a sanctioned Iranian supplier, even if the transaction took place in euros or sterling.

Crucially for the many banks that have found themselves subject to OFAC scrutiny in recent years, simply possessing a branch in the US is enough to bring the entire wider business structure under the reach of US law. It is irrelevant, therefore, that a London-based bank processes transactions to Sudan in London, if that bank also maintains a branch in New York City; even a UK payment to a sanctioned entity where none of the parties have anything to do with the US could be caught by the OFAC regime. Given the international popularity of the dollar and the high likelihood that large multinational companies will have a US presence, it is easy to grasp the overreaching influence that the US regime has on global finance, and the wide reach of its punishments. The US's reach with regard to individuals, not simply corporations, is illustrated by the case of the UK businessman Christopher Tappin. He stood accused of aiding and abetting others to illegally attempt to export batteries designed for use in Hawk missiles from the US to Iran, via the UK, between 2005 and 2007. As a designated defence article on the US Munitions List, exporting the batteries from the US required special clearance, which Tappin and his associates did not have. After a failed attempt through the UK courts, Tappin appealed to the European Court of Human Rights to block an extradition order against him based on a delay of nearly three years in the US submitting its request and because of his responsibilities in taking care of his sick wife. He was extradited to the US in 2012 where he reversed a not-guilty plea and entered into a plea bargain with prosecutors. He was subsequently handed a 33-month sentence.[8]

Sanctions can be breached in a number of ways. At their simplest, breaches may occur when a financial institution which has not conducted thorough checks is unaware that an entity with which it is asked to transact is subject to sanctions. If the transaction goes ahead, the institution concerned will have committed an inadvertent breach. A common feature of cases which have resulted in action being taken, however, is a more deliberate practice known as 'stripping'. US banks are aware that they must not make any payments which breach the OFAC regime and that they are required to freeze and report any transaction that appears to concern a sanctioned entity. In order to avoid this, financial institutions may 'strip' incriminating details from the wire transfer form sent to their US correspondent bank as part of the transaction in the hope that by doing so they will disguise the true (sanctioned) nature of the transaction (often this relates to the ultimate origin or destination of the funds or the identity of the parties concerned). The very filtering software to prevent such payments being processed through the US was, on some occasions, used as a first step in identifying the information to be stripped ahead of being sent to the US. A more elaborate practice has also been seen on some occasions by which the financial institution concerned encourages its (sanctioned) customer to set up a shell company in a less conspicuous jurisdiction and to route funds to be transferred through this company, thus disguising further the true origin of the funds concerned. Both of these methods involve a degree of planning and management approval that is likely to aggravate the nature of the offences committed by the financial institution involved.

Most observers would agree that at least some of the countries, entities, and individuals currently subject to sanctions present a real risk to global security. Financial services providers ought to be alive to the identities of persons on sanctions lists and to the risks that they run by breaching their stipulations. Not only do they risk assisting regimes, persons, or organisations that endanger global security, but they also (in theory at least) risk their professional reputations. However, up to this point, penalties imposed by the US authorities have stopped short at actually imprisoning the executives of offending institutions, and many feel that so long as the banks are disciplined only by fining them what amounts to a tiny fraction of their annual profits, little is likely to change, particularly as the reputational damage to the finance industry has already been done.

Proof of OFAC's power and wide remit can be found in its investigations in recent years of some of the largest names in international banking, such as HSBC, Standard Chartered Bank, RBS, and BNP Paribas. And it is not only banks which are being targeted by OFAC: the department is casting its net more widely to snag other operators in financial services, as demonstrated by a recent settlement with investment fund firm Genesis Asset Managers LLP for an apparent violation of Iranian sanctions. The OFAC regime provides for the prosecution of the offending institution or person, with penalties ranging from a fine to custody. However, the US authorities have historically shown themselves as reluctant to launch actual prosecutions of sanctions busters by typically relying instead on deferred prosecution agreements under which the threat of prosecution is deferred provided that specified actions are taken, usually involving a financial penalty and the implementation of remedial measures by the institution concerned. One factor that may influence the US authorities not to prosecute large financial institutions is that a conviction of an organisation may in theory cause counter-parties to stop doing business with them potentially causing destabilisation. This raises the question of whether some financial institutions enjoy effective immunity owing to their systemic importance. This local difficulty could be at least partially be addressed by prosecuting the responsible individuals.

The year 2010 saw hefty fines paid by Dutch bank ABN AMRO (acquired by RBS in 2007) and Barclays for similar actions. Barclays agreed to pay a $298 million forfeit in connection with violations of US law after systematically skirting OFAC filters to conduct transactions on behalf of sanctioned subjects. It is inconceivable that an individual involved in this form of conduct would be offered a DPA rather than a swift prosecution and a long prison sentence. As its stands, a mugger who steals a few dollars will be dealt with more harshly than a financial institution that facilitates billions of dollars of wire transfers in respect of sanctioned activity. Barclays was found to have moved hundreds of millions of dollars through the US financial system over the course of a decade for, amongst others, Cuban, Iranian, Libyan, and Burmese banks. The Barclays DPA recounted the particular perks of abusing a 'cover' payment processing system – whereby it was essentially easier to strip information – when an employee pointed out that in using that mechanism 'the US Treasury [would] remain blissfully unaware of [the payment's] existence'.[9] The culturally embedded industry-wide acceptability of breaching sanctions could not have been expressed any better than by the author of an internal memo who wrote: 'risk exists if we carry on using cover payments but that is what the industry does'. The author advised that the practice of using cover payments continue, whilst accepting 'that there is a risk of these being used on occasion to hide true beneficiaries'.

ABN agreed to forfeit $500 million the same year in connection with a conspiracy to violate US laws in its facilitation of dollar transactions on behalf of OFAC-sanctioned countries. The US authorities said that the bank had violated the country's Banking Secrecy Act by wilfully failing to have adequate anti–money laundering procedures in place.

The one-year DPA described how between 1995 and 2005 ABN AMRO stripped relevant information from payment messages to circumvent OFAC filtering, and employed similar methods in processing dollar traveller's cheques, letters of credit, and foreign exchange transactions linked with sanctioned countries. The stripping, involving Iran, Libya, Sudan, and Cuba, allowed hundreds of millions of dollars to pass undetected through the US financial system.[10]

The DPA recounted that in 1995 – the year that President Clinton toughened up US sanctions against Iran – ABN AMRO in Dubai had set about convincing HQ of the benefits of a request from an Iranian bank to (secretly) act on their behalf in dollar transactions:

Our relations with [an Iranian bank] are excellent and they frequently help us with our Overnight dirham funding. They also maintain an average of USD 20 mio [million] in call balances with us. Apart from this relationship angle, we will derive the following benefits: (a) from the interest free balances with us; (b) management fees; and (c) TT/DD charges, etc. There is also the possibility of cash backed L/Cs [Letters of Credit] of approx. USD 20 mio being routed through us in the future.

Around the same time, another Iranian bank circulated a telefax to instruct certain UAE banks (including ABN AMRO in Dubai) to process dollar payments with the involvement of a European financial institution 'WITHOUT MENTIONING OUR BANK'S NAME' conspicuously included in the instructions. After seeking legal advice, ABN AMRO decided to proceed with the Iranian dollar business. With substantial profits at stake, the bank was eager to reassure its Iranian counterparts of their commitment in colluding to circumvent US law, with one bank official in Dubai writing to an executive of an Iranian bank in 2000 as follows: 'We understand the special nature of your US$ transactions and will ensure that all operations departments concerned are properly briefed regarding this'. Reference to a Libyan bank in one SWIFT message flagged by ABN in New York was boldly attributed to a 'typographical error'. The Dubai branch told New York that the Libyan bank had been 'wrongly mentioned' and politely sent its 'regret [ ... ] for the inconv[enience]'. New York refused the payment in any case, only to find that it had later wormed its way through the US system after reference to Libya had been stripped. Further demonstrating its defiance in the face of OFAC rules, ABN in Dubai even had a special code word ('SPARE') that it told sanctioned entities to include in its payment messages. In that way, those particular messages would be re-routed for manual processing where the relevant details would be stripped.

The US Department of Justice said that 'over $3.2 billion dollars involving shell companies and high risk transactions with foreign financial institutions flowed through ABN AMRO's New York branch' between 1998 and 2005. One of the most interesting nuggets from the DPA in this respect clearly set out the bank's historic willingness to compromise the law in the frantic pursuit of targets. Desperate to attract business from small and medium-sized Russian financial institutions, despite widely recognised and serious concerns about their suspicious activities, an ABN New York employee wrote to a colleague in Moscow in 1999, begging them to '[P]lease phone them [potential Russian clients], push really hard, we need new accounts on our books. I must make my projections of $500,000 in revenues for 1999 from all russian banks. Please lend me your HAND!' The same New York employee would later receive an email from Moscow voicing concerns over the potential for 'trouble' in opening accounts for 'all those half-dead tiny Russian banks kicked out of [US financial institutions]'.

Fast-forward to 2012 and a cluster of DPAs were entered into by three major banks – ING, Standard Chartered, and HSBC. Dutch bank ING came to a settlement with the US authorities concerning breaches of sanctions involving Cuba, Burma, Libya, Sudan, and Iran in a period lasting more than a decade.[11] It agreed to pay what was then a record forfeit of $619 million to avoid criminal charges being pressed. These concerned transfers of over $1.6 billion to Cuba, $15 million to Burma, almost $2 million to Sudan, $26,803 to Libya (those sanctions have now been repealed), and $1.3 million to Iran. There were other allegations of deliberate steps that had been taken to assist with breaching the sanctions, including the use of shell companies, false stamps that would enable Cuban banks to forge US travellers cheques, and advice on concealment of dollar transactions. Introducing a new entry to the legal lexicon, ING Group Legal department even catalogued the actions of one ING branch purposely deceiving a US correspondent bank as a 'little white lie'. Threats were made to employees who refused to participate in the breach actions. Clearly, none of these actions could be called accidental or inadvertent.

Also in 2012, UK bank Standard Chartered settled with US authorities over billions of dollars of transactions with Iran. The bank paid

$340 million to the Department of Financial Services, $100 million to the Federal Reserve and $227 million to the US Justice Department and became subject to two years of monitoring as part of a DPA.[12] Initially, the bank's representatives disputed the sums involved and said that the conduct related to transactions in the millions, but the statement made by Superintendent of Financial Services for New York State Benjamin Lawsky claimed that 'The parties have agreed that the conduct at issue involved transactions of at least $250 billion'.[13] The case was memorable for an accusation that one of the heads of the bank had responded to warnings about sanctions breaches with the words 'You fucking Americans ... who are you to tell us, the rest of the world, that we're not going to deal with Iranians?' This suggested not only that the British bank felt aggrieved at the US's restrictions and the extent of their reach, but also that they had been determined to make the transactions despite being aware that the US prohibited them. As consultant to Standard Chartered, Deloitte Financial Advisory Services was hauled into the offices of the New York State Department of Financial Services and was accused of having 'apparently aided' Standard Chartered's illegal behaviour through its provision of services. The consultancy was fined $10 million and banned from new consulting work in New York State for a year.[14]

RBS and BNP Paribas are the most recent banks to have had their sanctions-busting behaviour unveiled. In December 2013, RBS group counsel Chris Campbell signed legal documents committing RBS to part with $100 million in civil penalties for violating US sanctions. Half this amount was ordered by New York State's Department of Financial Services, which found that between 2002 and 2011 RBS had channelled $523 million in over 3,500 transactions involving Iranian and Sudanese customers and beneficiaries through New York banks, unbeknownst to the US correspondent banks it utilised. RBS stumped up the remainder to the Federal Reserve, which placed various sanctions misdemeanours between 'at least 2005 to 2008'. The US Treasury's settlement agreement detailed various breaches between 2005 and 2009 which involved Burma, Iran, Sudan, and Cuba, although its $33 million fine was deemed satisfied by the Federal Reserve's civil penalty.[15] All three authorities found that RBS had systematically manipulated data involved in processing payments to conceal the identity of US-sanctioned subjects.

The story is an interesting one and starts over 15 years ago when NatWest Bank (acquired by RBS in 2000) struck up a correspondent banking relationship with Bank Melli Iran and UK subsidiary Melli Bank Plc in 1997. As a correspondent bank, NatWest would process US dollar payments on behalf of the Iranian banks via SWIFT payment messages by utilising 'cover' payments (as seen in the ABN AMRO case) which allowed for the exclusion of certain key pieces of information when sent to the US. It appeared to continue with the practice for five years at which point, fed up with the 'heavy operational burden' of the relationship, NatWest – by then part of RBS – closed the Iranian bank's accounts altogether.

Disgruntled customers started complaining that they were unable to send US dollar payments to Iran. This, coupled with the fact that the introduction of a new internal 'ProPay' system at RBS made it harder to remove Iran-specific data from SWIFT messages, left the British bank in a predicament, but not for long. A savvy group of banking staff put their heads together and figured out a way to use ProPay such that RBS could still wire dollar payments to Iran by omitting information that would alert the US clearing banks to a possible breach of OFAC sanctions. Firstly, RBS would use the services of a 'third country' non-US bank. In its payment instructions to the non-US bank, RBS would insert the Great Britain country code along with the name of the Iranian beneficiary bank, rather than using the Iran bank's unique identifier code (known as the 'BIC' – Bank Identifier Code). The non-US intermediary bank could identify the Iranian bank from this particular message, but, because of the way RBS had formatted the data, any references to Iran mysteriously disappeared by the time it made its way into a message processed by the US correspondent bank. Thus, the payment instruction to the US clearing bank contained no reference to Iran or the Iranian beneficiary bank.

This was not a secret guarded by a select few. RBS made the practice crystal clear to its payment operators, circulating a memo, part of which included the following instructions:

> IMPORTANT: FOR ALL US DOLLAR PAYMENTS TO A COUNTRY SUBJECT TO US SANCTIONS, A PAYMENT MESSAGE CANNOT CONTAIN ANY OF THE FOLLOWING: 1. The sanctioned country name, 2. Any name designated on the Office of Foreign Assets Control (OFAC) restricted list, which can encompass a bank name, remitter or beneficiary.

US investigators found that RBS boldly published these ProPay instructions in its 'Business Support Manual' and on its intranet in 2003. Although the instructions were apparently only meant to apply to certain Iranian banks, employees took the liberty of interpreting the guidance as applying to other countries sanctioned by the US. Legal filings reference

Libya in this respect and describe how a memo was circulated to the effect that RBS' Global Banking Services division 'as a matter of routine, advises that the name of the Libyan bank and beneficiary is not to be quoted on any SWIFT messages in order to avoid blocking in the US under OFACs sanctions'.

Brazenly flouting the bank's own November 2003 revised policy on sanctions ('Group businesses with US relationships and US$ payments must comply with US regulations'), some RBS divisions carried on processing payments to Iran and other US-sanctioned countries. A further explicit statement on the bank's policy regarding OFAC in 2006 was similarly ignored. In December of that year, the CEO's advisory group told the bank's anti–money laundering division that it had adopted a policy of 'no US Dollar business with Iranian counter-parties'. Still, RBS continued to channel payments through the US, contravening various sanctions regulations.

The New York Department of Financial Services determined that 'RBS's conduct was at odds with U.S. national security and foreign policy and raised serious safety and soundness concerns for regulators, including the obstruction of governmental administration, failure to report crimes and misconduct, offering false instruments for filing, and falsifying business records'. Whilst four RBS employees were dismissed in 2010 when RBS started its own investigation, and eight others were ordered to repay bonuses, no prosecutions were pursued; the sum total of these repercussions would hardly register a heartbeat on a scale of banking anxiety.

Most recently slammed by US enforcement was BNP Paribas, which, it was found, had processed billions of dollars worth of transactions on behalf of Iranian, Cuban, and Sudanese parties between 2002 and 2012. This particular case stands out for three reasons: the size of the financial settlement ($8.9 billion); the bank's guilty pleas to criminal charges; and the New York regulator's decision to ban the bank from carrying out certain dollar transactions for a year. Despite this relatively unusual combination of punishments, no criminal charges were brought against any banking executives, despite the collusion of high-ranking personnel in the deception. This was made particularly apparent from the narrative surrounding a 2005 meeting in Geneva attended by a number of BNP Paribas executives. According to legal documents, the meeting was convened after Swiss compliance officers voiced serious concerns over Sudanese transactions being executed by the bank. Not only were these serious concerns dismissed at the meeting by people who should have known better, but the (then) group chief operating officer requested that no minutes of the meeting be taken.[16]

These banks were all found to have failed to apply adequate analysis to the true nature of the accounts which they held and to have deliberately colluded in the evasion of sanctions by the 'stripping' of electronic banking records in order to erase all traces of the true origin or destination of the money concerned. It is plain that for them, the self-declared international jurisdiction of the US was an annoyance to be circumvented rather than a law to be upheld. The banks were content to take the risks of discovery and punishment, as the fines imposed do not, in the wider scale, represent a large dent in their profitability. The most concerning aspect of the breaches is the attitude that financial and ethical risks are worth taking; when one considers the number of banks (sometimes the same names) who have also admitted systematically ignoring and evading anti–money laundering regimes designed to evade corruption or money laundering, it is clear that a lax approach to sanctions can be a signpost to potential involvement in other dangerous behaviours.

## SCENARIO

Much effort is expended by the finance industry in screening payments in and out of bank accounts for the purpose of identifying whether they involve sanctioned parties. However as the following scenario highlights, sanctions risk can manifest itself in a variety of ways other than simply through payments, and stripping is by no means the only way in which sanctions legislation is breached.

A syndicated loan facility involving UK and foreign banks has advanced a loan in the sum of $100 million to the offshore parent company of a large commercial aviation leasing company. The loan is secured against two Boeing cargo planes which are acquired by the parent company (let's call it 'Aviation Leasing Parent Co') each through discrete subsidiary holding companies. It is a term of the facility that a majority of the syndicate members agree to the lease of either of the aeroplanes. With the agreement of the syndicate members, one of the planes is leased to a multinational couriering company and the other is leased to an offshore company with an onshore US parent company incorporated in Delaware with US directors provided by a registrant agent. Before agreeing to the leases, the syndicate members undertake some due diligence on the lessee companies but the focus of the questions pertain to credit risk. The syndicate members are primarily interested in whether the lessees can satisfy the lease costs in order that the lessor company (the syndicate's client, Aviation Leasing Parent Co) can repay the facility. Sanctions compliance is not a risk that registers on the radar of the credit risk departments of any of the banks concerned in conducting their due diligence checks.

The leases are each for a term of five years. Everything runs normally. The lessee companies transfer monthly funds in satisfaction of the lease to the bank account of the holding companies of the aircraft and those accounts are then swept on a quarterly basis in satisfaction of the facility.

Two years into the lease, international tensions are heightened by concerns that Iran may be closer than was thought to developing a nuclear weapon and UN, EU, and OFAC sanctions against Iran are intensified. The measures prevent the carrying on or the facilitation of any trade with the government of Iran or any organs of the state of Iran.

An internal review by one of the syndicate member banks raises questions about the facility and the quality of due diligence held by the bank in relation to the offshore lessee company and its US parent. Details are not held on the ultimate beneficial owners of the US parent. Those concerns are shared with other members of the syndicate and it is jointly decided that an external firm specialising in the conduct of corporate investigations be instructed to analyse the relationship and obtain the missing information. Shortly into the engagement, the external firm raises the question 'on whose behalf does the lessee company transport goods?' The syndicate members do not hold that information and are further unable to assist in identifying flight log details to help establish those countries to which the plane has travelled. After a protracted investigation, it is revealed that the plane has made several journeys to and from the Bishe Kola Airfield in Amol, Iran, a military airbase in the north of the country. Unbeknownst to either the syndicate members, the lessor company, or the US based 'nominee' directors of the Delaware parent company of the lessee, the lessee has been transporting cargo on behalf of another offshore company registered in another offshore centre. This company is ultimately controlled by representatives of the Iranian Revolutionary Guard. A full-scale internal investigation is launched by each of the banks. They know that at best they would through the syndicated loan have facilitated sanctions breaches and at worst (depending on the nature of the cargo) have facilitated nuclear proliferation activity. Unable to identify what the plane's cargo had been on its trips to Northern Iran, the banks do learn that the bank acting on behalf of the offshore company owned ultimately by the Iranian Revolutionary Guard stripped remitter details from the payment messages, thus allowing the lessee company to be paid in dollars.

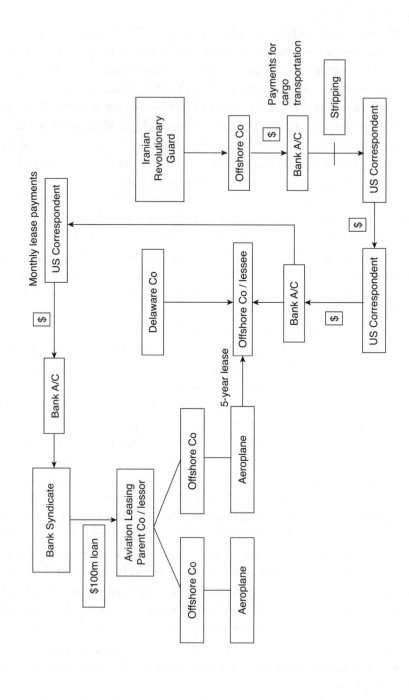

What does the scenario reveal about the exploitation of banks for criminal purposes? Firstly, that there was no identifiable placement, layering, or integration activity notwithstanding that the banks were clearly in receipt of the proceeds of crime. Instead, the syndicate banks were abused as parties to a facility that was used ultimately to breach sanctions. The scenario further reveals the abuse of ownership structures by a sanctioned state to circumvent the sanctions provisions to pursue its aims. In focusing purely upon the management of credit risk the banks failed to appreciate the other risks inherent in the relationship posed ultimately not by their customer, but by their customer's *customer's customer.* The absence of concern on the part of the syndicate banks would be embarrassing at worst in normal circumstances but in this instance they are faced with the uncomfortable reality that their basic due diligence requirements were not followed leading the authorities to question whether those compliance failures contributed to the perpetration of the underlying crimes.

# 10

# TAX EVASION/AVOIDANCE

In 1998, Starbucks opened its first outlet in the UK. Since then, it has opened over 750 coffee shops across the British Isles. To anybody with even a basic grasp of economics, it may come as a surprise that, despite such growth, Starbucks claims that it has 'found making a profit in the UK difficult'.[1] It is a wonder that a business would continue to operate hundreds of outlets if it were failing to make any money, least of all in a recession. The turnover may suggest differently: in 2012 it was reported that since 1998, Starbucks had recorded sales of over £3 billion in the UK. Tax paid in the same timeframe amounted to £8.6 million, or 0.3% of its turnover. After significant public pressure, not to mention a grilling by MPs, Starbucks has since congratulated itself on deciding not to claim tax deductions for royalties or payments related to intercompany charges for interest and mark-up on the coffee it buys.[2] From beneath the warm glow of its halo, it says that the move is 'unprecedented', but will allow the chain to 'contribute more'. Whilst it has chosen to pay around £10 million in corporation tax in 2013 and 2014, its example seriously undermines the clout of revenues collectors and lawmakers.

The fact of the matter is that Starbucks is right when it claims that technically it has abided by the letter of the law in 'optimising' the amount of tax it pays – or does not pay. Starbucks, like almost every other large multinational, engages in a complex system of internal financial contortions, designed to minimise its tax bill. It utilises structures that permit it to eliminate profits in high-tax jurisdictions and inflate them in low-tax jurisdictions. Nothing that Starbucks is alleged to do is in any way illegal. It does not lie on its balance sheets or deceive the taxman. It simply structures itself to ensure the most efficient distribution of its assets and liabilities, and despite being a hugely successful, globally recognised brand charging a healthy mark-up for every cup of coffee sold, it escapes the requirement to pay the same rate of tax as companies unable to take advantage of sophisticated tax structuring.

As unpalatable as this may seem to many hard working people who diligently pay their taxes and for whom tax mitigation is an alien concept, the reality is that tax optimisation is a fundamental component of free trade and the market economy. The idea that nakedly aggressive commercial enterprises will voluntarily choose to pay more tax than they need to, is delusional. The concept of tax optimisation has found support in the courts in both the US and the UK. In a landmark decision concerning US tax law, the US Supreme Court concurred with Judge Learned Hand who said: 'Any one may so arrange his affairs that his taxes shall be as low as possible; he is not bound to choose that pattern which will best pay the Treasury; there is not even a patriotic duty to increase one's taxes.'[3]

But the techniques used to minimise tax bills employed by individuals or by corporations can consist of legal or illegal activities and the desire to minimise the proportion of one's income that is paid over to state authorities exists at all levels, in all parts of the world. As a result, numerous and varied techniques are used to prevent treasuries from receiving what they are owed. Tax *evasion*, where deliberately deceptive steps are taken to reduce a tax liability, is generally illegal; currently, it is generally legal to *avoid* tax by taking steps that are within the boundaries of the law. However, in recent years a sizeable grey area has grown up between the two that consists of the more creative and tortuous methods of tax reduction, which, whilst not illegal per se, are under increasing fire for being unethical. The recent global recession has decreased the public and political tolerance for those who pay less than the spirit of the law suggests that they owe. This situation has been exacerbated by recent revelations concerning multinational corporations who manipulate their financial structures to avoid paying billions of dollars in tax, and offshore banks which provide accounts that are beyond the reach of their domestic revenues.

There is, of course, a legal and ethical conflict involved: providing these services is a lucrative business for many bankers, lawyers, financial consultants, and accountants, whether onshore or offshore. Further, governmental criticism of activities that are not outside the law is seen by many as compromising the relationship between state and individual, and there is the inevitable balance to be struck between attracting businesses and wealthy residents to an economy and being seen to permit such groups financial liberties simply because they can afford to pay handsomely for them. The result is that governments make up the shortfall by imposing greater burdens on those who are least able to afford it. The last few years have seen the beginnings of a legislative sea change as politicians battle to crack down on abusive financial models and to close easily exploited loopholes. Inter-governmental tax information sharing agreements are proliferating, heralding a new era of tax transparency intended to end the possibility of accounts kept hidden from the revenue inspectors. The coming into force of the Foreign Accounts and Tax Compliance Act (FATCA), which effectively destroys the concept of financial sovereignty by forcing foreign banks to provide account details for US clients or face exclusion from the US financial system, will change the landscape of tax legislation forever. Yet problems still exist. Experts will still be able to dream up ways for their clients to evade or avoid tax, and for many, despite the threatened penalties, the profits may still be worth the risk.

Tax evasion and tax avoidance are methods by which individuals and corporations can minimise the proportion of their income or assets that they pay to revenue authorities each year. Avoidance is generally seen as using methods that obey the letter, but not the spirit, of the law in order to minimise a tax bill. The UK's HM Revenue & Customs (HMRC) defines tax avoidance as 'using the tax law to get a tax advantage that Parliament never intended'. At its soft end, it includes standard and acceptable practices such as family tax planning and wealth management; at the more aggressive end, it involves taking more creative steps that are quite legal in themselves, but have as an end the significant and artificial reduction of a tax bill. As long as no tax rules are specifically broken and no active deception or fraud takes place, tax avoidance may attract public criticism but remains basically legal and subject to some restrictions on the precise methods used that may be imposed by the taxman.

Tax evasion, however, typically involves misrepresentation of the true value of assets, the concealment of ownership, and the underreporting of income. It does not operate within the furthest limits of the law, but deliberately goes outside them. False accounting, the failure to declare profits on foreign investments, or the construction of elaborate schemes to disguise the ownership of assets, either at home or abroad, and thereby evade paying tax or other charges, all constitute evasion.

Tax avoiders and evaders tend to be wealthy individuals or large multinational corporations. The structures used to maintain complicated illegal evasion methods require expensive investment in the services of finance professionals. The sums erased from tax bills are extremely high. Governments are deprived of a significant chunk of the revenue that would otherwise flow to them, but since the 2008 economic crash, they are aware that asking recession-hit taxpayers and small businesses to accept public spending cuts and higher tax rates is at odds with widespread inactivity concerning the lost tax owed by wealthy individuals and multinationals. Pressure groups such as the Tax Justice Network have been vocal in criticising the deficient regulation of tax structures, and successfully so: the international attitude to jurisdictions popular with tax evaders is increasingly censorious.

Although the numbers of persons and companies engaged in active avoidance and evasion may be low compared to taxpayers overall, the deficits that result are immense. According to HMRC estimates, the UK's tax gap (i.e., the difference between what is owed and what is collected) in 2011–2012 was around £35 billion of which 43% (£15.2 billion) was accounted for by tax evasion, the hidden economy, and criminal attacks on the tax system such as VAT fraud; whilst another 11% (£4 billion) was lost to legal tax avoidance. The EU's annual tax gap is estimated to be around €1 trillion, particularly significant when one considers the ongoing Eurozone crisis. In the US, the tax gap amounts to an estimated $385 billion annually with something like $150 billion of this lost to offshore tax schemes.[4] Billions are therefore being removed from national economies at a time when many governments are facing cuts which have a measurable effect on the welfare of ordinary people. The levying of higher personal tax rates is becoming a feature across much of Europe to make up for the shortfalls. Individuals who have moved abroad in order to escape the taxation burden of their home countries include the French actor Gerard Depardieu, now a Russian citizen following the announcement of a 75% 'millionaire tax', which was approved by France's constitutional court in December 2013.

Domestic tax reduction methods usually take the form of avoidance schemes. Some of these are as simple and uncontroversial as using a pension investment scheme, putting family assets into a trust, or passing on high-value assets such as real estate whilst the owner is still alive in order to avoid the payment of inheritance tax. Individuals may seek to lessen their bill by employing a family member in some capacity, thereby decreasing the overall income of the primary earner and allowing both to claim the tax-free personal allowance. Other methods are more complex, involving investment and charitable schemes. In his 2014 Budget speech, the UK chancellor made clear that the government is clamping down on these schemes. A partner in one private wealth firm described the news as 'a further bayonet into the dying corpse of aggressive and abusive tax avoidance schemes in the government's anti-avoidance battlefield'.[5]

Film investment schemes promoted in the early 2000s by the UK government, ostensibly to boost British cinema, permitted tax offsets through lucrative leveraged leaseback and loan arrangements. Enterprise investment schemes offer tax relief incentives for the making of a high-risk financial investment in a fledgling company. Ostensibly the tax relief is a happy side-effect of assisting British enterprise, but HMRC sees differently. Investment schemes involved in the financing of films such as *Avatar* and *Life of Pi* were described by HMRC's former head as 'scams for scumbags'.[6] The authority believes that the purpose of the investments is tax relief rather than genuine investment. One of the financial services firms behind the investments, Ingenious Media, denies that its partnerships are tax avoidance schemes but warned its investors in July 2014 that they should prepare for tax demands totalling at least £520 million.

A widely exploited method of avoiding tax concerns the tax relief from charitable donations. A recent and controversial example of such a scheme came to light in the UK in early 2013 and concerned The Cup Trust, a registered charity which purports to raise money for children and young people, whose sole corporate trustee was registered in the British Virgin Islands. It has no public profile, but it raised £176 million in 2010–2011 which made it one of the most successful (if unheard of) charities in Britain. However, up to 31 March 2013, it had only donated £152,292 to charitable causes.[7] It is alleged that the Trust, registered in 2009, is in fact a tax avoidance scheme which has allowed members to submit claims for £46 million from HMRC in 'gift aid' (as yet unpaid) by using an offshore bank loan to buy gilts which it sold to members at a significant undervalue. The Trust then donated a small sum to charity, and the members sold the gilts on the open market for their real, considerable, value. This money was then 'donated' to the Trust by the members, which allowed them to claim tax relief on it, and was then spent on paying back the loan. The Cup Trust therefore allows tax relief on the full value of the sum 'donated' to charity even though the scheme member only spent a tiny sum. The concept of 'charity' appears to be thoroughly abused, and a Public Accounts Committee concluded that the Trust did not meet public expectations of a charity. Despite this, the Charity Commission said it was unable to intervene as the charity itself was properly constituted. The Committee has questioned the Charity Commission's lack of authority by saying that it was unacceptable that it could not stop such an abuse of charitable status, and questions were raised around the regulatory effectiveness of the charity watchdog. The Cup Trust itself refuted allegations that its purpose was tax avoidance and denied any misconduct or mismanagement by its trustee's directors.

Many personal tax avoidance schemes involve the use of offshore accounts, and providing advice on such schemes is a lucrative line of business for many finance professionals. In the UK, such schemes have to be registered with HMRC and may be subject to review and court proceedings to determine whether they actually have any purpose outside of tax abuse. They are very popular: over 100 schemes have been registered between 2008 and 2012, with prominent schemes including K2 and Highlands. In the K2 scheme, a participant becomes an 'employee' of a company based in Jersey. This company 'seconds' the person to his actual employer who in turn pays a fee to the company in Jersey. The company then 'lends' this money to the participant who, because it is a 'loan' which could technically be recalled, does not need to pay tax on it. In February 2013, a court's ruling shut down the Highlands scheme which used artificial losses generated through offshore centres to save almost £400 million in tax, on the basis that it was a 'tax avoidance scheme with no underlying purpose whatsoever'.[8]

Whilst the Highlands, K2, and Cup Trust disputes centre upon technicalities in tax law, other tax-related schemes have depended upon blatantly fraudulent claims. In the US, a Seattle court handed out convictions to two men for a tax shelter scam which involved over $9.6 billion in 'phony' stock sales.[9] The 'POINT' (Personally Optimised Investment Transaction) scheme was promoted by Quellos Group LLC, and cost the public $240 million in tax losses. Wealthy clients were told that they could offset the capital gains of the participants by mingling their gains with losses from the sale of depreciated stock sitting in an offshore investment fund, which turned out to be nonexistent. Unbeknownst to investors the POINT scheme was 'predicated on a sham' and its two executives were sentenced for conspiracy to defraud the US and aiding and assisting with the filing of a false tax return. Fees paid by members of the scheme totalled $65 million, an example of how financial advisers engaging in this sort of work make vast sums for the risks they run.

Corporate exploitation of the tax differences between different countries has normalised the use of complex and artificial structural relationships which are designed to minimise the tax burden and offer 'tax optimisation' opportunities for the customer. The use of foreign subsidiaries has increased dramatically in the past decade and there is no sign of it slowing down. Indeed, many companies say that tax codes actively encourage them to exploit the onshore/offshore relationship in this manner.

Mindful of the amount of tax kept offshore by US companies that are only taxed on foreign income when it is repatriated to the US, the US Senate tried an experiment in 2004 which was intended to increase investment and jobs on home soil. As part of the American Jobs Creation Act, US corporations were briefly permitted to repatriate income held outside

the US at a tax rate of 5.25% rather than 35%, albeit with strictures applying to how it was actually spent. Overall, corporations repatriated $312
billion, mostly from tax havens, and avoided $3.3 billion in tax payments,
but the expected growth did not follow. Ironically, since the 2004 tax holiday, US multinationals have actually increased their offshore funds, leading the Senate to conclude that the tax break increased the use of offshore
accounts.

Offshore profit shifting is a common method by which multinational
corporations are able to relocate their tax burden around the globe according to where it is most favourable to make profits and losses. In general, it
involves ensuring that profits are recorded by subsidiaries located in low-tax
jurisdictions, and losses are recorded in high-tax jurisdictions. The subsidiary in the tax haven may be little more than a name on an office door; many
have virtually no employees and no active commercial purpose. Profit shifting can occur with tangible goods or intangible goods, such as intellectual
property, management guidance, or business plans. Therefore, a company
may sell 'royalties' in low-tax areas to subsidiaries located in high-tax ones,
so that large chunks of the actual profits made in high-tax locations appear
to be 'spent' on the royalties and become 'profits' where there is no or little
tax to be paid. Transfer pricing is a common component of such activities:
a parent company can sell assets or produce to its subsidiary for a price that
does not reflect its true value but enables the profit to be booked in the lowest
tax jurisdiction.

In a Public Accounts Committee hearing, UK MPs questioned Starbucks'
payments of royalties on gross revenues to its branch in the lower tax-rate
jurisdiction of the Netherlands, which holds the brand's European IP licensing rights. Starbucks justified the Dutch positioning in terms of a roasting
plant being located there and believed the royalty rates were reasonable. In
scenarios such as these, it is argued that a company's subsidiaries, based in
locations such as the UK with its relatively higher corporate tax rate, are
required to expend a sizeable sum on the 'rights' to the intellectual property:
the company appears to make less money in the UK, but the subsidiary in
the tax haven can make unlimited profit and still pay little or no tax. Some
attempts are being made to combat the problems that arise from the tan-
gible/intangible assets issue: the OECD is currently attempting to produce
guidelines on intangible assets to try to prevent companies from shifting
profits to tax havens on specious grounds such as for trademark royalties.

Through loan shifting practices, companies are also able to exploit
tax rules that govern the repayment of debts to organise a constant flow of
loans across international borders, thus managing to repatriate money to

the home country without it being subject to standard taxes. The US Senate Subcommittee of Investigations looked at the methods used by which numerous short-term loans, which are not subject to taxation, were staggered so that they covered the appropriate periods of the accounting year and were therefore not subject to revenue demands. The corporations were still succeeding in repatriating income to the US but just in a manner that on paper meant that they were not required to pay any tax on it.

The examples of the use of the offshore system range across the corporate board and include many of the biggest names in household goods and technological services. According to a statement made by Senator Carl Levin in 2012, Microsoft shifted 47% of its sales proceeds in the US to Puerto Rico (hardly the company's largest market) through the transfer pricing model.[10] Levin described how Microsoft sells rights to market its intellectual property in the Americas (including the US) to its Puerto Rico arm. Microsoft US buys back the distribution rights for the US from its Puerto Rico subsidiary by agreeing to pay the latter a percentage of the revenues it generates from the distribution of Microsoft's wares in the US. Microsoft US shells out a significantly higher sum for the US rights than it collected from Puerto Rico for a more extensive set of rights. According to Levin's calculations, by doing so Microsoft saved a whopping $4.5 billion in taxes on products sold in the US in the three years examined by the Senate subcommittee ('That's $4 million a day in taxes Microsoft isn't paying', as he pointed out). Bill Sample was heard by the Senate subcommittee, and said in his statement that Microsoft abided by 'US and foreign tax laws as written', at the same time recognising that there was a scope for improvement in the rules, communicating Microsoft's view that US tax rules are 'outdated' and 'not competitive with the tax systems of our major trading partners'.[11]

A *Financial Times* journalist described how, in 2012, Google reportedly shifted €8.8 billion of royalty revenues into a Bermuda company which owns the group's non-US intellectual property rights.[12] This was accomplished, apparently, by charging royalty payments from higher tax countries and routing them through states with decreasing tax liabilities. Royalties are paid from certain Google companies in higher tax countries to an Irish subsidiary enjoying a lower rate of corporate tax. These payments are then funnelled to the Netherlands, which, in turn, sends the sums to another company incorporated in Ireland, but controlled from Bermuda. In 2012 the company had a UK tax bill of $55 million, despite sales in the country of $4.9 billion. The same year, it paid a 2.6% tax rate on $8.1 billion in non-US income.[13] Google chairman Eric Schmidt has been decidedly less eager to pacify the public compared with his counterpart executives at Starbucks, saying that he was 'proud of the structure we set up', and equally 'proudly capitalistic'. In a similar vein, the head of Google in the UK has denied that the company is 'immoral' and that the responsibility lay with the politicians who set tax rates.[14]

In 2002, the US Permanent Senate Subcommittee on Investigations initiated a review of the development, marketing, and implementation of 'abusive tax shelters', following concerns about the growth of an entire financial industry devoted to assisting American taxpayers to reduce the sums paid to the IRS. The resulting report considered 'potentially abusive' transactions and focussed on four schemes that were provided by the accounting multinational KPMG, which it said generated over $124 million in fees between 1997 and 2001.[15] The report said that KPMG had not only organised such schemes but had actively marketed and promoted them as part of the evolution of the tax shelter from something produced by 'shady' and unaccountable backstreet firms into a standard provision of the mainstream accountancy world. The fact that the firm was fully aware of the 'potentially abusive' nature of the schemes on sale was plain from an email in which the writer enquired whether they were 'being paid enough to offset the risk of potential litigation' given that 'the transaction is clearly one that the IRS would view as falling squarely within the tax shelter orbit'. Having concluded that the potential profits that stood to be made far outweighed the risk and cost of the comparatively tiny and rarely imposed penalties imposed by the IRS, KPMG proceeded with them and assisted in the evasion of large sums of tax. The firm had actually taken deliberate steps to avoid detection in what it was doing by never registering or disclosing to the tax authorities any of its tax products, despite being aware of its obligations and the likely attitude of the IRS if they were discovered. In 2005, KPMG admitted its wrongdoing in relation to fraudulent tax shelters and agreed to pay $456 million in settlement to New York prosecutors.

Since 2008, there have been significant breakthroughs in the fight against deliberate tax evasion strategies, secrecy laws, and the number of citizens holding undeclared offshore bank accounts implicating financial institutions. Cases which stand out in this respect involve Lichtenstein-based bank LGT and three Swiss banks UBS, Wegelin, and Credit Suisse.

The LGT case came to light after a former employee of a trust company publicised a list containing data about clients of the Lichtenstein bank; it was subsequently discovered that LGT was using methods that resulted in its clients evading tax. Around a dozen countries, including the US and Germany, launched investigations into LGT accountholders. A US Senate report described how LGT employed methods which could facilitate – and sometimes resulted in – tax evasion in the US.[16] The Senate investigation found that these practices included: advising clients to open accounts in the name of Lichtenstein foundations, thereby disguising their beneficial ownership; establishing offshore structures; and creating transfer corporations to hide asset transfers. In what the Senate report called 'a culture of secrecy and deception', steps were taken that enabled clients to undertake a range of schemes to hide their money, including the hiding of one client's assets totalling $49 million simply by not reporting it as required by the Qualified Intermediary (QI) programme (introduced in the US in 2001 to encourage foreign financial institutions to report US-source income in their accounts and to withhold the relevant tax). Other practices reported by the Senate included: the disguising of the ownership of property by setting up a complex structure that made it look as if the property had been sold when in actual fact it was still controlled by its original owner; the deliberate wooing of a high-value customer on the basis that he would benefit from what Lichtenstein has to offer in terms of bank secrecy; the secreting of money to evade creditors in the US; and the creation of a Lichtenstein foundation that possibly hid money that the client had been ordered to pay out as part of a divorce settlement. Significantly, the data was used to prosecute tax evaders in Germany, including Deutsche Post's former CEO, and in 2011 LGT reached a €50 million settlement with German prosecutors over charges of abetting tax evasion. An LGT spokesman emphasised that the settlement did not imply an admission of guilt and said the decision had been taken to avoid protracted litigation proceedings.

The second concerned the Swiss bank UBS: a banker named Bradley Birkenfeld provided a list of US account holders to the IRS, whilst admitting that he had helped numerous Americans evade taxes on $200 million of offshore assets whilst working for the bank. Birkenfeld agreed to an offer from the US government which granted him immunity so long as he disclosed everything he knew. He was charged and imprisoned when he breached the agreement by failing to disclose the name of a US citizen whom he assisted in evading millions in taxes. As a result of the information, the bank was investigated by the US Senate Subcommittee on Investigations. According to the *Tax Haven Banks And U.S. Tax Compliance* report into their findings, UBS made deliberate efforts to attract US clients and employed practices which resulted in US tax evasion. The Senate report said that UBS maintained around 19,000 undeclared accounts which had not been disclosed to the IRS and systematically circumvented a QI agreement in part with the connivance of both clients and bankers, which carried certain obligations to report US client accounts. The Senate report recounted that UBS also promoted the use of offshore structures and took steps to ensure that the bank's activities relating to clients' securities could not be detected by telling employees to avoid email, US mail, couriers, or faxes on the subject. UBS estimated, according to the Senate report, that between the 1,000 declared and 19,000 undeclared accounts that it held for US clients were total deposits of nearly $18 billion; Birkenfeld estimated that the undeclared accounts were earning the bank up to $200 million every year in fees. The US Department of Justice took steps towards prosecution which concluded with UBS signing a deferred prosecution agreement in February 2009. The agreement meant that the bank admitted to assisting its clients to evade tax in the US by help-ing them to evade reporting requirements and to take steps to disguise the ownership of accounts. UBS paid $780 million as part of a settlement and was required to provide identities and account information for numerous other US customers who banked with it offshore. The then chairman of UBS responded to the news by saying, 'Client confidentiality, to which UBS remains committed, was never designed to protect fraudulent acts or the identity of those clients, who, with the active assistance of bank personnel, misused the confidentiality protections'.[17] The previously inviolable rule of Swiss bank secrecy had been dealt a powerful blow by the US.

Shortly afterwards, Birkenfeld was released from prison and awarded a payment of $104 million by the IRS for the assistance he had provided. Financial institutions that continue to provide offshore opportunities to US citizens should take note of the immense power and reach of the US's extra-territorial jurisdiction: the mere threat of legal action succeeded in obtaining the sort of information that the Swiss bank secrecy rules had prevented from being made public for decades. Birkenfeld was ultimately rewarded hand-somely for his short spell in prison, a clear incentive for other whistleblowers and those currently awaiting trial in connection with the UBS case. Should any of those charged, including Birkenfeld's former boss, be convicted and decide to cooperate, the lid may be well and truly blown off Swiss banking protocol which has remained impenetrable to outsiders for so long.

The fallout of the UBS case, and further evidence of the mindset of the offshore European banking world, came in 2013 when it was announced that the Swiss bank Wegelin was to close after it had pleaded guilty to helping US citizens evade tax on around $1.2 billion over the course of a decade.[18] This activity had apparently increased dramatically after the events of 2008; following its disastrous exposure that year, UBS, like other offshore banks, began to turn away US clients, meaning that many people settled on Wegelin as an alternative. Wegelin's senior management, clearly undeterred by what had happened to UBS and unconcerned by the growing risk run by such behaviour, took steps to scoop up the business that UBS had exited. Clients filed false tax returns with the IRS and the bank opened and serviced undeclared accounts in the name of sham entities in tax havens to evade scrutiny, apparently believing that its Swiss location meant that it was bound by national secrecy laws. In the end, this made no difference: Wegelin agreed to pay $57.8 million and was forced to close, the first foreign bank to plead guilty in the US since the crackdown began. In addition to its guilty plea and acceptance of responsibility for its conduct in conspiring to help US taxpayers evade taxes, Wegelin also submitted a reply to a government's sentencing memo in which it stated among its responses to the state that the US government had been 'incorrect in attempting to paint Wegelin as a rogue institution behaving in ways far worse that its peers', and that it had 'missed the point' over coming to certain of its conclusions.[19] The response highlights the fact that a bank may genuinely not realise that offering some of its ordinary banking services would risk criminal prosecution in the US.

The dominos will keep tumbling yet as the Department of Justice has opened investigations into over a dozen Swiss banks suspected of similar antics since 2008. One of the most recent banks to come to the public's attention is Credit Suisse, which was the Permanent Subcommittee on Investigations' 'Case Study in Swiss Secrecy' in its February 2014 report.[20] The investigation found that Credit Suisse held bank accounts for over 22,000 US customers, collectively containing around $13 billion, understanding that 'the vast majority' of these accounts were undeclared. Crucially, the investigation found that Credit Suisse had 'either turned a blind eye to the accounts' undeclared status', or 'actively assisted' clients wishing to dodge their US tax obligations.

The bank apparently enticed would-be tax evaders in one of several ways: bankers were sent to the US to 'secretly' recruit clients; a New York outfit was set up with the express purpose of supporting Swiss activities; clients were signposted to intermediaries to form offshore shell accounts; and a branch office was conveniently established at Zurich Airport to greet US clients after touch down. Official documents show how one banker told a customer wishing to send money to the US that they needed to do so in transfers of less than $10,000 to sidestep regulatory reporting requirements. Some clients were provided with a 'personal touch' delivery service: with a number of clients requesting that their bank statements were not mailed to them on US soil, Swiss bankers played courier with account documentation.

In 2011, seven former Credit Suisse employees and the founder of a Swiss trust were indicted for conspiring to defraud the US. As of May 2014, two of the eight individuals – Andreas Bachmann and Josef Dörig – have pleaded guilty to the charges against them. The Statement of Facts in *USA v Andreas Bachmann* is a fascinating read and details a particularly hairy 'incident' for Bachmann serving to underline the collusion between bankers and tax-evading customers. In this particular scenario, which took place in the early 2000s, Bachmann travelled to the US to meet with clients. In one of his New York meetings, a client handed Bachmann $50,000 in cash to deposit into an undeclared account. Sticking to a policy of never carrying cash over the US border, Bachmann had a meeting lined up with another client in South Florida who wished to make a withdrawal from his undeclared account in the same sum. A slight glitch occurred after a police officer found the cash in Bachmann's cabin luggage ahead of his meeting in South Florida. Bachmann was only briefly questioned and left to continue his journey, but the customer's feet took a chilly turn after hearing of Bachmann's close brush with law, and he decided not to accept the cash. Probably rather anxiously, Bachmann packed the money into his hold luggage and made his way back to Switzerland. The statement describes Bachmann's superiors condoning his practices, whilst a February 2014 statement by the bank to the Senate Permanent Subcommittee on Investigations said that misconduct had been 'centered on a small group of Swiss-based private bankers' and executive management had not been aware of the actions of those individuals.[21]

In May 2014, Credit Suisse entered a guilty plea to one count of conspiracy to assist US customers in presenting false income tax returns to the IRS. The CEO said in a public statement that they 'deeply regret the past misconduct' which led to the plea and fines and restitution totalling $2.6 billion.[22] Unlike other banks that have entered into deferred prosecution agreements, the agreement considers Credit Suisse a convicted bank.

To the surprise of many observers the Justice department did not require as part of the settlement that the bank disclose the names of their US clients with Swiss bank accounts. It now remains to be seen whether the names of the undisclosed account holders, will, in any case, be disclosed via the new and powerful piece of US legislation, FATCA. Enacted in 2010, FATCA effectively puts the onus on foreign financial institutions to comply with US financial disclosure laws and report to the IRS US-resident account holders along with the details of their accounts as well as withholding income. Institutions that fail to comply face being shut out of the US banking system by denying them access to correspondent banking services, thereby rendering the bank unable to take part in the global financial system. Several countries have already signed up, and despite significant opposition, an agreement on the implementation of FATCA was signed between Switzerland and the US in 2013.

If the US succeeds in imposing FATCA across the world, financial institutions in every jurisdiction will have to comply with its requirements to assist the IRS, whatever their domestic laws. Despite the discontent in some countries concerning the invasion of their sovereignty and the new compliance burden, the reality is that the penalties imposed by the US authorities for failing to comply are highly punitive and go beyond the purely monetary fines normally imposed to date in matters of this sort, which historically many institutions have been prepared to risk rather than lose the income that they gain by flouting the rules. It of course remains to be seen whether FATCA compliance will be similar to QI compliance, with banks working hard to find ways around the requirements, whilst appearing to fulfil their obligations. FATCA's progress will provide strong evidence for the risk appetite of institutions as well as individual states. Institutions that were once content to provide services to those who wished to evade tax through the classic methods will face far greater penalties and run much larger risks if they do choose not to comply.

Increased interest in preventing tax evasion has not been restricted to the higher echelons of politics alone. The growing sense of public injustice has been harnessed by pressure groups and is being exploited by politicians, who are increasingly condemnatory of those who take even licit steps to minimise tax. In 2012, when it was revealed that the British comedian Jimmy Carr participated in the wholly legal Jersey-based K2 tax avoidance scheme, the media reaction was so hostile that Carr (who had not broken any laws) decided to issue an apology for his conduct, and rescind his membership of the scheme. Prime Minister David Cameron branded Carr's arrangements as 'morally wrong'.[23] Later that year, Margaret Hodge, the chair of the UK Public Accounts Committee, said that the public would consider tax avoidance methods 'completely and utterly immoral', a view echoed by Cameron at the 2013 Davos World Economic Forum when he put addressing tax avoidance at the top of the agenda for the G8 group and criticised the conduct of companies who use 'an army of clever accountants' to get round the tax rules. When it emerged in May 2014 that former Take That member Gary Barlow had invested in a scheme which was found by a judge to be primarily for tax avoidance, Cameron again went on record calling them 'aggressive tax avoidance schemes', but he rejected claims that Barlow should be stripped of his OBE.[24] Whilst Barlow's actions may have been branded immoral and he (along with 1,000 other investors in similar partnerships) is likely to face a hefty tax bill, there is no suggestion of criminal wrongdoing on his part.

The concept of 'ethical' banking is clearly having an effect. In February 2013, it was announced that Barclays was to disband its Structured Capital Markets business. This was a division responsible for making the vast majority of its investment banking profits through complex structured international deals and schemes intended to avoid tax. Despite the fact that Barclays was not accused of illegal activity in relation to these schemes, the bank faced criticism in the press and from a number of members of the political establishment, which was particularly pointed given its recent implication in the LIBOR rigging scandal. In a speech explaining the move, the Barclays chief executive Anthony Jenkins stated: 'Although this [the use of the tax structures] is legal, going forward such activity is incompatible with our purpose, and incompatible with the new tax principles we are publishing today. We will not engage in it again'.[25]

## SCENARIO

That said, ethics hold very little sway for those prepared to go way beyond the merely questionable to engage in outright criminal activity. This is demonstrated in the following scenario, which describes the illegal activities of a tax consultant who colludes with a sports agent that has a number of wealthy, high profile sports clients all of whom are eager to reduce their liability to pay tax on their income from both their sporting activity and their lucrative endorsements. As an adjunct, the scenario also includes the corruption of one of the stars by an Asian betting syndicate. This particular sportsman is a snooker player who has his palm greased by the syndicate in return for deliberately losing some of his matches.

The backdrop is that the UK government increases the rate of income tax for the highest earners to 50%, prompting the tax consultant to approach the sports agent with a simple proposition. The consultant explains to the agent that he has a foolproof and 'above board' way of allowing the agent's clients to reduce their tax bills significantly by allowing them to claim tax relief at the same time as donating to charity. It is, the consultant says, a 'win, win' because the stars pay less tax whilst being seen to do their bit for charity, and the agent will be on to a good thing because his clients will be delighted at having to pay less tax. As an additional inducement, the consultant, who operates on a contingency fee of 10% of the tax saved, will share that income with the agent fifty, fifty. The deal is struck. The sports stars, none of whom are particularly adroit in relation to the finer details of revenue law, but all of whom want bigger houses and flashier cars, agree to participate. Welcoming the sums to be saved, and the opportunity for some positive PR, they are happy for the agent to hammer out the finer details and stick their signature to any paperwork.

Two offshore companies are set up, each ostensibly involved in oil and gas research in Eastern Europe. Both companies are administered by a law firm in an offshore centre with 28 employees and 1,850 structures that it 'manages and controls'. Critically, despite operating a conveyor belt business model, the law firm is a listing sponsor for a small but internationally recognised stock exchange.

The athletes are directed to purchase penny shares in the two companies purporting to operate in the oil and gas research sector. They do so, momentarily bemused by their foray into the energy industry, but looking forward to the benefits it promises. Some buy the shares in their own name and others buy them through companies that have been established to own their image rights. Once all of the share acquisitions are made, the corporate service provider successfully organises the listing of the two companies on the local stock exchange. From that point on, the shares in the two companies trade alongside shares in thousands of others.

The price of the shares in the companies remains stagnant for the first four months at which point within a two-week period both companies issue press releases claiming that their research activities are yielding what appear to be positive results. Both releases hint at the possibility of significant oil and gas discoveries. The news is positively received by investors, and the share price of both companies moves steadily upwards. In actuality there is no substantive news about either company and the share price is being manipulated to an artificially high level (this is known as 'pumping' or 'ramping').

The tax consultant directs the agent to instruct his clients to donate the shares to any UK-registered charity of their choice. The question of whether they publicise their donations is left to them. The players donate the shares at between 50 and 68 pence, many multiples higher than the original purchase price. They then go knocking on HMRC's door to claim tax relief on the shares based on their value at the point of donation. In total the stars donate shares valued in excess of £20 million to various charities including a children's home and an organisation promoting sport participation among teens. Over £19 million of tax relief is claimed back from HMRC from income and company profits calculated on the donated shares, the real value of which was significantly lower than the value claimed. Just like that, fictitious values have been conjured, materialising in the form of tax relief destined for the pockets of the tax consultant, agent, and athletes.

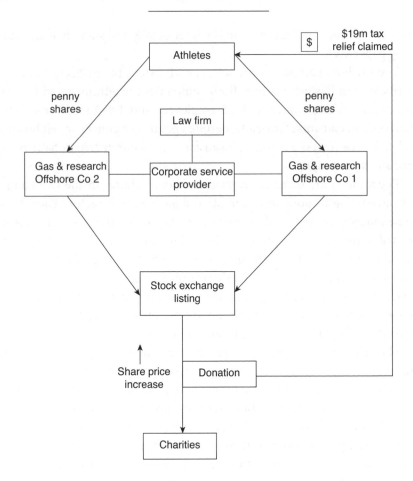

One of the stars participating in the scheme is a snooker player, who channels his funds through the structure displayed overleaf. He claims relief in an offshore company into which his image rights in the Asian market have been parked. Two years previously he had been approached by a gambling syndicate in Kuala Lumpur, Malaysia, with the promise of significant inducements for attempting to throw matches. When the desired results were achieved he was paid. The bribes were represented as payments from a Malaysian hair product company whose product he falsely claims to be endorsing. In fact no such endorsement contract actually exists. Nevertheless, the player is eager to participate in the scheme in the belief that it will help to give the funds a further patina of legitimacy. Like many other criminals who represent their illicit funds as having been legitimately generated, he is eager to pay as little tax on the funds as possible.

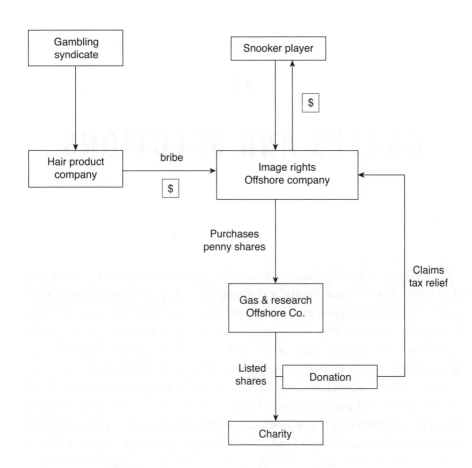

# 11

# CAUSES AND SOLUTIONS

A new chapter in social and economic history was opened on 15 September 2008 when Lehman Brothers Holding Inc. collapsed under debts of $613 billion in the US's largest ever bankruptcy. Ripples swelled to waves and one by one the major names in international finance became engulfed by the threat of total ruin. Governments across the globe pumped trillions into the global financial system to calm the waters and halt contagion. Six years after the crisis started and the dominos are still falling: job seekers, evicted homeowners, and users of public health and education systems worldwide continue to experience the daily effects of cuts and austerity. As the spotlight has remained on the industry other harmful and abusive practices have been revealed, with new scandals emerging with monotonous regularity. Despite this, the discourse around preventing a repeat of the events of 2008 appears to be sliding down the agenda, especially with recent figures indicating that economies are in recovery and the World Bank proposing that the global economy had reached a 'turning point' in 2014.

I opened this book by proposing a commonality of causal factors underlying a spectrum of harmful conduct, from excessive risk taking of the type seen in the run-up to the Lehman collapse, to mis-selling, fixing, sanctions evasion, and the finance industry's role in money laundering and the facilitation of crime. I said that an aversion to identifying, examining, and remedying the causes of the global recession was mirrored in the treatment of financial crime. Now that we are at the stage where legislation and regulatory action risks reaching a point of diminishing returns, further reform is called for – not only to avoid another 2008-style meltdown, but also to specifically address money laundering and the facilitation of crime by the finance industry.

Nobody could dispute that an unprecedented amount of time, energy, and money has been poured into understanding the gremlins in the system, and there have, of course, been some significant developments as a consequence. The Financial Services Act has overhauled the UK regulatory system, calling time on the FSA and instituting the Prudential Regulation Authority and the Financial Conduct Authority; the Banking Reform Act has separated high street banking from investment banking, and in the US, the Dodd Frank Act has resulted in the largest reforms to the regulation of the banking industry since the Great Depression. But there can be no denying that what remains is a tangible sense that the sum total of measures taken globally since 2008 fall short, and motivation is flagging as economic recovery gathers pace. In May 2014, Christine Lagarde, managing director of the IMF, said of banking reform: 'The bad news is that progress is still too slow, and the finish line is still too far off. Some of this arises from the sheer complexity of the task at hand. Yet, we must acknowledge that it also stems from fierce industry pushback, and from the fatigue that is bound to set in at this point in a long race'.[1]

Given the interconnectivity between all of the parties involved in oiling the money machine, plotted against a host of jurisdictional variables, knowing how to approach risk and effectively anticipate impacts can seem a little like joining a game of three-dimensional chess halfway through. Set against a backdrop of lobbyist rhetoric, regulatory capture, and other kinds of conflicts of interest, the task sometimes seems almost impossible. Certainly it is not just a few rogue overpaid bankers operating beyond the wit of legislators, regulators, and the banks themselves who pose the greatest threat; although approached from the view that greed is to blame, bankers and their bonuses are commonly painted bullseye red. Clearly the pursuers of profit are prominent actors in shaping the behaviours of the financial industry, but financial institutions and their employees do not operate in a vacuum. Uprooting the underlying causes of institutional weakness turns up a tangle of responsibilities borne not only by the banks themselves, but also by lawmakers and regulators.

Meaningful reform is dependent on robust and properly enforced regulation and legislation which is meshed with systems within financial institutions that are adequately designed, implemented, and governed – these are the subject of the remainder of this chapter. I do not claim to be exhaustive in my analysis, but I hope to present a summary of the most pressing changes that need to be made.

# HUMAN FACTORS

Billions of dollars have been expended by the finance industry on the design and implementation of internal systems of risk control as the regulatory compliance burden has increased. Yet, nobody appears to have stopped to question why there seems to have been no perceptible parallel decrease in harmful behaviour. The reason for this is very simple: the industry has neglected to account for the fact that most of its problems occur from the neck up. It is a happy marriage between the right *people* and the right systems which is critical to successful reform, but despite 'human factors' being every bit as important as systems in managing risk they have to a very large extent been overlooked by the finance industry and by regulators.

The misplaced emphasis on systems solutions has been compounded as lawmakers have reacted to every scandal by passing new rules requiring, you guessed it, more systems. The effect has been similar to that of the electronic calculator upon our powers of arithmetic with employees of financial institutions increasingly unable or unwilling to think, reliant instead upon 'the system'. It is way past time for us to take stock and remember that finance is first and foremost a people business. That we have failed to do so is all the more extraordinary given the advances made in human factors analysis in other industry sectors, including aviation and medicine. Human factors have been studied for years in the aviation sector as evidence demonstrates that errors in human judgement, rather than mechanical failure, are the underlying cause of most aviation accidents. At best, human error results in time wasted or minor inefficiencies; at worst, it costs lives. Having learned some very painful lessons, the pilot recruitment process now actively 'selects out' applicants that display those characteristics which appear to be the most highly prized within the finance industry. So why, in an industry that wields such extraordinary amounts of power, has the human aspect to risk taking and harmful behaviour been so overlooked? Does the genuine fear of social breakdown following the Lehman collapse not merit the attention that is extended to the factors influencing the behaviours of pilots, doctors, and other professionals engaged in daily encounters with risk?

One of the reasons for the lack of focus on human factors in finance is undoubtedly because jobs in the industry have the status of vocation and not profession. While the industry is littered with professional service providers – lawyers, accountants, trust practitioners, chartered secretaries, securities brokers, and so forth – none of the key functions in finance such as board director, compliance officer, money laundering reporting officer, or chief risk officer are regarded as constituting a professional discipline in their own right that require a corresponding level of professional training, qualification, and on-going assessment. Progress has been made in recent years to require regulatory approval for individuals to fulfil what are referred to as 'controlled functions' and a more stringent approval regime of senior bankers is now in place in the UK but it is a long way from according those functions professional status through the imposition of stringent professional qualification requirements. The necessity to professionalise the banking industry to achieve higher standards appears to be at odds with the view of Mark Carney, Governor of the Bank of England, who said as late as May 2014: 'To build this sense of the systemic, business ultimately needs to be seen as a vocation, an activity with high ethical standards, which in turn conveys certain responsibilities'.[2] Nobody could take issue with his stated aims but it is precisely because banking has been regarded as a vocation, a calling to pursue riches, that the industry has become so diseased. Technical skill and high ethical standards must be taught and inculcated. For this to be done effectively banking must be regarded as a profession that incorporates various strands across different professional banking functions. At its core then, ignorance of human factors in finance has been symptomatic of the absence of professionalism within the finance industry.

In consequence, there are a variety of human factor weaknesses in evidence that range from sheer technical incompetence at board level to the personality types and characteristics that seem to be most highly rewarded. Unsurprisingly, business go getters, generally in the guise of Gordon Gekko Alpha personalities, reap the biggest rewards and what that communicates to everybody else is that aggressive and sometimes unethical behaviour pays. Very quickly such examples begin to contaminate and eventually dominate the culture of an organisation. Other consequences include the elevation of dominant personality types to key management positions and the development of threatening rather than supportive working environments in which employees with vital information about wrongdoing often remain mute.

Of course, financial institutions are in the business of making money, and there is obviously a need and a place for ambitious and brash Wall Street stereotypes in order for that to happen. But it is the blend of personality types within an organisation and the apportionment of authority and power between them that really matters. Consider the bridge of a cruise liner – in one seat is a brilliant fly-by-the-seat-of-his-pants captain prepared to cut corners to save on fuel in order to make the shipping company more money. As a passenger who would you want to have sitting next to him with the power of veto? The answer of course is a more analytical, calmer co-captain with his eyes firmly focused on where the icebergs are. For too long, risk takers within the financial services industry have held the whip hand whereas those charged with the responsibility for the management of risk have been treated – and thus regarded internally – as second class employees. It will always be the case that taking risk is sexier than abstinence, particularly when it pays off and the corks start popping. It behoves directors responsible for the stewardship of institutions to recognise this fundamental internal status discrepancy and to redress the balance. Directors need to acknowledge that business getters will always be able to quantify the value of business that has been turned away because of internal policies and controls, whereas risk managers are never able to quantify the cost savings of disasters averted. The difficulty is that many directors are themselves former Gekkos unlikely to be willing to embrace such change without a significant new stick: the prospect of handcuffs, interviews, and the dock or at the very least stiff regulatory censure. This status discrepancy reinforces the 'back office' stereotyping of risk, compliance, and ethics functions. Understaffed, out of sight, and per-ceived as an irritant to those in the 'front' office drumming up the business, these operatives urgently require a large injection of status, authority, and resources. That will not begin to happen until such time as financial insti-tutions are stewarded by professional directors, who, like pilots, are skilled and qualified in the art of balancing risk and reward and by recognising that culture is not only to be found in the bottom of a yoghurt pot.

There can be no doubt that the culture of many financial institutions has been fundamentally flawed. It would be convenient to assume that LIBOR rate riggers, mis-sellers, and relationship managers were wilfully blind to the criminality of their customers but such behaviours are in fact frequently the product of the environments in which they work. Too often, the inves-tigations that follow result in blame being attached to employees who are conveniently exited from the business without the organisation being forced to confront the fundamental question – *to what extent was the employee a product of our environment?* Perhaps this explains why we observe repeated wrongdoing by so many large financial institutions. Businesses must be led by directors and policed by regulators who appreciate that culture (not only organisational wide culture but also sub-cultures within business divisions or units) shapes attitudes to risk and ethics. Each instance of toxic behaviour must be followed by an objective assessment of the environment in which an employee operated. Dismissing or sanctioning a hapless employee who went along with conduct that was not openly condoned by management but was covertly encouraged and rewarded, is the equivalent of sticking a finger in the dam. How then to positively influence culture? The answer does not lie in mission statements but from example. Boards get the organisational behaviours they deserve. An old proverb has it that 'a fish rots from the head'. If directors and members of senior management display the wrong behaviours, either in terms of their interactions with colleagues, the paucity and quality of information they rely upon to run the business, or the frequency with which they sanction the non-application of internal due diligence controls to high value customers, they will contaminate attitudes throughout the entire organisation. Here again the importance of professionalising the finance industry is relevant – a profession is about more than mere competence – good professions also embody, nurture, and encourage the correct ethos and ethical standards among their practitioners.

Directors are a legal component of corporate structures – from the UK's 'Limited' company, the Luxembourg's 'Société Anonyme', to the US's 'Inc', and many more. Boards governing the sorts of large financial institutions to which I have made reference throughout this book tend to have less than 20 directors: JP Morgan Chase & Co. has 11, and Goldman Sachs Group Inc. and Credit Suisse Group AG both have 13. In each case, the board of directors is the beating heart of the bank's governance structure. Among a host of responsibilities and powers, the board signs off on a company strategy and objectives and has the capacity to set the culture, ethos, and transparency of an organisation. It then quickly becomes clear that an institution's success or failure often correlates with a board's performance.

There are directors of financial institutions across the globe who are technically incompetent. This should come as no surprise because until relatively recently, boards were to a very large extent self-selecting. The ignorant selecting the ignorant can give rise to a homogenous group of individuals insufficiently equipped to collectively identify the most pressing risks to an organisation. Regulators have in recent years sought to play a role in approving the appointment of directors of financial institutions but their involvement has largely backfired as the wrong appointments have continued to be made by institutions which now feel vindicated in their appointment decisions because they had regulatory approval to proceed. It beggars belief that even after the 2008 crisis a person can be approved to sit on the board of a systemically important financial institution without sitting and passing an examination that assesses technical competence in areas such as risk, conflicts of interest, governance, and human factors. You need to pass written and practical tests to drive a car, but not to run a bank. This was highlighted during the interviews conducted by the UK Parliament's Treasury Select Committee in its 2009 enquiry into the banking crisis. HBOS former chairman Lord Stevenson, RBS former CEO Fred Goodwin, and RBS former chairman Sir Tom McKillop were asked whether they had any formal banking qualifications and, although they could all point to relevant experience, the Committee's questioning revealed that none of them had one.

The fact that there are ill-equipped directors dotted about the industry's boardrooms evidences the fact that there is a gross underestimation of the professional nature of being a director of a financial institution, and the only way to remedy this is to enforce qualifications, training, and professional standards. There are certifications issued by bodies such as the UK's Institute of Directors – but none of these is compulsory or indeed specifically geared to banking. Equipping directors to ensure that responsibilities are understood and met requires a statutory obligation for training and professional certification. Pilots, lawyers, accountants, surgeons, and nurses all do this, and I cannot see anyone saying it should be any different. How then can individuals sitting at the helm of a bank holding billions in assets saunter into the position without an accreditation evidencing that they hold the appropriate skills and knowledge specific to the role of being a director of that institution?

The pace of innovation within financial services is so rapid that continuing professional development for directors is also vital, by which I mean more than reading the *Financial Times* on a daily basis as a means of demonstrating continuing professional development but meaningful on-going training relevant to the products, services, markets, and risks of whichever organisation the director stewards. In commercial aviation, the skills of pilots are tested on average 100 times throughout their careers. In finance and banking, once a director gets his feet under the boardroom table, barring any regulatory investigation, his skills will never be tested by an objective third party. The cosiness at the top is fundamentally at odds with the public interest in the way that financial institutions are run. Of course, the holding of professional qualifications of itself does not guarantee that expert and faultless stewardship of financial institutions will result. Professional bodies can never entirely prevent bent lawyers and incompetent doctors from practising. But by setting a sufficiently high bar to entry, and taking swift action to suspend or revoke the professional status of those whom they adjudge to be unworthy of it, they are arguably the best means we have of seeking to ensure that the right people are selected to do the job and that they continue to be the right people to do the job throughout the durations of their appointments.

Outside of technical competence, the most important characteristics of an effective director are a willingness to ask probing and difficult questions and to 'rock the boat'. The reluctance to do both of these things appears part of a general practice in the industry by which directors fail to devote sufficient attention to the difficult agenda items for fear of exposing their ignorance once they have hit the boardroom big time. Hans Christian Andersen's fable 'The Emperor's New Clothes' holds as much relevance now as it did when he wrote it 180 years ago. How many board directors at the large banks immediately before the 2008 crisis hit knew exactly what a CDO was, how it worked, and what the risks were associated with them? Were there executives who had an inkling that something was not right at Barings, but did not want to ruffle any feathers by asking the question and anyway assumed that someone more qualified had their eye on the ball? Certainly it became very clear throughout the Treasury Select Committee's 2009 interviews that board directors did not understand the complex financial products their banks were using. A director being able to identify what he *doesn't* know, and having the courage to demand the information which is going to fill that knowledge gap, is worth more than hundreds of pages of bland board pack papers.

Home-grown executive directors can be the product of the inadequate structures they oversee, which renders them ill-equipped to recognise what is often patently wrong internally. Every fibre of their being is calibrated to impressing their fellow board directors, justifying their appointment, and maintaining their status. Having climbed the ladder, they are eager not to slide back down it by asking questions about detail they assume they should know. Even executive directors with sharper objectivity can be caught in the invidious position of being an employee of the organisation they seek to hold to account. Not all executive directors have the stomach to ask tough questions of their employer particularly if they have ambition. Structurally then, boards that have majority executive director representation can be inherently flawed – the more likely a question is to blow the lid on something big and toxic internally, the less motivated an executive director may be to ask it, assuming that he has the wherewithal to interrogate it in the first place. Here then the role of non-executive directors is critical. A non-executive director must be fearless in speaking truth to power. Apart from the necessary intelligence and technical know-how to allow for an understanding of the intricacies of every product or service, information about which comes before the board, the non-executive director must lead the way in calling attention to information that he does not understand. It may seem counter-intuitive but being able to reveal ignorance is one of the greatest attributes of a board director. Instead what repeated scandals and failures in the finance industry reveal is that when directors do not understand something they do nothing.

None of this is just theoretical. A direct link between a bank's operating failures and poor governance was clearly demonstrated by the independent review, published in May 2014, into the oversight functions of the UK's

Co-operative Group and, albeit comprising a somewhat lesser focus, its banking business. (As if the group needed any further negative publicity, on the same day that the damning report was released, the Co-operative Bank's former chairman appeared in court pleading guilty to possession of cocaine and crystal meth).

The 'Co-op' group, founded over 150 years ago, operates across several industries in addition to banking and is owned by its eight million members. In 2013, the group chalked up its largest losses in its history – £2.5 billion – largely accounted for by the gaping holes in the Co-operative Bank's finances. The Co-operative Bank was saved from complete collapse by a rescue plan which saw external investors collectively take 70% of its ownership.

The review, led by Lord Myners, found that the governance of both the Co-operative Group and its bank was riddled with serious deficiencies.[3] Whilst some of the report's content is specific to running an organisation with a membership base (which is not the case for most of the banks mentioned throughout this book), many of Myners' findings and conclusions are pertinent to governance structures found throughout the financial sector and, ultimately, support the thesis that radically reforming those existing frameworks is a critical factor in protecting the financial sector from future crises.

Myners highlighted, in particular, an unacceptable lack of relevant skills, competencies, qualifications, and experience at the helm of the Co-operative Group, which, he found, meant that management staff were insufficiently monitored, motivated, challenged, and directed. One of his proposed solutions included board appointments which would depend upon recruits fulfilling an objective set of criteria determined by an in-depth examination of the board's existing and missing skills and experience. The report also lamented a failure to embed the Group's values and principles into the governance structure; a suggested response lay, again, in the appointing process of board members who would be obliged to demonstrate a commitment to the Group's values from the outset of their tenure. An examination of the Co-op's governance culture found, furthermore, that evading responsibility, silencing opposition, and divisiveness were pervasive, and that the Group's board members carried on their business without fully understanding the scope of their duties.

The Co-operative Group is embarking on a long road to recovery, and there are probably tough challenges ahead, not least because investigations have been instigated by the FCA, the PRA, and the Financial Reporting Council in light of the disasters that have befallen the Co-operative Bank. The Myners report no doubt makes for uncomfortable reading for many of the financial institutions whose governance structures are unfit for purpose, and whose executives may wonder whether meaningful change can be implemented before they may themselves be brought to account.

# SYSTEMS

Many books have been written on the design and implementation of effective systems of internal risk control within financial institutions, and it is beyond the remit of this book to rehearse them. Models vary between those in which business units are encouraged to be autonomous and 'own' their own risk decisions to models in which internal risk functions are required to sign off on new products, new customers, and transactions with certain characteristics. There are, believe it or not, several hybrid versions in-between. There is no 'right model'. Whatever model is employed, the same or similar weaknesses tend to lead to disaster.

The purpose of an internal system of financial crime risk control is to prevent and detect the abuse of an institution in the facilitation of crime and the laundering of the proceeds of crime by customers. These outcomes should be the starting point in designing any new system of internal control or in assessing the suitability of an existing system, especially as more and increasingly sophisticated financial products are brought to market and financial crime adapts to its new environment; the systems must be met with fresh analysis and evolving methods of detection need to be crafted. It rarely works that way in practice, as illustrated by the widespread continuing reliance by the finance industry on the 'placement, layering, and integration' model of money laundering in the development of systems and employee training programmes. In the rush to comply nobody seems to have paused to consider what the internal control mechanisms are supposed to achieve and whether they are capable of helping an institution to avoid being abused in the facilitation of crime and the laundering of the proceeds of crime. I hope this will have been clear by now in having presented the role that the finance industry plays in the execution of several predicate crimes – drug trafficking, bribery, corruption, piracy, trafficking of human beings, smuggling of migrants, terrorist financing, sanctions busting, and tax evasion. Most of the scenarios at the end of the earlier chapters show that the existing paradigm in money laundering is ill-suited to protect banks and other types of financial institution from criminal abuse. The conduct is too often hidden in plain sight.

To be effective, a system needs to be risk-based in the sense that it must be capable of distinguishing between those customers, products, or transactions that pose greater risks and subject them to an enhanced level of control and monitoring. Critically, the system must be robust enough to withstand

pressure to flex the controls when their application is deemed to be preju-
dicial to valuable customer relationships. As numerous laundering scandals
involving high net worth politically exposed persons have revealed, institutions that wax lyrical about the efficacy of their control environments can
make exceptions for their most highly prized (and highest risk) customers
rendering their control environments virtually worthless.

Beyond implementing risk-based controls that apply to customers and
transactions, an effective system must be capable of generating information about its performance so that those with responsibility for it can make
informed decisions on how it should be reformed or adapted. Knowing how
effective (or not) an existing system is represents a critical component of an
effective governance regime. The situation is not dissimilar to that of an aeroplane pilot. For the pilot there are many factors that need to be taken into
account in assessing whether risk is being properly managed – the weather,
the passengers (particularly since 9/11), the crew, the particular characteristics of the destination runway, and of course the aeroplane systems. The
pilot will be constantly checking whether the systems are operating normally, having been taught to take nothing for granted about how the system
is operating in practice. He wants the system to alert him to abnormalities
and defects but, by contrast, within the finance industry systems are not
designed to produce the 'bad news'. Instead, they are designed to produce
information for the consumption of more senior members of an organisation and as a result what is communicated 'upwards' from the system is more
often than not, good rather than bad news.

Recognising that no one within a system of risk control wants to reveal
to colleagues further up the food chain that the system for which they have
operational responsibility is defective is an obvious danger. It takes courage
to deliver a message that a boss does not want to hear. The directors of a
financial institution to whom ultimately information about the efficacy of
a system should flow, must primarily be interested in being told not what
they know more junior colleagues want to tell them (the good news) but the
data that reveals the weaknesses in the system (the bad news). Managing risk
effectively is an information-critical exercise, and a control system must be
capable of producing bad news or at the very least information that equips
directors to ask difficult questions which teases out the bad news. If a system
does not do that, it is not fit for purpose. The bad news must also be welcomed and be seen to be welcomed throughout the organisation. If it is not,
then instead of being shared, it will be buried.

Paul Moore's experience at HBOS is a textbook case study of the dangers inherent in a system and culture that undervalues bad news. Moore,

who was the bank's head of Group Regulatory Risk between 2002 and 2005, said that he was dismissed from his position after expressing concerns over serious risks the bank was running, while HBOS claimed that he was made redundant following a restructuring. An unfair dismissal claim by Moore resulted in a settlement in which, Moore says, he was given 'substantial damages' but was subjected to a 'gagging order'.[4] In the memo Moore wrote in 2009, he recounted how he had urged the board to minute his concerns that the bank was 'going too fast'. As if to emphasise the board's appetite for good news, the bank's auditors were appointed to examine the points Moore had raised with nobody at the bank stopping to question whether the auditors were conflicted from giving a truly objective assessment on the issues raised by Moore who had, by then, left the building.

The growing pressure on compliance departments to detect the kinds of dubious customers, behaviours, and transactions described throughout this book has prompted an increase in the *quantity* of controls while sacrificing their *quality* and, therefore, the efficacy of those controls. The increase in the quantity of controls no doubt results from risk and compliance departments trying to keep a handle on the ever expanding legion of laws and regulations. But plugging this information into systems in such a way as to yield quality output depends on a number of interrelated factors: the design of automated systems, a system's ability to identify relevant anomalies, and whether or not information is intelligently integrated so as to build a picture whose significance is greater than the sum of its parts.

Board packs can be symptomatic of the emphasis on quantity and not quality. Funnelling information to boards often takes the form of reams of reports, the majority of which a director may only skim. Papers which contain little to no analysis of internal weaknesses and which are characterised by the judicious inclusion of what the board wants to hear, are worthless. Minutes can often read as an anodyne rehashing of board papers that give limited insight into the factors which have been considered in forming an opinion or reaching a decision, and how those factors have been weighed against one another. They lack the 'bad news' factor, often because of the fear of litigation risk or the risk that fuller board minutes will prove to be incriminating in the eyes of the regulator. Regulators providing further guidance and enforcing tighter rules around minute taking would ensure an audit trail of the deliberations at the board level that could serve to promote a better quality of discourse, replete with the bad news and recorded examples of challenge. Such simple reforms to minute-taking obligations could genuinely shift the tone and dynamic of board meetings and focus the minds of directors who, in their quiet moments, probably know they do not merit a place at the boardroom table. For this to

happen, prosecutors and regulators need to do more to communicate a recognition that finance is not a zero failure environment. Accidents and losses
will inevitably occur but blame should only be apportioned if institutions have
failed to take adequate measures to prevent them. Board minutes that demonstrate institutional awareness of the risks, calculations and decisions of directors will enable regulators to more appropriately assess whether an institution
has taken satisfactory measures. Where they have, even if they reach the wrong
answer, credit must be given.

However, an institution can only hope to implement a system capable
of producing bad news if the system promotes a relatively flat authority gra-
dient. When a board fosters an environment in which operations staff are
fearful of reporting painful-to-digest information in a frighteningly steep
upward fashion, that particular control becomes impaired. Board meetings
become staid with complacency, and lack the dynamism to identify and dis-
sect vulnerabilities of the type that need to be minuted. Some argue that
a cultural shift towards a greater communication of the bad news lies in
the promotion of a stronger whistleblowing culture. While the necessity of
whistleblowing procedures is obvious, an emphasis on whistleblowing actually detracts from the opportunity to establish a norm whereby the negative
news regularly becomes part of the company-wide agenda. Approaching a
manager or company executive with unwelcome information should be normalised and promoted (perhaps by means of internal reward) as a healthy
way of managing operations within finance.

## THE ROLE OF LAWMAKERS AND REGULATORS

Andy Hornby hit the pinnacle of his banking career when he was appointed
CEO of HBOS in 2006. Three years later, he was sitting before the Treasury
Select Committee and called to account for his role in the UK banking sector crisis. Hornby hung his head and admitted the widespread and calamitous effects of HBOS' demise, saying: 'it has affected shareholders, many of
whom are colleagues; it has affected the communities in which we live and
serve; it has clearly affected taxpayers; and we are extremely sorry for the
turn of events that has brought it about'.[5] Others taking their turn in the hot
seat shared similarly contrite sentiments. Lord Stevenson, Fred Goodwin,
and Sir Tom McKillop all agreed that it was terrible, it should never have
happened, and they were all very sorry.

You would be forgiven for thinking that regulatory and legal proceedings were in the offing, a fine at the very least, who knows, possibly disquali-
fication. As it turned out, Hornby was greeted with open arms to head up the

FTSE 250 betting and gaming company Coral. He is also the non-executive chairman of Pharmacy2U, which champions his addition to the board as bringing 'a wealth of experience from working across a number of blue chip organisations'.[6] Lord Stevenson is a non-executive director of Waterstones Holdings Limited; Goodwin sauntered into early retirement; McKillop flits between the boards of the biotech company Evolva Holding SA, healthcare business Alere Inc, and biopharmaceutical company UCB SA. Stephen Green, who was the group chairman of HSBC Holdings Plc between June 2006 and December 2010, was created a life peer as Baron Green of Hurstpierpoint, and in 2011 he became a UK government minister of state for trade and investment. Green remains a government minister despite the fact that in 2012 his former bank was fined $1.9 billion dollars for its lax anti–money laundering controls that allegedly enabled Mexican drug cartels to launder their money leading the new group chief executive of HSBC, Stuart Gulliver, to comment that 'between 2004 and 2010, our anti–money laundering controls should have been stronger and more effective and we failed to spot and deal with unacceptable behaviour'.[7] What does all this tell us? It tells us that there is something seriously wrong with the lack of personal cost to the most senior individuals of institutions involved in wrongful behaviour. There is certainly a discussion to be had about the ethics of discredited executives accepting potentially lucrative and prestigious appointments, but their position is similar to that of the tax avoider: if it is not illegal and there is a benefit to be had, they will go ahead and do it anyway. Such high rewards only serve to reinforce the image of the executive who ultimately 'gets away with it', rapped across the knuckles, dabbing his brow in relief as he scurries from the boardroom, thanking his lucky stars it was not any worse. This then begs the questions, *why* is it not worse, and how *can* it be made worse? Precisely what *will* prompt directors – along with chief risk officers, relationship managers, and so forth – to make good decisions founded on the right criteria? What will *deter* them from defective decisions based on ignorance and poor judgment? And finally, how can discussions around risk and ethics be consistently woven into the discourse on turning a profit?

In broaching these questions, let's start with the current approach by lawmakers to the 'human factor' in apportioning responsibility. It goes like this: not a single human being sitting on the board of a bailed out bank or a bank found to have been engaged in mis-selling, rate fixing, sanctions evasion, aiding tax evasion, or money laundering has been sweating it out in a dock charged with breaking the law, nor have any of the actions taken against banks for failures relating to criminal capital flowing through the financial system resulted in an executive donning prison garb.

A number of the Andy Hornbys of the financial system have been paraded before parliamentary and Senate committees in London and Washington DC to examine various aspects of the financial crisis. Each 'examination', has been a case study in missed opportunity as politicians ill-equipped to interrogate the witnesses have played to the gallery, but has adequate consideration really been given to whether any of these executives should have been prosecuted or stripped of their right to be a director? Or, indeed, is the current legal and regulatory environment calibrated in such a way as to really hold senior executives to account? I believe that the concept of the deferred prosecution agreement is evidence enough to suggest that the answer is 'no'. If you were not acquainted with the notion of a DPA before, you certainly are familiar with it by now: you complain a bank is misbehaving; you wait a while; you complain again; you knock on the door; you ask for millions of documents; maybe you issue a few subpoenas; you grill the bosses; you sift the documents; you spot the violations; the bank agrees; you talk criminal charges; you defer the charges; you tell them how to behave; they agree; they pay a settlement. You throw in a few law firms and auditors, and it all takes a very long time. So the problem becomes that it is these inanimate companies which are bearing the brunt of the 'punishment'. Just as drug dealers and tax evaders take shelter behind anonymous shell companies, so are executives able to leave the ramparts exposed to attack as they scuttle deep inside their organisations, beyond the reach of the law.

True, there is merit to issuing pecuniary punishments and entering into rehabilitation agreements, and there are many advantages to this approach. DPAs pay for themselves, they encourage self-reporting and can be resolved more quickly than criminal proceedings. But critics are on to something when they point out the lack of deterrent this poses, saying executives walk away scot free while shareholders and consumers foot the bill. The DPA just becomes a cost of doing business. A petty thief gets a criminal record, a bank gets an invoice. The same limitations also appear now to have contaminated criminal prosecutions of institutions that are too big to fail. Credit Suisse pleaded guilty to aiding tax evasion in May 2014, and BNP Paribas pleaded guilty for its sanctions busting activities shortly afterwards, but US prosecutors have been at pains to ensure that these prosecutions did not destabilise the banks or the wider financial system. If an individual is convicted of a criminal offence it sticks. It has a material impact on their prospects and future. Yet in the case of Credit Suisse, instead of connoting pariah status on the bank, its chief executive, Brady Dougan, is reported to have said on a conference call shortly after the conviction was announced that it would not cause 'any material impact on our operational or business capabilities'.[8]

In consequence of these two convictions none of the banks' senior executives were held accountable for the banks' actions and none were fired from their positions. This begs the question, what was the point of the criminal conviction over a deferred prosecution agreement? Can it possibly represent progress for a bank and its executives to so easily weather the bank becoming a convicted felon?

Prosecutions or regulatory action not against institutions but against directors therefore present an unparalleled opportunity to demonstrate just how serious the consequences are of board-level incompetence, and would lend the most credence yet to repeated claims from lawmakers that harmful behaviours will not be tolerated. There otherwise simply is not the incentive for executives to ensure that quality internal systems are in place to spot the excesses and harmful behaviours. The threat of action against directors is all the more important as we enter an era in which reputational risk has become meaningless. Public opprobrium is not enough. Not only is it impossible for consumers to keep track of which banks have been up to no good, but they do not vote with their feet. Even if they did, where would they go?

In proposing alternatives to deter bad behaviour, some have fiercely argued for bonus claw backs and bonus ceilings. There can be no doubt that remuneration strategies can help to drive behaviours but to try and determine the financial industry's conduct in a free market by seeking to influence operational decisions of the type that sets pay and bonus structures is likely doomed to failure. The institutions themselves, hotbeds of financial ingenuity, will circumvent the rules to meet their end goal in any case. Bonuses morph from lump sums into share options and other fringe benefits. There are other problems too; meddling with bonuses not only generates bad will within an industry with which we need to engage constructively in order to achieve meaningful reform but even more worryingly it creates arbitrage opportunities because jurisdictions not willing to curb bankers' bonuses attract more business to their shores, encouraging a rush to the bottom.

So if the bonus question is thrown out, and criminal or regulatory action is called for, what exactly would a prosecution against an executive look like, and what needs to change in order for that to happen? The UK Banking Reform Act introduced a criminal offence applicable only to senior managers of making a decision causing a financial institution to fail. The narrow applicability of the offence to decisions relating to bank failure attests either to the power of the UK's banking lobby or the naïvety of its lawmakers or both. Why was the opportunity presented by the crisis not taken for a new criminal offence to be introduced that captured egregious conduct with less calamitous consequences such as mis-selling or rate rigging?

Former FSA chairman Lord Adair Turner has suggested that an offence be introduced in which the burden of proof shifts from judge to director. A director called to account for his allegedly negligent activities in a court of law would be obliged, under such a regime, to prove that he adequately scrutinised the risks and likely outcomes of events taking place under his governance against an objective set of criteria. In such a way, it would no longer fall to a judge or jury to subjectively assess whether or not a director was genuinely ignorant of the activities of others. Despite its merits, I am doubtful that lawmakers will introduce criminal law reform that makes it easier to prosecute a bank director than a common criminal, but there is mileage in the application of a burden of proof reversal in the application of regulatory penalties. Setting a benchmark by which directors are required to demonstrate that the absence of concern on their part was reasonable, would emphasise the need for directors to *have the concern* in the first place and support their work in providing sharply defined responsibilities in the discharge of their duties. Any failure to demonstrate concerns and an adequate process to address them would result in regulatory censure against a director which would include fines, public statements, and dis-qualification. These criteria would capture the clearly egregious activities that simply cannot be rationalised – stripping activity or a banking execu-tive defending the decision to do business with a PEP whose official salary is a tiny fraction of the millions of dollars he banks each year. There is no doubt in my mind that if a director knew that he could be required to positively justify why he had not been concerned about a particular aspect of a business, he would exit stage left if he knew he was not up to the task, or he would up his game significantly by holding the business to greater account.

Perhaps it seems somewhat unfair to suddenly start bringing regulatory action or criminal charges against executives who will claim they were doing their best and that they simply cannot be expected to know what is going on in all corners of the world – is a director in the UK really supposed to know what a compliance officer is doing in the Cayman Islands? Well, the answer is yes and no. Of course a director cannot know the intricacies of everyday operations undertaken by thousands of staff members across the globe, but he can certainly set a strategy; identify and agree on the risks inherent in that strategy; influence the quality of information he receives; dictate the questions staff ask and influence the quality of the discourse around risk, ethics, and culture. Integrating these improvements with measures to ensure technically competent directors and fit-for-purpose risk management sys-tems, and the industry starts to look a lot less blameworthy. Of course bad things will continue to happen, but they will happen in spite of, and not because of, poor governance.

Law reform that paves the way for criminal or regulatory charges to be brought against bankers is not a panacea. The distinction between such consequences and their likelihood of coming to pass is key and is set against the deeper question of whether there is the political will to pursue senior executives of financial institutions at all. Would any newly introduced laws or regulations be used and enforced? Would the agencies charged with responsibility for doing so be adequately resourced and staffed by professionals at least as talented as the legions of regulatory and criminal lawyers lined up on the other side to defend the executives, paid for by institutions with limitless resources? In truth, we are a very long way from being in that position. If lawmakers are unwilling even to contemplate professional qualification and meaningful continuing professional development requirements for bank directors there is very little hope that they will create the conditions necessary to make senior executives nervous about the consequences for them personally of the conduct of their businesses. The signs do not look good as lamer initiatives are being pursued. Mark Carney, Governor of the Bank of England, has welcomed the creation of the Banking Standards Review Council, a banking industry funded body with no disciplinary powers and no teeth headed by the former chairman of the Confederation of British Industry. Carney said:

> A meaningful change in the culture of banking will require a true commitment from the industry. That is why a second initiative, the creation of the Banking Standards Review Council (BSRC), is particularly welcome. This new independent body, again proposed by the Parliamentary Commission, is designed to create a sense of vocation in banking by promoting high standards of competence and behaviour across the UK industry.[9]

The idea that public naming and shaming of banks (the only punishment that can be meted out by the BRSC) by an industry funded body will somehow drive up standards within the banking industry is one of the clearest indications to emerge from the post-crisis analysis that the opportunity for meaningful reform is being missed. It beggars belief given the international nature of all systemically important UK banks that the BRSC's standards will apply only to banks' UK operations.

It is in all of our interests to encourage the finance industry to strike a better balance between risk and reward in the future. There is much good to be derived from well-run financial institutions; indeed they are essential to the functioning of a mature market economy. Whilst bad press on the finance industry is not difficult to find and much of it is well deserved, the industry is in fact positioned to provide enormous social and economic benefit. In addition to providing valuable intelligence to law enforcement through the mechanism of Suspicious Activity Reports, banks and allied businesses provide essential services to the wider economy and generate taxes and jobs, while also contributing to the arts, entertainment, and charitable causes. This observation does not, of course, give the industry carte blanche to operate as it wishes; it is, rather, a motivation for ensuring that the sector is reformed in a sustainable and meaningful manner so that it may continue to serve society as a whole.

On one count, the financial services sector was reported to employ 1,045,500 people in Great Britain in 2012. In the same year, the financial services and insurance sectors in the US employed 5.8 million people.[10] Measuring the output of financial firms is notoriously challenging, but there are some useful statistics to be found in the public domain. Data collected by PricewaterhouseCoopers showed that for the year ending March 2013, the UK financial services sector made a total tax contribution of £65 billion that represented 11.7% of the total tax revenue.[11] While in the US, the finance sector generated around 6.4% of the country's GDP.[12]

There is then much to be gained, economically, socially, and culturally from a reformed industry that better balances risk and reward and does less harm.

You may well reflect on why none of the suggestions for reform outlined in this final chapter have or are likely to be implemented despite the urgency created by the 2008 financial crisis and the many scandals surrounding conduct within the finance industry since. Here we return to the mobility of capital. Despite the risks of another crisis and the inevitability of more toxic behaviours involving the proceeds of crime, rare is the jurisdiction that will act unilaterally in a way that disadvantages it economically by alienating its finance industry. In the 'race' for finance sector reform, governments do not want to be ahead of the peloton, preferring the safety to be found in collective inaction. What has resulted then is a paralysis, a status quo borne of regulatory capture. We sit, we wait for the next catastrophe, all the while watching institutions write more cheques in settlement of fines that represent a fraction of their annual profits, whilst the feet of senior executives remain comfortably under boardroom tables across the globe. Capital, whether criminal or not, is power.

# NOTES

## 1 HARMFUL PRACTICES

1  'Wall Street and The Financial Crisis: Anatomy of a Financial Collapse', a report published by the US Permanent Subcommittee on Investigations on 13 April 2011 (www.hsgac.senate.gov//imo/media/doc/Financial_Crisis/FinancialCrisisReport. pdf?attempt=2)
2  'JPM Trade "Flawed, Complex, Poorly Reviewed, Executed, Monitored"', *Forbes*, 12 May 2012 (www.forbes.com/sites/robertlenzner/2012/05/12/flawedcomplexpoorly-reviewed-executed-monitored)
3  The FSA's Final Notice to Barclays Bank Plc, 27 June 2012 (www.fsa.gov.uk/static/pubs/ final/barclays-jun12.pdf)
4  Deferred Prosecution Agreement, *USA v The Royal Bank of Scotland* 5 January 2014 (www.justice.gov/atr/cases/f292500/292555.pdf)
5  'RBS fined £87.6 million for significant failings in relation to LIBOR', FSA notice, 6 February 2013 (www.fsa.gov.uk/library/communication/pr/2013/011.shtml)
6  'The Wheatley Review of Libor: final report', published in September 2012 (www. gov.uk/government/uploads/system/uploads/attachment_data/file/191762/wheatley_ review_libor_finalreport_280912.pdf)
7  Andrew Lo was quoted by *CNN*, on 10 July 2012 (http://money.cnn.com/2012/07/03/ investing/libor-interest-rate-faq/index.htm); Martin Wheatley, CEO of the FCA, was quoted in a *BBC News* article, dated 4 February 2014 (www.bbc.co.uk/news/business-26041039).
8  'Secret Currency Traders' Club Devised Biggest Market's Rates', *Bloomberg*, 19 December 2013 (www.bloomberg.com/news/2013-12-19/how-secret-currency-traders-club-devised-biggest-market-s-rates.html)
9  'Forex claims 'as bad as Libor', says FCA', *Financial Times*, 4 February 2014 (www. ft.com/cms/s/0/6d2f697a-8da8-11e3-bbe7-00144feab7de.html#axzz2slPlhGhc)
10  'Are we having fun yet?', *London Review of Books*, 4 July 2013 edition (www.lrb.co.uk/ v35/n13/john-lanchester/are-we-having-fun-yet)
11  Payment protection insurance case studies ('case study 8'), published by the Financial Ombudsman (www.financial-ombudsman.org.uk/publications/technical_notes/ppi/ PPI-case-studies.html#cs8)
12  'Lloyds accused of short-changing PPI claimants', *BBC News*, 25 March 2014 (www.bbc. co.uk/news/business-26715982)
13  'Risk Management and Regulatory Failures at Riggs Bank and UBS: Lessons Learned', testimony by Thomas C Baxter, 2 June 2004 (www.newyorkfed.org/newsevents/ speeches/2004/bax040602.html)
14  Deferred Prosecution Agreement, *USA v Lloyds TSB Bank Plc*, 9 January 2009 (www.gib-sondunn.com/publications/Documents/LloydsTSB-DeferredProsecutionAgmt010909.pdf)
15  House of Commons, transcript from 12 February 2009 (www.publications.parliament. uk/pa/cm200809/cmhansrd/cm090212/debtext/90212-0014.htm)

16   Factual Statement forming part of the Deferred Prosecution Agreement, *USA v Credit Suisse AG*, 16 December 2009 (www.justice.gov/criminal/pr/documents/12-16-09-CreditSuisse-factualstatement.pdf)

17   Deferred Prosecution Agreement, *USA v American Express Bank International*, 6 August 2007 (www.justice.gov/criminal/pr/2007/08/08-06-07amex-charge-agremnt.pdf)

18   'U.S. Vulnerabilities to Money Laundering, Drugs, and Terrorist Financing: HSBC Case History', a report released by the US Permanent Subcommittee on Investigations on 17 July 2012 (www.levin.senate.gov/download/?id=90fe8998-dfc4-4a8c-90ed-704bcce990d4)

19   Deferred Prosecution Agreement, *USA v UBS AG*, 18 February 2009 (www.justice.gov/tax/UBS_Signed_Deferred_Prosecution_Agreement.pdf)

20   'Swiss Bank Pleads Guilty In Manhattan Federal Court To Conspiracy To Evade Taxes', US Attorney's Office for the Southern District of New York press release, 3 January 2013 (www.justice.gov/usao/nys/pressreleases/January13/WegelinPleaPR.php)

21   Deferred Prosecution Agreement, *USA v JP Morgan Chase Bank NA*, 6 January 2014 (www.justice.gov/usao/nys/pressreleases/January14/JPMCDPASupportingDocs/JPMC%20DPA%20Packet%20(Fully%20Executed%20w%20Exhibits).pdf)

22   'Farewell to the FSA – and the bleak legacy of the light-touch regulator', *The Guardian*, 24 March 2013 (www.theguardian.com/business/2013/mar/24/farewell-fsa-bleak-legacy-light-touch-regulator)

## 2   MONEY LAUNDERING MODELS

1   'Bitcoin Soars While Liberty Reserve Draws Guilty Plea', *Forbes*, 8 November 2013 (www.forbes.com/sites/robertwood/2013/11/08/bitcoin-soars-while-liberty-reserve-draws-guilty-plea/); 'Co-founder of Liberty Reserve Pleads Guilty to Money Laundering in Manhattan Federal Court', US Department of Justice press release, 31 October 2013 (www.justice.gov/opa/pr/2013/October/13-crm-1163.html)

2   United Nations Convention Against Illicit Traffic in Narcotic Drugs and Psychotropic Substances, 1988 (www.unodc.org/pdf/convention_1988_en.pdf)

3   www.fincen.gov/news_room/aml_history.html

4   www.fatf-gafi.org/pages/faq/moneylaundering

5   '"The crime of the century": The story of the Great Train Robbery', *Daily Express*, 18 December 2013 (www.express.co.uk/news/uk/449356/The-crime-of-the-century-The-story-of-the-Great-Train-Robbery)

6   See 'Correspondent Banking: A Gateway for Money Laundering', a report released by the US Permanent Subcommittee on Investigations Committee, dated 5 February 2001 (www.hsgac.senate.gov/download/report_correspondent--banking-a-gateway-for-money-laundering)

7   'The World's 500 Largest Asset Managers', Year end 2012 (www.towerswatson.com/en-GB/Insights/IC-Types/Survey-Research-Results/2013/11/The-Worlds-500-Largest-Asset-Managers-Year-end-2012)

8   'Of waffle and remittances', *The Economist*, 20 September 2013 (www.economist.com/blogs/baobab/2013/09/somalia)

## 3   ONSHORE/OFFSHORE DICHOTOMY

1   'A crisis of confidence', *The Guardian*, 22 October 2008 (www.theguardian.com/commentisfree/cifamerica/2008/oct/22/economy-financial-crisis-regulation)

2   www.cayman.com.ky/the-cayman-islands-a-premiere-offshore-banking-center

3   According to: 'UK tax take on wealthy 'non-doms' rises 6%', *Financial Times*, 3 February 2014 (www.ft.com/cms/s/0/1fd89cde-8ce3-11e3-ad57-00144feab7de.html#axzz2vxSXyOCb)

4   According to figures in: 'Citizenship-for-Cash Program in Malta Stirs Security Concerns in European Union', *The New York Times*, 5 April 2014 (www.nytimes.com/2014/04/06/world/europe/citizenship-for-cash-program-in-malta-stirs-security-concerns-in-european-union.html?_r=0); http://spainresidencepermit.com/; www.second-citizenship.org/permanent-residence/immigration-and-permanent-residency-in-mauritius/

5   'Bono defends U2's tax set-up', *USA Today*, 5 December 2013 (www.usatoday.com/story/life/people/2013/09/23/bono-u2-taxes/2858283/)

6   www.cia.gov/library/publications/the-world-factbook/rankorder/2004rank.html

7   'The Price of Offshore Revisited', a report published by the Tax Justice Network in July 2012 (www.taxjustice.net/cms/upload/pdf/Price_of_Offshore_Revisited_120722.pdf)

8   www.cimoney.com.ky/stats_reg_ent/stats_reg_ent.aspx?id=200&ekmensel=e2f22c9a_14_72_200_6

9   A statement by Senator Carl Levin, presented at a US Permanent Subcommittee on Investigations hearing on 14 November 2006 (http://frwebgate.access.gpo.gov/cgi-bin/getdoc.cgi?dbname=109_senate_hearings&docid=f:32353.pdf)

10  Cited in: 'Gordon Brown says world must 'take action' on tax havens', *The Telegraph*, 19 February 2009 (www.telegraph.co.uk/finance/personalfinance/tax/4695513/Gordon-Brown-says-world-must-take-action-on-tax-havens.html)

11  Group 1 jurisdictions were described as being perceived as having legal infrastructures and supervisory practices, and/or a level of resources devoted to supervision and cooperation relative to the size of their financial activities, and/or a level of cooperation that are largely of a good quality and better than in other offshore financial centres.

12  'Mutual Evaluation Report, Anti Money Laundering and Combating the Financing of Terrorism', a report published by FATF, dated 9 April 2008 (www.fatf-gafi.org/media/fatf/documents/reports/mer/MER%20UAE%20full.pdf)

13  'Global Shell Games: testing Money Launderers' and Terrorist Financiers' Access to Shell Companies', by Michael Findley, Daniel Nielson and Jason Sharman, published in 2012 (www.griffith.edu.au/__data/assets/pdf_file/0008/454625/Oct2012-Global-Shell-Games.Media-Summary.10Oct12.pdf)

14  According to: 'Offshore Tax Evasion: The Effort to Collect Unpaid Taxes on Billions in Hidden Offshore Accounts', a report released by the US Permanent Subcommittee on Investigations on 26 February 2014 (www.hsgac.senate.gov/download/report-offshore-tax-evasion-the-effort-to-collect-unpaid-taxes-on-billions-in-hidden-offshore-accounts-5-22-14-update)

15  'Tax: Trouble abroad for the City?', *Financial Times*, 9 September 2013 (www.ft.com/cms/s/2/dbc8af56-0fc5-11e3-a258-00144feabdc0.html#axzz39neYdtzt)

16  See: 'China's princelings storing riches in Caribbean offshore haven', *The Guardian*, 21 January 2014 (www.theguardian.com/world/ng-interactive/2014/jan/21/china-british-virgin-islands-wealth-offshore-havens)

# 4   DRUG TRAFFICKING

1   Statistics from: 'Five years of London murder victims listed', *The Guardian*, 5 October 2011 (www.theguardian.com/news/datablog/2011/oct/05/murder-london-list) and www.osac.gov/pages/ContentReportDetails.aspx?cid=14380

2   'Mexico violence: Monterrey police find 49 bodies', *BBC News*, 13 May 2012 (www.bbc.
    co.uk/news/world-latin-america-18052540)
3   Figures cited in: '200 million people use illegal drugs; what is the toll on health?', *Los
    Angeles Times*, 5 January 2012 (http://articles.latimes.com/2012/jan/05/news/la-heb-
    worldwide-drug-use-20120105)
4   '2005 World Drug Report' Volume 1 (www.unodc.org/pdf/WDR_2005/volume_1_web.
    pdf)
5   'Treasury Targets Major Money Laundering Network Linked to Drug Trafficker
    Ayman Joumaa and a Key Hizballah Supporter in South America', US Department of
    the Treasury press release, 27 June 2012 (www.treasury.gov/press-center/press-releases/
    pages/tg1624.aspx)
6   See: UNODC's 'World Drug Report 2013' (www.unodc.org/documents/wdr/World_
    Drug_Report_2013.pdf)
7   See: UNODC's 'Estimating Illicit Financial Flows Resulting from Drug Trafficking and
    Other Transnational Organized Crimes', October 2011 (www.unodc.org/documents/
    data-and-analysis/Studies/Illicit_financial_flows_2011_web.pdf)
8   Statistics from: 'The Economic Impact of Illicit Drug Use on American Society', pub-
    lished by the US Department of Justice National Drug Intelligence Center in April 2011
    (www.justice.gov/archive/ndic/pubs44/44731/44731p.pdf) and 'No Quick Fix', pub-
    lished by the Centre for Social Justice in September 2013 (www.centreforsocialjustice.
    org.uk/UserStorage/pdf/Pdf%20reports/addict.pdf)
9   'Mexican ex-governor gets 11 years in U.S. for money laundering', *Reuters*, 28 June
    2013    (www.reuters.com/article/2013/06/28/us-usa-mexico-villanueva-idUSBRE95R
    14720130628)
10  See: www.forbes.com/profile/joaquin-guzman-loera/
11  See: UNODC's 'Financial Flows linked to the Illicit Production and Trafficking of
    Afghan Opiates', November 2008 (www.unodc.org/documents/afghanistan//Rainbow_
    Strategy/Orange_Paper_12_December_2008.pdf)
12  'Gang jailed after laundering £20m of drugs money for criminals', *Manchester Evening
    News*, 16 January 2014 (www.manchestereveningnews.co.uk/news/greater-manchester-
    news/gang-used-banks-chorlton-longsight-6520358)
13  'Moving Illegal Proceeds', a report released by the US Government Accountability
    Office on 9 March 2011 (www.gao.gov/new.items/d11407t.pdf)
14  '2 women arrested for attempting to smuggle U.S. dollars into Mexico', *Arizona Daily
    Star*, 6 January 2014 (http://azstarnet.com/news/local/women-arrested-for-attempt-
    ing-to-smuggle-u-s-dollars-into/article_24c45d16-774c-11e3-a579-001a4bcf887a.
    html)
15  The information on Wachovia in this chapter is primarily sourced from: Deferred
    Prosecution Agreement, *USA vs Wachovia Bank NA*, 16 March 2010 (www.justice.gov/
    usao/fls/PressReleases/Attachments/100317-02.Agreement.pdf)    and    corresponding
    Factual Statement (www.justice.gov/usao/fls/PressReleases/Attachments/100317-02.
    Statement.pdf)
16  'How a big US bank laundered billions from Mexico's murderous drug gangs', *The
    Guardian*, 3 April 2011 (www.theguardian.com/world/2011/apr/03/us-bank-mexico-
    drug-gangs) ,
17  'Wachovia Enters Into Deferred Prosecution Agreement', US Drug Enforcement
    Administration press release, 17 March 2010 (www.justice.gov/dea/pubs/pressrel/
    pr031710.html)
18  The information on HSBC in this chapter is primarily sourced from: 'U.S. Vulnerabilities
    to Money Laundering, Drugs, and Terrorist Financing: HSBC Case History', a report
    released by the US Permanent Subcommittee on Investigations on 17 July 2012 (www.

levin.senate.gov/download/?id=90fe8998-dfc4-4a8c-90ed-704bcce990d4), and the Statement of Facts which formed part of the Deferred Prosecution Agreement between HSBC Bank USA NA/HSBC Holdings Plc and the US Department of Justice, the US Attorney's Office for Eastern District of New York, and the US Attorney's Office for the Northern District of West Virginia, filed 11 December 2012 (www.justice.gov/opa/documents/hsbc/dpa-attachment-a.pdf)

# 5  BRIBERY AND CORRUPTION

1  See: Stolen Asset Recovery Initiative entry for Teodoro Nguema Obiang Mbasongo/ Teodoro Nguema Obiang Mangue (http://star.worldbank.org/corruption-cases/ node/18586) and *USA vs One White Crystal-Covered "Bad Tour" Glove and Other Michael Jackson Memorabilia*, Second Amended Verified Complaint for Forfeiture *in rem*, filed 11 June 2012 (www.globalwitness.org/sites/default/files/library/Second%20 Amended%20Complaint%206.11.12.pdf). Much of the information in this chapter regarding Teodorin originates from these two sources (and the additional complaint cited below).

2  See: *USA vs One Gulfstream G-V Jet Aircraft Displaying Tail Number VPCES, Its Tools and Appurtenances*, Verified Complaint for Forfeiture *in rem*, filed 25 October 2011 (www.foreignpolicy.com/files/fp_uploaded_documents/111025_DDC_1.pdf) and 'Teodorin Obiang: The Dictator's Son with a Malibu Mansion and Warrant for His Arrest', *Time*, 16 July 2012 (http://world.time.com/2012/07/16/teodorin-obiang-the-dictators-son-with-a-malibu-mansion-and-a-warrant-for-his-arrest/)

3  GDP statistics available at: http://data.worldbank.org/indicator/NY.GDP.PCAP.CD

4  'SEC Charges Baker Hughes With Foreign Bribery and With Violating 2001 Commission Cease-and-Desist Order', SEC press release, 26 April 2007 (www.sec.gov/ news/press/2007/2007-77.htm)

5  See: 'Siemens AG and Three Subsidiaries Plead Guilty to Foreign Corrupt Practices Act Violations and Agree to Pay $450 Million in Combined Criminal Fines', US Department of Justice press release, 15 December 2008 (www.justice.gov/opa/pr/2008/ December/08-crm-1105.html) and 'Siemens AG reaches a resolution with German and U.S. authorities', Siemens AG press release, 15 December 2008 (www.siemens. com/press/en/pressrelease/?press=/en/pressrelease/2008/corporate_communication/ axx20081219.htm)

6  See: 'EU joins national donors in freezing aid to Uganda over graft', *Reuters*, 4 December 2012 (www.reuters.com/article/2012/12/04/us-uganda-aid-idUSBRE8B30 DA20121204)

7  See: 'Commission unveils first EU Anti-Corruption Report', European Commission press release, 3 February 2014 (http://europa.eu/rapid/press-release_IP-14-86_en.htm)

8  See: 'Six Questions on the Cost of Corruption with World Bank Institute Global Governance Director Daniel Kaufmann' (http://web.worldbank.org/WBSITE/ EXTERNAL/NEWS/0,,contentMDK:20190295~menuPK:34457~pagePK:34370~piPK: 34424~theSitePK:4607,00.html)

9  See: Transparency International's 'Global Corruption Report 2004' (www.transparency.org/whatwedo/pub/global_corruption_report_2004_political_corruption)

10  'Illicit Financial Flows from Developing Countries: 2000-2009', a report published by Global Financial Integrity in January 2011 (www.gfintegrity.org/wp-content/ uploads/2011/12/GFI_2010_IFF_Update_Report-Web.pdf)

11  The South African case is cited in: 'Keeping Foreign Corruption Out of the United States: Four Case Histories', a report released by the US Permanent Subcommittee on

Investigations on 4 February 2010 (www.hsgac.senate.gov/download/report-psi-staff-report-keeping-foreign-corruption-out-of-the-united-states-four-case-histories)

12    'Former DOD Contractor Sentenced in Case Involving Bribery, Fraud and Money Laundering Scheme in al-Hillah, Iraq', US Department of Justice press release, 29 January 2007 (www.justice.gov/opa/pr/2007/January/07_crm_055.html)

13    'BAE fined in Tanzania defence contract case', Serious Fraud Office press release, 21 December 2010 (www.sfo.gov.uk/press-room/press-release-archive/press-releases-2010/bae-fined-in-tanzania-defence-contract-case.aspx)

14    'The Transparency of National Defence Budgets', published by Transparency International in October 2011 (www.ti-defence.org/publications/20-category-publications/publications-dsp/124-dsp-pubs-transparency-defence-budgets.html)

15    See: 'Riddle of sheikh's £100m secret fund', *The Guardian*, 2 June 2002 (www.theguardian.com/politics/2002/jun/02/uk.armstrade); a statement published on *The Guardian* website (and assumed to have been issued by the Jersey Attorney General) (http://image.guardian.co.uk/sys-files/Guardian/documents/2007/05/29/qatardoc01.pdf); and *Jersey Evening Post Limited v His Excellency Sheikh Hamad Bin Jassim Bin Japer Al-Thani*, 2 December 2002 (www.jerseylaw.je/Judgments/UnreportedJudgments/Documents/Display.aspx?url=02-12-02_JEP-v-Qatar_227.htm&JudgementNo=2002/227)

16    See: 'BAE accused of secretly paying up to £1bn to Saudi prince', *The Guardian*, 7 June 2007 (www.theguardian.com/world/2007/jun/07/bae1) and ' "National Interest" halts arms corruption inquiry', *The Guardian*, 15 December 2006 (www.theguardian.com/uk/2006/dec/15/saudiarabia.armstrade)

17    'US Seizes Ex-Ukrainian Prime Minister's Mansion', *The Wall Street Journal*, 7 November 2013 (http://blogs.wsj.com/riskandcompliance/2013/11/07/us-seizes-ex-ukrainian-prime-ministers-mansion-picasso-lithograph/)

18    ' "Biens mal acquis" case: French Supreme Court overrules Court of Appeal's decision', Transparency International press release, 9 November 2010 (www.transparency.org/news/pressrelease/20101109_biens_mal_acquis_case_french_supreme_court_over-rules_court_of_appe)

19    See: 'Former Nigeria state governor James Ibori receives 13-year sentence', *The Guardian*, 17 April 2012 (www.theguardian.com/global-development/2012/apr/17/nigeria-governor-james-ibori-sentenced) and 'Former Nigeria governor James Ibori jailed for 13 years', *BBC News*, 17 April 2012 (www.bbc.co.uk/news/world-africa-17739388)

20    Information regarding Dipreye Alamieyeseigha was sourced from: 'Nigeria governor to be impeached', *BBC News*, 23 November 2005 (http://news.bbc.co.uk/1/hi/world/africa/4462444.stm); Stolen Asset Recovery Initiative, sourced from 'Kleptocrats' Portfolio Decisions, or realities in State Asset Recovery cases' by Tim Daniel and James Maton (https://star.worldbank.org/corruption-cases/node/18620); 'Nigeria Pardons Goodluck Jonathan ally, Alamieyeseigha', *BBC News*, 13 March 2013 (www.bbc.co.uk/news/world-africa-21769047); *Federal Republic of Nigeria v Santolina Investment Corporation*, 3 December 2007 (available at: http://star.worldbank.org/corruption-cases/node/18493); 'British Police ask FG to extradite Alamieyeseigha', *Oyibos Online* (www.oyibosonline.com/cgi-bin/newsscript2.pl?record=2562); 'We're still waiting for Alamieyeseigha in UK – Envoy', *The Sun*, 28 March 2013 (http://sunnewsonline.com/new/?p=21879 )

21    'Money Laundering and Foreign Corruption: Enforcement and Effectiveness of the Patriot Act: Case Study involving Riggs Bank', a report released by the US Permanent Subcommittee on Investigations on 15 July 2004 (www.hsgac.senate.gov//imo/media/doc/ACF5F8.pdf?attempt=2)

22    Available at: www.fsa.gov.uk/pubs/other/aml_final_report.pdf

23    'Coutts fined £8.75 million for anti-money laundering control failings', FSA press release, 26 March 2012 (www.fsa.gov.uk/library/communication/pr/2012/032.shtml)

and FSA's Final Notice to Coutts & Company, 23 March 2012 (www.fsa.gov.uk/static/pubs/final/coutts-mar12.pdf)

# 6  PIRACY

1   Cited in: 'Somali pirates free UK couple Paul and Rachel Chandler', *BBC News*, 14 November 2010 (www.bbc.co.uk/news/uk-11752027)
2   'Pirate Trails', a report published by the World Bank, in collaboration with UNODC and Interpol, in 2013 (https://openknowledge.worldbank.org/handle/10986/16196)
3   See: 'Reports on Act of Piracy and Armed Robbery Against Ships Annual Report - 2011', a report published by the International Maritime Organization on 1 March 2012 (www.imo.org/blast/blastDataHelper.asp?data_id=31023&filename=180.pdf)
4   'Piracy and Armed Robbery against Ships' a report by ICC International Maritime Bureau for the 1 January – 31 December 2013 period (www.harbourmaster.org/downloadfile.php?df=images/upload/files/news-maritime_news_file_419.pdf&dfn=MjAxMyBBBbm51YWwgSU1CIFBpcmFjeSBSZXBvcnQgQUJSSURHRUQucGRm&decode=y)
5   'Al Shabab Fights the Pirates', *The New York Times*, 22 October 2013 (www.nytimes.com/2013/10/23/opinion/international/al-shabab-fights-the-pirates.html?_r=0) and 'Organised Maritime Piracy and Related Kidnapping for Ransom', a report published by FATF in July 2011 (www.fatf-gafi.org/media/fatf/documents/reports/organised%20maritime%20piracy%20and%20related%20kidnapping%20for%20ransom.pdf)
6   'Shabaab-Somali pirate links growing: UN adviser', *Reuters*, 20 October 2011 (www.reuters.com/article/2011/10/20/ozatp-somalia-shabaab-pirates-idAFJOE79J0G620111020)
7   'Somali sea gangs lure investors at pirate lair', *Reuters*, 1 December 2009 (uk.reuters.com/article/2009/12/01/us-somalia-piracy-investors-idUSTRE5B01Z920091201)
8   'Somali Hostage Negotiator in S/V Quest and M/V Miranda Marguerite Piracies Sentenced to Multiple Life Sentences', FBI press release, 13 August 2012 (www.fbi.gov/newyork/press-releases/2012/somali-hostage-negotiator-in-s-v-quest-and-m-v-miranda-marguerite-piracies-sentenced-to-multiple-life-sentences) and 'Highest-ranking Somali pirate in U.S. custody loses appeal to overturn 12 life sentences for killing 4 American tourists', *NY Daily News*, 12 July 2013 (www.nydailynews.com/news/world/convicted-somali-pirate-loses-appeal-article-1.1397564)
9   Relevant excerpt available at: www.publications.parliament.uk/pa/ld200809/ldselect/ldeucom/132/13208.htm
10  'Treasure Mapped: Using Satellite Imagery to Track the Developmental Effects of Somali Piracy', a report published by Chatham House in January 2012 (www.chathamhouse.org/sites/files/chathamhouse/public/Research/Africa/0112pp_shortland.pdf)

# 7  TRAFFICKING OF HUMAN BEINGS AND SMUGGLING OF MIGRANTS

1   '14 years for Dover tragedy lorry driver', *The Guardian*, 5 April 2001 (www.theguardian.com/uk/2001/apr/05/immigration.immigrationandpublicservices); ' "Death Truck" Driver Pleads Innocent', *CBS News*, 30 November 2000 (www.cbsnews.com/news/death-truck-driver-pleads-innocent/); and *R v Perry Wacker*, 2002 (www.lccsa.org.uk/r-v-perry-wacker-2002/)
2   Cited in: 'Driver jailed over immigrant deaths', *BBC News*, 5 April 2001 (news.bbc.co.uk/1/hi/uk/1258240.stm)

3   See: 'Money Laundering Risks Arising from Trafficking in Human Beings and Smuggling of Migrants', a FATF report published in July 2011 (www.fatf-gafi.org/media/fatf/documents/reports/Trafficking%20in%20Human%20Beings%20and%20Smuggling%20of%20Migrants.pdf)

4   See: www.unodc.org/unodc/en/treaties/CTOC/

5   'The Mexican Drug Cartels' Other Business: Sex Trafficking', *Time*, 31 July 2013 (http://world.time.com/2013/07/31/the-mexican-drug-cartels-other-business-sex-trafficking/)

6   'Lampedusa boat tragedy: Migrants "raped and tortured"', *BBC News*, 8 November 2013 (www.bbc.co.uk/news/world-europe-24866338)

7   Available at: www.state.gov/j/tip/rls/tiprpt/2013/index.htm

8   See: 'Cockle gangmaster gets 14 years', *BBC News*, 28 March 2006 (http://news.bbc.co.uk/1/hi/england/lancashire/4851194.stm); 'Man guilty of 21 cockling deaths', *BBC News*, 24 March 2006 (http://news.bbc.co.uk/1/hi/england/lancashire/4832454.stm); 'Morecambe Bay cocklepicker gangmaster freed after serving just four months for each life lost', *The Mirror*, 9 February 2014 (www.mirror.co.uk/news/uk-news/morecambe-bay-cocklepicker-gangmaster-lin-3126508);   and   'Going   under', *The Guardian*, 20 June 2007 (www.theguardian.com/uk/2007/jun/20/ukcrime.humanrights)

9   'ILO Action Against Trafficking in Human Beings', published in 2008 (www.ilo.org/wcmsp5/groups/public/@ed_norm/@declaration/documents/publication/wcms_090356.pdf)

10  See: 'Children Trafficked and Exploited inside Europe by Criminal Gangs', 11 January 2011 (www.europol.europa.eu/content/press/children-trafficked-and-exploited-inside-europe-criminal-gangs-501)

11  See: 'Smuggling of migrants: the harsh search for a better life' (www.unodc.org/toc/en/crimes/migrant-smuggling.html)

12  'Snakehead empress who made millions trafficking in misery', *The Guardian*, 6 July 2003 (www.theguardian.com/uk/2003/jul/06/immigration.china)

13  'The Case of the Snakehead Queen', FBI news story, 17 March 2006 (www.fbi.gov/news/stories/2006/march/sisterping_031706)

14  See: Settlement Agreement, *State of Arizona v Western Union Financial Services Inc.*, February 2010 (www.sec.gov/Archives/edgar/data/1365135/000119312510030898/dex101.htm)

15  'Western Union, Arizona to Cooperate to Combat Money Laundering', *The Wall Street Journal*, 3 February 2014 (http://online.wsj.com/article/BT-CO-20140203-706961.html#printMode)

16  FATF's 'Money Laundering Risks Arising from Trafficking in Human Beings and Smuggling of Migrants' report (See note 3 above).

## 8   TERRORISM FINANCING

1   'Three British Islamists convicted of plotting "another 9/11"', *Reuters*, 21 February 2013 (http://uk.mobile.reuters.com/article/topNews/idUKBRE91K0SK20130221?i=2)

2   'The Numerous Federal Legal Definitions of Terrorism: The Problem of Too Many Grails', by Nicholas J Perry, Journal of Legislation (2004)

3   See: www.refworld.org/cgi-bin/texis/vtx/rwmain?docid=42c39b6d4

4   Cited in: 'What's In A Name? How Nations Define Terrorism Ten Years After 9/11', by Sudha Setty (2011) (www.law.upenn.edu/live/files/139-setty33upajintll12011pdf)

5   'When does Reuters use the word terrorist or terrorism?', *Reuters*, 13 June 2007 (http://blogs.reuters.com/blog/archives/7146)

6  See: http://govinfo.library.unt.edu/911/staff_statements/911_TerrFin_Monograph.pdf

7  'Terrorism and tobacco', 29 June 2009 (www.icij.org/project/tobacco-underground/ terrorism-and-tobacco)

8  'The 9/11 Commission Report' released by the 9/11 Commission on 22 July 2004 (www.9-11commission.gov/report/911Report.pdf)

9  See: www.gov.uk/government/uploads/system/uploads/attachment_data/file/228837/1087. pdf

10 'Twin brothers jailed for raising money for terrorism', *The Guardian*, 1 August 2012 (www.theguardian.com/uk/2012/aug/01/twin-brothers-jailed-money-terrorism)

11 See: US Department of the Treasury's entry for 'The Holy Land Foundation for Relief and Development' (www.treasury.gov/resource-center/terrorist-illicit-finance/Pages/ protecting-charities_execorder_13224-e.aspx)

12 'Five Convicted in Terrorism Financing Trial', *The New York Times*, 24 November 2008 (www.nytimes.com/2008/11/25/us/25charity.html?_r=0)

13 See: 'Combating the Abuse of Non-Profit Organsations', a FATF Guidance Document published on 11 October 2002 (www.fatf-gafi.org/media/fatf/documents/ recommendations/11%20FATF%20SRIX%20BPP%20SRVIII%20October%202003%20 -%20COVER%202012.pdf)

14 See: www.loc.gov/rr/frd/pdf-files/NarcsFundedTerrs_Extrems.pdf

15 'South America drug gangs funding al-Qaeda terrorists', *The Telegraph*, 29 December 2010 (www.telegraph.co.uk/news/worldnews/southamerica/colombia/8230134/South-American-drug-gangs-funding-al-Qaeda-terrorists.html)

16 'Somalia fears as US Sunrise banks stop money transfers', *BBC News*, 30 December 2011 (www.bbc.co.uk/news/world-africa-16365619)

17 'Looking in the wrong places', *The Economist*, 20 October 2005 (www.economist.com/ node/5053373)

18 See: *Brief and special appendix for plaintiffs-appellants* (available at: www.mm-law.com/ wp-content/uploads/2013/12/Weiss-v.-National-Westminster-Bank-Appeal-Brief.pdf)

19 '2nd Circuit Oks Israeli terrorism victims' suit against Lebanese bank', *Thomson Reuters* blog, 19 November 2013 (http://blog.thomsonreuters.com/index.php/2nd-circuit-oks-israeli-terrorism-victims-suit-lebanese-bank/)

20 'Family of American teen killed by suicide bombing in Israel wins $332 MILLION law-suit against Iran and Syria ... but will they ever see the money?', *Daily Mail*, 17 May 2012 (www.dailymail.co.uk/news/article-2145621/Family-Daniel-Wultz-awarded-332M-judgement-Iran-Syria-Israeli-suicide-bombing.html)

21 'Member of Afghan Taliban Sentenced to Life in Prison in Nation's First Conviction on Narco-terror Charges', US Department of Justice press release, 22 December 2008 (www.justice.gov/opa/pr/2008/December/08-crm-1145.html) and *United States v Mohammed*, decided 4 September 2012 (https://casetext.com/case/united-states-v-mohammed-5/)

22 'Haji Bagcho Sentenced to Life in Prison on Drug Trafficking and Narco-Terrorism Charges', US Department of Justice press release, 12 June 2012 (www.justice.gov/opa/ pr/2012/June/12-crm-744.html)

23 See: www.treasury.gov/resource-center/sanctions/Programs/Documents/tar2012.pdf

24 Following the investigation into the financing of 9/11, it emerged that in the week prior to the attacks an unusually high level of put options were placed on airline and insur-ance company stocks with the result that some speculators made significant gains when the stock prices of these companies plummeted. The *9/11 Commission Report* concluded that the trades were not conducted by parties with foreknowledge of the attacks and were thus not suspicious.

# 9   SANCTIONS-BUSTING

1   'UN Sanctions', a Security Council Special Research Report published in November
    2013 (www.securitycouncilreport.org/atf/cf/%7B65BFCF9B-6D27-4E9C-8CD3-CF6E4
    FF96FF9%7D/special_research_report_sanctions_2013.pdf)

2   'Mabey & Johnson directors made illegal payments to Sadam Hussein's Iraq to
    gain contract', SFO press release, 10 February 2011 (www.sfo.gov.uk/press-room/
    press-release-archive/press-releases-2011/mabey--johnson-directors-made-illegal-
    payments-to-sadam-hussein's-iraq-to-gain-contract.aspx)

3   See: announcement regarding *HMA v Weir Group PLC (www.scotland-judiciary.org.
    uk/8/695/HMA-v-WEIR-GROUP-PLC)*

4   Paddy Power gifts to Kim Jong-un could have broken UN sanctions', *The Telegraph*,
    10 January 2014 (www.telegraph.co.uk/news/worldnews/asia/northkorea/10564722/
    Paddy-Power-gifts-to-Kim-Jong-un-could-have-broken-UN-sanctions.html)      and
    'Irish Whiskey and a handbag: Paddy Power denies breaking UN sanctions with gifts
    for Kim Jong-un', *Independent*, 10 January 2014 (www.independent.ie/world-news/
    irish-whiskey-and-a-handbag-paddy-power-denies-breaking-un-sanctions-with-gifts-
    for-kim-jongun-29905910.html)

5   See: Regulations concerning restrictive measures against the Democratic People's
    Republic of Korea: http://eur-lex.europa.eu/LexUriServ/LexUriServ.do?uri=OJ:L:2007
    :088:0001:0011:EN:PDF

6   See the FSA's Decision Notice, 2 August 2010 (www.fsa.gov.uk/pubs/other/rbs_group.pdf)

7   '£750,000 fine for Royal Bank's rules breach', *The Guardian*, 18 December 2002 (www.
    theguardian.com/business/2002/dec/18/royalbankofscotlandgroup)

8   'British Businessman Christopher Tappin Sentenced To Federal Prison For Aiding
    and Abetting The Illegal Export of Defence Articles', US Attorney's Office for Western
    District of Texas press release, 9 January 2013 (www.justice.gov/usao/txw/news/2013/
    Tappin_El%20Paso_sen.html)

9   Deferred Prosecution Agreement, *USA v Barclays Bank Plc*, filed 16 August 2010 (avail-
    able at: http://legaltimes.typepad.com/files/dpa_barclays.pdf)

10  Deferred Prosecution Agreement, *USA v The former ABN Amro Bank NV now known
    as The Royal Bank of Scotland NV*, filed 10 May 2010 (available at: www.gibsondunn.
    com/publications/Documents/ABNAmroDPA.pdf)

11  Deferred Prosecution Agreement, *USA v ING Bank NV*, filed 12 June 2012 (available at:
    www.frank-cs.org/cms/pdfs/DOJ/DOJ_ING_12.6.12.pdf)

12  Deferred Prosecution Agreement, *USA v Standard Chartered Bank*, 7 December 2012
    (available   at:   www.steptoe.com/assets/htmldocuments/1.%20114-1-Standard-Char-
    tered-Bank-DPA(2).pdf)

13  See: Statement from Benjamin M. Lawsky, Superintendent of Financial Services,
    Regarding Standard Chartered Bank, 14 August 2012 (www.dfs.ny.gov/about/press/
    pr1208141.htm)

14  Agreement in the Matter of Deloitte Financial Advisory Services LLP, 18 June 2013
    (www.dfs.ny.gov/about/press2013/pr20130618-deloitte.pdf)

15  Settlement Agreement with Department of the Treasury, 11 December 2013 (www.
    treasury.gov/resource-center/sanctions/CivPen/Documents/12112013_rbs_settle.pdf);
    Department of Financial Services Consent Order in the Matter of The Royal Bank of
    Scotland Plc, 11 December 2013 (www.dfs.ny.gov/about/press2013/131211-rbs.pdf);
    and Federal Reserve Order of Assessment of a Civil Penalty in the Matter of Royal Bank
    of Scotland Group Plc, 11 December 2013 (www.federalreserve.gov/newsevents/press/
    enforcement/enf20131211a2.pdf)

16  Statement of Facts, *USA v BNP Paribas SA*, 28 June 2014 (www.justice.gov/usao/nys/pressreleases/June14/bnppsupportingdocs/BNP%20Paribas%20Statement%20of%20Facts.pdf)

# 10   TAX EVASION/AVOIDANCE

1   See: www.starbucks.co.uk/our-commitment
2   'Starbucks "pays £8.6m tax on £3bn sales"', *The Guardian*, 15 October 2012 (www.theguardian.com/business/2012/oct/15/starbucks-tax-uk-sales) and 'Starbucks, Amazon and Google grilled by MPs on tax', *Channel 4 News*, 12 November 2012 (www.channel4.com/news/starbucks-amazon-and-google-grilled-by-mps-on-tax)
3   *Helvering, Com'r of Internal Revenue v Gregory* (1935) (available at: www.uniset.ca/other/cs5/69F2d809.html)
4   'Measuring tax gaps 2013', HMRC report available at www.hmrc.gov.uk/statistics/tax-gaps/mtg-2013.pdf ; European Parliament's 'Draft Report on Fight against Tax Fraud, Tax Evasion and Tax Havens', dated 29 January 2013 (www.europarl.europa.eu/sides/getDoc.do?pubRef=-//EP//NONSGML+COMPARL+PE-504.066+01+DOC+PDF+V0//EN&language=EN); 'Offshore Tax Evasion: The Effort to Collect Unpaid Taxes on Billions in Hidden Offshore Accounts', a report released by the US Permanent Subcommittee on Investigations on 26 February 2014 (www.hsgac.senate.gov/subcommittees/investigations/hearings/offshore-tax-evasion-the-effort-to-collect-unpaid-taxes-on-billions-in-hidden-offshore-accounts)
5   Cited at: www.saffery.com/news-and-events/press-releases/2014/19-march-2014-1.aspx
6   'Osborne plans to take "pay now, argue later" approach with rich tax avoiders', *The Guardian*, 19 March 2014 (www.theguardian.com/uk-news/2014/mar/19/osborne-pay-now-argue-later-tax-avoiders)
7   'The Cup Trust', a report by the Comptroller and Auditor General, 4 December 2013 (www.nao.org.uk/wp-content/uploads/2013/11/10299-001-Cup-Trust-Book-Copy.pdf)
8   'Court shuts down £400m tax avoidance scheme', *CityWire*, 28 February 2013 (http://citywire.co.uk/new-model-adviser/court-shuts-down-400m-tax-avoidance-scheme/a662151)
9   'Former Quellos Executives Sentenced in Offshore Tax Shelter Scam Involving More Than $9.6 billion in Phony Stock Sales', a US Attorney's Office for the Western District of Washington press release, 28 January 2011 (www.justice.gov/usao/waw/press/2011/jan/quellos.html)
10  Senator Carl Levin's Opening Statement at the Permanent Subcommittee on Investigations' Hearing: www.levin.senate.gov/newsroom/speeches/speech/opening-statement-at-psi-hearing-offshore-profit-shifting-and-the-us-tax-code
11  Bill Sample's Statement at: www.hsgac.senate.gov/download/?id=602db197-1a9b-4b3b-89dd-86bacd82eb83
12  ' "Dutch sandwich grows" as Google shifts €8.8bn to Bermuda', *Financial Times*, 10 October 2013 (www.ft.com/cms/s/0/89acc832-31cc-11e3-a16d-00144feab7de.html#axzz2ySxUZwwK)
13  'Google pays $55 million tax in Britain on 2012 sales of $5 billion', *Reuters*, 30 September 2013 (http://uk.reuters.com/article/2013/09/30/us-google-tax-britain-idUKBRE98T0L120130930)
14  'Google boss: I'm very proud of our tax avoidance scheme', *The Independent*, 13 December 2012 (www.independent.co.uk/news/uk/home-news/google-boss-im-very-proud-of-our-tax-avoidance-scheme-8411974.html) and 'Google UK boss Matt Brittin fights back over tax payments', *The Telegraph*, 27 November 2012 (www.telegraph.

co.uk/finance/personalfinance/tax/9707121/Google-UK-boss-Matt-Brittin-fights-back-over-tax-payments.html)

15   'U.S. Tax Shelter Industry: The Role of Accountants, Lawyers, and Financial Professionals – Four KPMG Case Studies', a report released by the US Permanent Subcommittee on Investigations on 18&20 November 2003 (www.levin.senate.gov/imo/media/doc/suppo rting/2003/111803TaxShelterReport.pdf)

16   'Tax Haven Banks And U.S. Tax Compliance', a report released by the US Permanent Subcommittee on Investigations on 17 July 2008 (www.hsgac.senate.gov/download/ report-psi-staff-report-tax-haven-banks-and-us-tax-compliance-july-17-2008)

17   See UBS press release, 18 February 2009: www.ubs.com/global/de/about_ubs/media/ global/releases/news_display_media_global.html/en/2009/02/18/2009_02_18a.html

18   'Swiss Bank Pleads Guilty In Manhattan Federal Court To Conspiracy To Evade Taxes', US Attorney's Office for Southern District of New York press release, 3 January 2013 (www.justice.gov/usao/nys/pressreleases/January13/WegelinPleaPR.php)

19   'Wegelin & Co.'s Reply To the Government's Sentencing Memorandum' (www.wenag. ch/documents/Wegelin_Reply_Memorandum.pdf), 28 February 2013

20   'Offshore Tax Evasion: The Effort to Collect Unpaid Taxes on Billions in Hidden Offshore Accounts', a report released by the US Permanent Subcommittee on Investigations on 26 February 2014 (www.hsgac.senate.gov/subcommittees/investigations/hearings/ offshore-tax-evasion-the-effort-to-collect-unpaid-taxes-on-billions-in-hidden-off-shore-accounts); and see: USA v Andreas Markus Bachmann submitted 11 March 2014 (available at: www.woodllp.com/Publications/Articles/pdf/Bachmann_Statement.pdf)

21   Statement of Credit Suisse available at: www.hsgac.senate.gov/download/?id=39a9fca2-2253-4d97-8116-51e87659dbdb

22   See Credit Suisse CEO Brady Dougan quoted in: www.credit-suisse.com/investors/doc/ csg_resultssummary_2q14_en.pdf

23   'Jimmy Carr tax affairs "morally wrong" – Cameron', BBC News, 20 June 2012 (www. bbc.co.uk/news/uk-politics-18521468)

24   'Tax avoidance schemes "utterly immoral", says Hodge', BBC News, 6 December 2012 (www.bbc.co.uk/news/business-20624848) and Prime Minister David Cameron's speech to the World Economic Forum in Davos found at: www.gov.uk/government/speeches/ prime-minister-david-camerons-speech-to-the-world-economic-forum-in-davos

25   See Barclays Group CEO speech at: www.barclays.com/content/dam/barclayspublic/ docs/InvestorRelations/IRNewsPresentations/2013Presentations/Antony-Jenkins-speech.pdf

# 11   CAUSES AND SOLUTIONS

1   'Economic Inclusion and Financial Integrity—an Address to the Conference on Inclusive Capitalism', a speech by Christine Lagarde, Managing Director of the International Monetary Fund, 27 May 2014 (www.imf.org/external/np/speeches/2014/052714.htm)

2   'Inclusive capitalism: creating a sense of the systemic', a speech by Mark Carney, Governor of the Bank of England, 27 May 2014 (www.bankofengland.co.uk/publica-tions/Documents/speeches/2014/speech731.pdf)

3   'The Co-operative Group: Report of the Independent Governance Review', by Paul Myners, 7 May 2014 (www.co-operative.coop/PageFiles/989348879/Report_of_the_ Independent_Governance_Review.pdf)

4   Paul Moore's memo published in Financial Times, 11 February 2009 (www.ft.com/ cms/s/0/fca6a706-f81d-11dd-aae8-000077b07658.html#axzz2x3zD3R3t )

5  See the Treasury Select Committee's Examination of Witnesses at: www.publications.
   parliament.uk/pa/cm200809/cmselect/cmtreasy/144/09021002.htm

6  See Andy Hornby's corporate profile at: www.pharmacy2u.co.uk/ourteam.html

7  'HSBC's money-laundering crackdown riddled with lapses', *Reuters*, 13 July 2012 (http://
   mobile.reuters.com/article/topNews/idUSBRE86C18H20120714?i=7&irpc=932)

8  'In Credit Suisse Settlement, a Question of Justice', *The New York Times*, 21 May 2014
   (http://dealbook.nytimes.com/2014/05/21/in-credit-suisse-settlement-a-question-of-
   justice/?_php=true&_type=blogs&_r=0)

9  'Inclusive capitalism: creating a sense of the systemic', a speech by Mark Carney,
   Governor of the Bank of England, 27 May 2014 (www.bankofengland.co.uk/publica-
   tions/Documents/speeches/2014/speech731.pdf)

10 See City of London's research at: www.cityoflondon.gov.uk/business/economic-re-
   search-and-information/statistics/Pages/Research%20FAQs.aspx and Select USA's
   research  at:  http://selectusa.commerce.gov/industry-snapshots/financial-services-
   industry-united-states

11 'Total Tax Contribution of UK Financial Services Sixth Edition', a research report
   prepared for the City of London Corporation by PwC, December 2013 (www.cityo-
   flondon.gov.uk/business/economic-research-and-information/research-publications/
   Documents/research-2013/total-tax-contribution-of-uk-financial-services-sixth-edi-
   tion.pdf)

12 'Wall Street less important to US economy than thought', *Financial Times*, 11 March
   2014  (www.ft.com/cms/s/0/c1ec53b4-a938-11e3-9b71-00144feab7de.html?siteedition=
   uk#axzz31RhKCyAj)

# INDEX

Printed and bound by CPI Group (UK) Ltd, Croydon, CR0 4YY